Date Due

WRITING IN AN AGE OF TECHNOLOGY

Writing

IN AN AGE OF

Technology

THOMAS E. KAKONIS
JOHN SCALLY

Ferris State College

MACMILLAN PUBLISHING CO., INC.
New York

Collier Macmillan Publishers
London

MACMILLAN PUBLISHING CO., INC.
866 Third Avenue, New York, New York 10022
COLLIER MACMILLAN CANADA, LTD.

Library of Congress Cataloging in Publication Data

Kakonis, Thomas E
  Writing in an age of technology.

  Includes index.
    1. English language—Rhetoric.   2.   College readers.
I. Scally, John, joint author.   II.   Title.
PE1408.K253   808'.042   77-1499
ISBN 0-02-361890-6

Printing: 1 2 3 4 5 6 7 8   Year: 8 9 0 1 2 3 4

PREFACE

Writing in an Age of Technology is written for students who expect an English composition course to provide them with a practical competence in writing that they can apply in other fields of study and in their future careers. It is written for those who recognize the ability to write clearly and correctly as an important qualification for employment. The approach to the principles of writing, the examples, and the readings place writing in a context that every student—regardless of vocational goals—can relate to. The text speaks to the student in a concerned, easy manner that overcomes hostility and leads to seeing writing as a useful skill, as something worth knowing about.

The student will find something more here than just another rehash of rhetoric with a smattering of grammar. We do talk a great deal about writing, but, unlike most English texts, this one also raises questions about living, about the harmony between man and nature, about the risks and benefits of technological progress. We try to bridge the gap the student often feels between English class and the concerns of the "real" world. The thematic threads running through the text are developed more fully in a collection of readings that differ dramatically from those found in most writing texts.

The English teacher using this text comes into direct contact with the values and concerns most important to a new generation of students; the teacher becomes a craftsman sharing the skills of a trade crucial to survival and success in the world of economic realities.

T. E. K.

J. S.

CONTENTS

Introduction

Writing in an Age of Technology approaches writing as a practical skill useful in every profession. The strategies and principles discussed in this book underlie every writing task, whether it consists of drawing up a letter of application for a job, describing a piece of equipment, or preparing a formal professional report. Knowing how to write effectively adds an important skill to the kit of tools you carry with you into the job market. Writing lets others know what you know. The principles of organization and the processes of thought required to write well are close relatives of the organizing and thinking abilities necessary to career success. But you will find something more in these pages than just another rehash of rhetoric and a conventional smattering of grammar.

The first unit of this text, "The Raw Materials," introduces sentences and paragraphs, the raw materials of which every piece of writing is formed. This section assumes you know a good deal about the language you have been using daily for years, although you may not, perhaps, know or remember all the formal rules and terminology of traditional grammar. We offer some practical suggestions for putting the knowledge you already have into action. We rely a great deal on common sense and explain some tactics for building paragraphs that work.

Unit II, "The Tools of the Trade," presents the basic principles of rhetoric. Writing can be divided into four categories: writing that describes (description), writing that explains (exposition), writing that tells a story (narration), and writing that tries to influence someone else's opinion (persuasion). In practice, these categories mingle, and one piece of writing may perform all four functions. We introduce each type of writing separately for the same reason a football coach trains his players first in blocking, then in tackling, before he sets the team to learning plays. The fundamentals must be mastered before the game.

That facts "speak for themselves" is a common cliché. It is important to realize how misleading this statement is. If facts are not interpreted through the strategies in Unit II, they do nothing more than exist; they do not "speak" at all. What you know—the facts, the skills you have mastered, the experience you have had—is of little value unless it can be communicated. Rhetoric gives you a playbook, a system of strategies and techniques for communicating facts to friends, colleagues, and associates.

The essays included in the third unit of this book express facts and opinions about the world we live in. These essays all deal with the same basic theme: the relationship between technological progress and man's well-being. We live in a technological age, and much of your future writing will concern technical subjects.

Unit IV, "Job-Related Writing," provides writing survival skills for anyone about to begin a career. Here you will find recommendations for writing a résumé and its covering letter, often the most important steps in finding a job. This section also presents the format and principles governing writing duties encountered in most professions. Many of the examples are drawn from real situations to demonstrate how valuable good writing is in carrying out a professional assignment. Study of this section and practice in following the models provided will help you to get the job you want and to perform it successfully.

The final unit of this book should be referred to over and over again as you develop your writing skill. The glossary defines particular points of style and usage; the information will suggest the final polish for your work that will eliminate those minor flaws that detract from good ideas and an otherwise functional organization.

I

The Raw Materials

SENTENCES

SENTENCES show the relationships between different things named or described by words. As we develop, we use more complicated sentence structures to express our thoughts and observations. This process begins very early in life. A child first learns to name certain objects; then, as awareness grows, words cluster in structures resembling sentences:

Daddy car go
Bow-wow cookie

An adult can understand these first utterances, and they can be classified as sentences, although they lack many of the elements necessary for clear communication. In the first example a variety of messages could be intended: "Daddy is going away in the car." "I want to go in the car with Daddy." "Daddy, the car is going away." Adults have a more complex language system that conveys meaning more exactly, thereby avoiding possible confusion.

In writing we strive to avoid confusing messages; we cannot use sign language or gestures, as the child frequently does, so the pattern of our sentences must convey the intended meaning clearly. Lack of clarity in sentences is called ambiguity, and one ambiguous sentence in a set of instructions or a report to a supervisor can create a multitude of potential problems.

The sentence "We need the parts for the compressor that broke down today" looks fine until we examine it a little more carefully. Does it mean that the parts are needed right now, urgently? Or is it simply telling when the compressor broke down? If the parts are needed right away, the person responsible for sending the parts could very well miss the urgency of the request because the sentence is ambiguous. Consequently, a job could be delayed unnecessarily; a dissatisfied customer might be the result of an unclear sentence.

The basis of clarity is simplicity. It is a fine talent to be able to write long, complicated sentences, but this talent is not necessary in the type of writing you will do. What is essential is clarity.

To be able to write clearly and accurately, you must know something about the structure of English sentences. You already know a great deal about our language simply because you have been speaking it for a number of years. You can read the following sentence, for example, and immediately recognize that something is wrong with it and also specify the problem:

The man whom the radio for was repaired left.

There is something wrong with the order in which the words appear. The meaning of a sentence depends on the pattern or order in which words are arranged. If we use a word order that others will not recognize, our sentences will have no meaning, no matter how accurate and specific individual words are. In fact, even sentences built from nonsense words seem familiar if the word order imitates a conventional pattern:

The brumble gogged liggily.

When used to build sentences, words fall generally into two large classes: meaning words and function words. Meaning words carry the message of the sentence. Accurate, clear writing requires some knowledge of the nature of these words, and the easiest way to discuss them is by describing the nature of nouns, verbs, adjectives, and adverbs. Function words are "little" words that help meaning words hang together in a sentence and connect one word or group of words with another. The function words are underlined in the following sentence:

A   may   this   to   with a
   machinist   connect   modified nozzle   any hose
                                        near
   standard mating coupling   his workplace.

To achieve clarity, good writers generally use far more meaning words in their sentences than they do function words. Function words often have no clear meaning (try to define the word *of*), so too many in one sentence can distract the reader's attention from the sentence's message.

UNCLEAR: *It is* believed *by* management *that there are not* many employees *who* fail *to* use their sick days.
CLEAR: Management believes most employees use their sick days.

Sentences are built from words, and words have specific tasks within a sentence. Three basic types of meaning words make up a sentence. The first class of words is the *noun*. Nouns name things, people, and ideas. *Verbs* are the second type of meaning words. Verbs show movement or action (He *worked* hard); they also show relationships among name words (John *loves* Mary). A large group of words called *modifiers* constitutes the third class of words used in sentences. Modifiers qualify or change the nature of names or relationships.

John loves Mary *deeply*.
Big John loves *little* Mary.

Verbs are the most important meaning words in a sentence. They tell us what action is being performed or precisely what the relationship is between two things. A very important group of verbs does not really show action but rather describes a state of being. These common words are listed below in their various forms:

PRESENT	PAST
am, are (aren't), is (isn't)	were (weren't), was (wasn't)
do (don't), does (doesn't)	did (didn't)
have (haven't), has (hasn't)	had (hadn't)
will (won't), shall	would (wouldn't)
can (can't)	should (shouldn't)
must (mustn't)	could (couldn't)
	might

Verbs change their form to signal time and number. A verb can show that an action or relationship is occurring in the present (*begin, run, drive, throw, love*). Verbs change their form slightly to indicate that an action or relationship took place in the past (*begun, ran, drove, threw, loved*). With the addition of the verb forms *will* or *shall*, an action or relationship can be placed in the future (*will begin, will run, will drive, will throw, will love*).

Verbs also change their form to signal the number of people, places, or things involved in an action or relationship. Verbs have singular (one) and plural (more than one) forms:

he hits, they hit
he runs, they run

he loves, they love
he drives, they drive
he begins, they begin
he throws, they throw

In a sentence, make certain you are using the correct form of the verb, especially with regard to number. The form of the verb is dependent on the subject (noun) of the sentence. If the subject is plural in number, then the verb should also be plural. If the subject is singular, then the verb should also be singular.

Nouns are also extremely important meaning words and deserve close attention. Again, nouns are words that name things, people, actions, ideas—in fact, anything that exists. Because nouns usually indicate what the sentence is all about, they are basic to the clear understanding of your message. To become more familiar with nouns, you need to know a few characteristics of these naming words.

Nouns can change form to indicate that more than one thing is being named; they have singular and plural forms:

one child   two children
one worker   two workers
one factory   two factories

Sometimes you can identify a noun simply by asking yourself if more than one of those things can exist. This is not always true, but most nouns have a plural form. Further, certain questions can be asked about nouns: How much? How many? What kind? Nouns will often have words (*adjectives*) associated with them that supply the answers to these questions:

five old men
four huge fires

Another characteristic that helps identify nouns is that they have a possessive form; in other words, a noun can own something:

Thompson's job
a *mechanic's* tools
a *craftsman's* pride
James's house

The possessive form of nouns is signaled by the use of the apostrophe. The word following a possessive word (including *my, our, your, their*) is a noun. If something can be possessed by something or someone, then it functions as a noun.

Almost all nouns can be preceded by a possessive word. Most nouns can be preceded by the articles *a, an,* or *the,* often called noun determiners. These words always signal the presence of a noun, although descriptive words sometimes appear between the determiner and the noun:

a superintendent
an excuse
the executive
a good *job*
a piston *engine*
the conveyor *belt*
a fuel injection *system*

In a sentence, a noun can be either a subject or an object. A subject is what the sentence is all about; or, put another way, a subject is doing the acting in a sentence. We have italicized the subjects in the following sentences.

Construction stopped.
Cars skidded.
Men laughed.
Rain fell.

Nouns can also function as objects in a sentence. An object is something being acted on, or the receiver of an action. In a sentence the noun used as an object usually follows the verb.

Bill lost the *ball.*
Joe operated a *crane.*
An accident halted *construction.*
My television blew a *tube.*

Objects also appear after a special group of function words called *prepositions.* We would very seldom say, for example, "He fell into." Obviously, he fell into something, and this something is the object of the preposition *into* (*into the lake, into the fire*). A list of some common prepositions follows:

to	under
into	until
of	after
for	behind
on	before
in	beneath
over	through
above	around
below	

We use these words often in English, and they are nearly always followed by a noun functioning as an object.

The two most important types of meaning words in our language are nouns and verbs. If we had only these two kinds of words to work with, we could communicate fairly effectively. But our language would be without essential elements that contribute precision and accuracy to our messages.

A class of meaning words called *modifiers* adds much of the clarity of meaning to a well-written sentence. This class of words and word groups contains adjectives and adverbs. Adverb and adjective modifiers contribute a great deal to the accuracy of your writing. They can describe, qualify, and locate an action or object in time or place.

The first and most important function of an adjective modifier is to tell your reader which one of a group of similar objects you are talking about. This can be extremely important information:

the *blue* wire
the *black plastic* cap
the *outer* surface

Adjectives also inform the reader how much of a certain material is to be used in a given situation or how many objects or ideas are involved:

fifty grams
two pistons
five pounds

Adjectives modify nouns, and more than one adjective can modify the same noun.

height adjustment screws
peak firing temperatures
a *sufficient, steady* flow
clean, uncontaminated air

Adverbs, like adjectives, can add a necessary dimension of clarity and accuracy to our writing. Adverbs can modify verbs, adjectives, or other adverbs. Their most important function is to tell us when an action occurs, in what way it happens, where it happens, and under what conditions it happens. Adverbs can be used just about anywhere in a sentence and can many times be recognized by the ending *-ly:*

Finally the job was finished.
Frequently the machine broke down.
Eventually we will replace the engine.

These adverbs appear first in the sentence, but they could also appear in other positions without changing the meaning of the sentence. Here are some further examples of *-ly* adverbs in various sentence positions.

The estimates varied *considerably.*
The operation was *efficiently* concluded.
The truck *quietly* slid into the ditch.

Not all adverbs end in *-ly*, however. Some of the most frequently used words in our language are adverbs indicating time, place, or manner. A partial list follows:

there	today
here	tomorrow
upward	yesterday
inside	now
outside	then
somewhere	often
anywhere	never
overhead	seldom
above	sometime
behind	

You can see the importance of these words in giving your reader a clear message. The nature of adverb modifiers will become clearer to you in the discussion that follows. For more information regarding all parts of the sentence, refer to Unit V of this book.

Adjective and adverb modifiers can also be groups of words, particularly groups of words beginning with one of those prepositions we discussed earlier. Prepositional phrases are the most useful and most widely used modifiers in our language, giving the writer an invaluable method for indicating time, place, location, and other qualities of an object:

> The upper section *of the shell* sets down *into the base.*
> The turbochargers can also be equipped *with air suction ducts.*
> An aluminum strip *across the open back* strengthens the structure.
> Ease *of maintenance* is a strong feature *of all National engines.*

Prepositional phrase modifiers add clarity and specific detail to your sentences. Prepositions are function words that connect one thing or idea to another; in other words, they can connect nouns with each other. Prepositions can also connect a naming word to an action (Joe works *for Harry*). Careful use of prepositional phrases adds precision to your writing and makes your writing more interesting to a reader. Prepositional phrases indicating time or place can begin a sentence to vary sentence structure or give important information:

> *For many years* the mountain people made their own clothing *with hand-spun thread.*

Notice the contribution modifiers can make when they are added to the sentence "Methods have improved."

methods	*what kind?*	of application
have improved	*how?*	tremendously
	where?	in the plastics industry
	when?	during the past ten years

Methods of application have improved tremendously in the plastics industry during the past ten years.

The modifiers limit, identify, and locate in time and place the basic elements of the sentence. You have been using these modifiers for years, ever since you learned to speak, answer questions, or explain your meanings. By making use of the things you already know about the English sentence, you can communicate your knowledge and skills clearly and effectively.

Assembling and arranging words into sentences involve as much care and precision as are demanded of a carpenter joining pieces of fine wood to form a cabinet. English syntax (the order of words in a sentence) can be very complex, but a working knowledge of certain basic structures can produce clear writing. These patterns carry the message of every English sentence. No matter how much elaborate detail a carpenter might add to a cabinet to make it more attractive or more interesting to look at, it still remains a piece of furniture designed to hold objects. Many problems with clarity in writing arise from adding decorations and clever finishing touches before establishing the basic message. You should first try to be clear and, to do this, become thoroughly familiar with the basic structures that form the backbone of all English sentences.

The examples that follow illustrate some basic sentence structures. Once you can consistently produce sentences like these, you can begin to add some interesting touches of your own.

1. The generator runs.
   Methods have improved.
   Adjustment screws are provided.
2. Mr. Harvey connected the wires.
   The discharge raises the temperature.
   The technician repaired the equipment.
3. The converter is a unit.
   Cost was a factor.
   The car is an Oldsmobile.
4. The shipment is heavy.
   The alloy is hard.
   The solar cell is simple, light, and reliable.

Obviously, you can write sentences like these; and if you can, then you can write clearly and accurately. Let's look a little more closely at each pattern.

Pattern 1 is very simple. In this case we have a naming word (noun) performing an action described by the verb. In formal writing situations, it is quite unusual to find sentences precisely like this one or like the other patterns. But, in many cases, if you take away all the elements added onto the sentence, you will find a basic structure similar to one of these. Part of our purpose here is to help you understand how these basic patterns can be expanded and modified in ways that clarify your meaning rather than obscure it.

The first modification or change that can take place in pattern 1 has to do with the verb *runs*. Verbs not only describe an action, but also can tell us when that action took place—this feature is often called *verb tense*. So we can change the verb *runs* to indicate changes in time and number:

The generator ran.
The generators run.
The generator is running.
The generators will run.

If we add the helping or *auxiliary* verb forms mentioned earlier, the verb can take on many different forms, each changing the time in which the action occurred:

The generator will run.

| The generator | is was will be has been | running. |

| The generator | has run. had | |

| The generator | could ought to might may | run. |

These are not all the changes the verb can undergo. Without even knowing the grammatical names for all these types of verbs, you can probably recognize them or recall having used them yourself, and you can probably think of many other verb forms that could fit this pattern.

This basic pattern (The generator runs) can help us approach a definition of an English sentence. Only two elements are necessary to form a good English sentence: a verb showing action or state of being and something doing the acting or being. With these two elements present (commonly called a *subject* and a *verb*), a sentence can say all sorts of things. In very loose terms, a sentence says something about a subject or tells a subject to do something. The single word *generator* carries a meaning, but we don't get a sense of anything happening. The verb *runs* by itself shows us an action, but anything or anyone could be performing that action. Put both words together, and you have a sentence that tells us that a subject is doing something: *The generator runs.*

This statement carries with it a sense of completeness, a sense that we have been told all there is to know. You must be careful, however, about adding other types of words, mainly function words, to this basic structure because they can ruin this sense of completeness and destroy clarity. One group of function words in particular presents problems in this regard. These are function words used as connectors to join one sentence to another. Notice what happens when the following connectors are added to the basic sentence:

when
while
if   the generator runs
because
although

Adding these words creates a sense that something is needed to complete the thought. What happens when the generator runs? What will happen if the generator runs? What happens while the generator runs? Clarity is destroyed in these cases because the message raises unanswered questions. Only certain types of words can be added to this basic sentence without creating the need for more information. These elements add information to the base; they make it more complete by telling us such things as which generator is running or how noisy it is or where it is located or when it runs.

We can add adjective and adverb modifiers to the base sentence to supply additional information, if that information is necessary to understand a situation. In the following example, we have labeled the kinds of modifiers usually found in certain positions, but you don't have to know their names to use them effectively:

Adverbs	*Adjectives*	*Adjectives and Adverbs*	*Adverbs*
The	generator		runs

Frequently, the large generator in the corner runs erratically.

Now this looks more like the type of sentences you are accustomed to reading. But notice how simple it was to create. Once we were sure that the base pattern said exactly the right thing, more information could be added by using modifiers to specify time, place, and other characteristics of the generator.

By understanding one of the simplest basic patterns of the English sentence, you have come close to knowing everything essential about the written language. You can learn some other things from this sentence. First, notice that the new sentence begins with an *-ly* word, an adverb indicating time (*frequently*). Writers often begin sentences with various types of adverbs, especially those that indicate time. Adverbs can move around in the sentence; in other words, no rule restricts them to one certain position; only the standard of clarity does. Beginning your sentences with adverbs, whether a phrase or a single word, can make your writing a little more interesting to the reader. Examine the following examples:

> *Eventually* the foundation will crack.
> *Finally,* the glue melted.

Once you understand a little about modifying words and phrases and can write good base sentences, you can build your own structures to communicate precisely the right message. Do not overload your sentences, however. No one expects you to be a great stylist; the person reading your writing simply wants clear, accurate information. If you wrote in only these basic patterns, your writing might not win any awards, but you would be doing your job efficiently and productively.

But the nature of the language makes it nearly impossible to rely on only one pattern. Look at the following groups of words, for instance:

> Bill Thompson connected.
> The discharge raises.

Immediately, unless Mr. Thompson is a boxer, questions arise: Connected what? Raises what? Some verbs must pass the action on to an object (much like prepositions) before the sentence can make sense.

Bill Thompson connected the wires.
The discharge raises the temperature.

These sentences show something or someone acting to influence or change something else. Basically, in this structure nouns interact with each other, and one thing does something to another: The action is passed across from one noun to another. But everything else true of our first example is also true of these. Modifiers can add more information to make the message more specific and clear.

Bill Thompson connected the *outside* wires *to the control box.*
The discharge *from the factory dramatically* raises the *water* temperature *of the lake.*

Once again, adjective and adverb word and phrase modifiers are added to the base, and you don't even have to think, "Should I use an adjective or an adverb?" because your common sense and instinct tell you which type of word fits where.

Our third and final pattern uses the various forms of the verb *to be.* These are sometimes called *linking* verbs because they act like an equals sign ("The sky is dark" means "The sky = dark"). Because they link nouns with nouns or nouns with adjectives, the various forms of the verb *to be* could very well be considered function words rather than meaning words. Many writers avoid using too many linking verbs in their sentences because these words don't carry any definite meaning. But you should know something about the sentence patterns associated with linking verbs.

1. The converter is a unit.
2. Cost was a factor.
3. Cost is high.
4. The shipment is heavy.

These sentences state that one named thing is the same as another. The linking verb *to be* can link one noun to another: (1) *The converter is a unit.* (2) *Cost is a factor.* Much of the time, this structure linking one noun with another places a particular thing in a class with other things so that we can more easily identify its nature or its function, much as we would say, "John is a man" or "This car is an Oldsmobile." The linking verb also links nouns with adjectives, in this way describing the noun: *The shipment is heavy.* This statement could be rewritten as a phrase: *the heavy shipment will arrive tomorrow.* Instead of an adjective, an adverb often appears after the linking verb, as in the statement *The delivery is here.*

Sentence patterns with linking verbs can be expanded in much the same way the other patterns are expanded. In the *noun is noun* structure, adjective modifiers can be added to say more about the nouns:

The *initial* cost of *construction* is an *important* factor *in our decision.*

And, of course, adverbs can be added, perhaps to specify time:

Finally, the initial cost of construction is *now* an important factor in our decision.

The most important words in any sentence—because they carry most of the meaning—are nouns and verbs. Consequently, you should build your sentence skills upon a mastery of the basic sentence patterns, adding word and phrase modifiers with care.

Combining Base Sentences

Writers often combine two or more base sentences into one complete sentence structure (incomplete sentence structures are discussed in Unit V under "Fragments"). Base sentences are combined to bring important ideas closer together and to show the relationship between two ideas. More than one base sentence can be included in a complete sentence structure. Two base sentences can be joined by connecting words called *coordinating conjunctions* (*conjunction* means "to join with"). Several words can join one base sentence to another:

and	nor
but	for
yet	so
or	

When used as conjunctions, these words should nearly always have a comma in front of them. Some examples of base sentences joined by these common conjunctions follow. Identify the base sentences in these examples.

> I've worked in industry, *and* management doesn't listen.
>
> The average successful engineer owes half of his success to his ability as a communicator, *so* engineers should become better communicators.
>
> The turbochargers are normally fitted with air filters and silencers, *but* they can also be equipped with air suction ducts.

Once you have practiced writing base sentences and combining them using conjunctions, you can easily add other elements to your sentence base. Adding beginners, interrupters, and enders to your sentences makes them more specific and clear.

Beginners

A *beginner* is a word or group of words added to the front of a sentence base. Writers use beginners to give more precise information, especially information about the time an action took place or special conditions influencing an action or idea. Beginners also help give your writing some variety by changing the shape of the sentence. This makes your writing more interesting to read. Beginners are usually joined to the base sentence with a comma, particularly if your beginner is more than a few words long. In the following examples we have italicized the beginners added to the base sentence.

> *In my job as foreman,* I am responsible for the smooth operation of the shop.
>
> *After the tenement was demolished,* the people looked for new homes.
>
> *In the years ahead,* environmental pollution is industry's biggest problem.
>
> *During the past five years,* I have been a computer programmer.
>
> *Because of excessive noise,* people in large cities turn deaf much earlier in life.
>
> *Yesterday morning,* Congress debated the new energy bill.

Each of these examples follows the same pattern: a beginner set off by a comma has been added to the sentence base. Note that none of the beginners can stand by itself (see "Fragments" in Unit V). Each beginner is dependent on a base sentence to complete its meaning.

> In my job as foreman . . .
> After the tenement was demolished . . .
> In the years ahead . . .

The easiest type of beginner to master consists of one word or only a few words. These short beginners give your reader invaluable help in following your thoughts. They show the relationship between the sentence they introduce and the ideas that have gone before. Here are some important short beginners and the relationships they signal:

TIME	CONTRAST
then	but
next	however
first, second, third	conversely
in addition	on the contrary
yesterday	yet
last month, last year	
suddenly	
recently	
occasionally	ADDITION
previously	and
formerly	in addition
	furthermore
RESULT	indeed
thus	in fact
as a result	for example
so	also
consequently	once again

This is not an exhaustive list of short beginners. We discuss these words further in the section on paragraphs, where we describe their function as transitional devices. These words, used with care, can make your information clearer to your reader.

Longer beginners usually require a comma to join them to the base sentence. Long beginners supply much more information than the short ones. Once again, these beginners show relationships between the sentence they introduce and information that has gone before. Long beginners are usually signaled by a key word that affects the meaning of the beginner. In the following examples, we use the same base sentence but change the signal words on the beginner:

After you have finished the job, you will be paid in full.
Because you have finished the job, you will be paid in full.
Although you have not finished the job, you will be paid in full.
When you have finished the job, you will be paid in full.
Before you have finished the job, you will be paid in full.
If you have finished the job, you will be paid in full.

An important type of long beginner is signaled by words ending in *ing*. These beginners result from combining two base sentences that naturally belong together:

1. He was carrying a heavy piece of equipment. He hurt his back.
   Carrying a heavy piece of equipment, he hurt his back.
2. The engine was missing a sparkplug. The engine would not start.
   Missing a sparkplug, the engine would not start.

Interrupters

As the word implies, an interrupter is placed within the sentence base, interrupting the order of the base sentence. An interrupter supplies information not important enough to isolate it in a sentence of its own. This additional information will usually clarify a single word, whereas a beginner can affect the meaning of an entire base sentence. A common type of interrupter has its own special class of signal words:

who	which
whom	whose
where	that

These signal words enable us to insert one base sentence inside another, as in the following example:

His first bid was much too high. The bid was in excess of $30,000.
His first bid [which was in excess of $30,000] was much too high.
His first bid, which was in excess of $30,000, was much too high.

Usually, commas set off the interrupter, one before and one after. More detailed information on the use of commas in this situation is available in Unit V. As a general rule, any element interrupting the base sentence should be surrounded by commas. In the following examples we have italicized the interrupters:

A relief valve, *which is an essential component in any hydraulic circuit*, is designed for almost any type of pump.
A funnel-shaped horn, *which is mounted at the open side*, catches the heat rays.
The city government, *which studied the many problems of urban renewal*, made some very good decisions.

Many writers eliminate the signal words from this type of structure for the sake of brevity and economy. In the first two of the preceding examples, the signal word *which* could very easily be eliminated from the interrupter:

A relief valve, *an essential component in any hydraulic circuit*, is designed for almost any type of pump.
A funnel-shaped horn, *mounted at the open side*, catches the heat rays.

There are, of course, many other types of sentence interrupters, most of which you use naturally in everyday speech. Most of the beginners can also be made into interrupters, once again set off by commas. In fact, it is common practice to insert many of the single-word beginners inside the base sentence:

The drought, *however*, will be over soon.
Many banks, *for example*, offer special interest rates on long-term savings accounts.

Long beginners can also be inserted into the sentence base:

A doctor, *although he earns a high income*, must give up much of his privacy.
Three men, *if they are strong enough*, can lift the capsule.
The local consumer's organization, *as a result of pressure from the citizens*, has begun investigating pricing practices at local supermarkets.

Enders

A base sentence may often require additional details to make its message clear. Many modern writers provide additional details through enders, elements added on to the end of a base sentence. Enders are joined to the base with a comma, as in our other examples.

Enders can be created in a variety of ways. One method is simply to add on more detail, perhaps to clarify the meaning of a vague word or words. In our example the enders are italicized:

The car was completely wrecked, *the engine torn from its mounts, the hood sticking through the windshield, the doors ripped from their hinges.*

A frequent technique relies on *-ing* words to pack more information into a sentence, especially when one is describing an action:

The legs of the "centipede" track are individually sprung, *giving* the machine a capability of climbing vertical objects.
The scientists demonstrated the transistor effect, *amplifying* and *controlling* the flow of electrons in a solid material.
A pacemaker can now be implanted into failing hearts, *producing* accurately timed electrical impulses, *helping* the patient maintain normal health.

After you have developed your native ability to write base sentences, the techniques we have introduced here can help you extend your writing skills. But everything depends on the base. If your base sentence is not clear and accurate, no amount of combination or addition will save it. Here are a few suggestions for writing good, clear sentences:

1. Say what you have to say right away or at the end of a sentence structure. In other words, avoid "sandwiching" your message between beginners and enders.
2. Keep subjects and verbs as close together as possible. In other words, use interrupters with care.
3. Rely on *meaning* words rather than *function* words. Meaning words are primarily nouns and verbs with an occasional ad-

jective or adverb. Function words are the "little" words that contribute very little to the meaning of your sentence structure.

EXERCISES

1. Identify the base sentences in the following:
   a. On July 1, Paul Brenner, an executive in the sales department, sent a large order to the plant's production department.
   b. He has had some college engineering training, but he is primarily a businessman.
   c. When we investigated the problem, we found eyelets made of two different metals with the same order number.
   d. The salesman will show you our newest products, pointing out their special characteristics.

2. In the four preceding sentences identify instances of combining base sentences with a conjunction and of adding beginners, interrupters, and enders to a base sentence.

3. Combine the following base sentences by using appropriate conjunctions:
   a. Scientific projects are now suffering severe budget cuts. The government has cut down all grants.
   b. Many people have never heard of a balanced diet. No amount of money will make these people healthy.
   c. A generator produces sufficient electricity when the engine is running fast. It produces no electricity when the engine is idling.

4. Add a suitable opener to the following base sentences:
   a. The construction was not a difficult process.
   b. This proposal could solve one of our most pressing problems.
   c. Our safety record is 36 per cent better.
   d. No criticism can be made of the part's quality.
   e. We can decrease chances of costly breakdowns.
   f. We shall cancel our order.

5. Add suitable interrupters to the following base sentences:
   a. Bill's job saps all of his creative energy.
   b. More nuclear power plants are a needed source of energy.

6. Add suitable enders to the following base sentences:
   a. He left work early.
   b. Economists foresee higher interest rates in the next few years.
   c. Most of the plant's employees are now on unemployment.
   d. The growth of the firm has been remarkable.

THE PARAGRAPH

THE paragraph is the foundation of all written communication. Put another way, a paragraph is like the individual walls of a house or the major components of an automobile (the body, the engine, the wheels). A paragraph is a collection of sentences working together to clarify and explain a single idea.

The sentences that form a paragraph relate to the paragraph much as each particular two-by-four relates to the wall it helps create or as a single piston relates to the entire function of an automobile engine. A single two-by-four all by itself doesn't have much value, but nailing a number of two-by-fours together results in a very functional wall. A single piston is interesting to look at, but it doesn't have much practical use except, perhaps, as a paperweight or as a doorstop; but when combined with other mechanical components, the piston takes on purpose and function in contributing to the operation of the engine. In the same way, one sentence by itself is often not very useful in explaining a complex idea; but when it is joined with other sentences to form a paragraph, a meaningful act of communication can result. A paragraph can be loosely defined as a purposeful unit of communication constructed from a varying number of sentences.

To illustrate further our point regarding the relationship between the sentence and the paragraph, let us consider the following sentence:

> The need for protection offered by a strong union was illustrated by the fate of the employees of the *Bigelow Record*.

The natural response to this perfectly clear sentence is one of confusion. Questions arise: What's the point? Why? Where? For what reason? A sentence by itself is like a piston divorced from its engine; it really doesn't perform a very useful function. Now put this sentence in a paragraph, and it becomes a vital piece of information.

> The need for protection offered by a strong union was illustrated by the fate of the employees of the *Bigelow Record*. Working conditions in the office had become unbearable. An underpaid janitorial staff neglected the washrooms. Equipment was so inadequate that re-

porters were forced to use their own typewriters. Employees had not received a raise in salary for three years. Complaints to management had no effect. As a last resort, employees picketed the newspaper office for three days. On the fourth day, the pickets arrived to find their desks occupied by a new staff.

In fact, if our sample sentence were left out of this paragraph, the entire message would be confusing and incomplete. Conversely, without the other sentences in the paragraph, that sentence resembles a discarded two-by-four lying around waiting for someone to give it purpose and function. As you can see, the "message" in our example depends on all the sentences working together to create a fundamental unit of communication—the paragraph.

To be a meaningful unit of communication, a paragraph must have two essential qualities: *unity* and *order*. There are, of course, other qualities that contribute to an effective paragraph—and you will become more aware of these qualities as you practice the rhetorical techniques presented in the next section of this book— but without unity and order a paragraph cannot communicate its message clearly and effectively.

Above all, a paragraph must have unity. All the parts (sentences) must work together in harmony to carry out the purpose of communicating your perceptions and your ideas clearly and accurately. Generally, before beginning to write, you will have a fairly good idea in mind of what you want to say; but to get your message across, you must have the ideas and the facts "hanging together."

To make all the elements hang together, a single paragraph should develop *one* idea and only one idea. In fact, the most effective way to gain unity is to tell the reader immediately the single main idea you want to present in the paragraph. This is usually done through a *topic sentence*, which, in most cases, will be the first sentence in the paragraph. The five-space indentation that signals the beginning of a paragraph means that a new idea is starting, and the writer's obligation is to state that idea and then stick to it throughout the paragraph. In a more practical sense, breaking your writing into paragraphs makes it much easier for your reader to follow your thoughts. In the paragraph you should include everything necessary for understanding the main idea and omit everything not needed for understanding the main idea.

As a general rule, a paragraph should begin with a topic sentence. Experienced writers don't abide strictly by this suggestion, but it is a good rule to follow at first in trying to establish unity in your paragraphs. A topic sentence simply states the main point of the paragraph; it could be compared to a neon sign flashing above a restaurant, telling the passerby what he or she can expect to find inside the building. The following topic sentences tell you what you can expect to find in the sentences of the paragraph that follows them.

The experiment yielded two findings that were surprising.

The interactions observed in matter can be grouped into four distinct categories.

Brakes and clutches serve very different functions in the automobile, but their principles of operation are the same.

We decided to investigate the effects on the employment situation here of the rapid growth in the use of computers.

The ring-wound armature is seldom used in modern generators.

The molecules of a gas are in a perpetual state of motion, constantly colliding with one another.

Each of these statements is a *generalization*. In each case, we rightfully demand more information, and each statement is, in effect, promising that more is coming. The type of information used to support or explain each of these topic sentences will be different in each case, ranging from precise facts and figures to detailed physical descriptions. But in every case these generalizations must be associated with facts that explain them or descriptions that show more clearly what the writer has in mind.

The selection of the information that will develop or support each topic sentence is dependent on the *controlling idea* contained in each of them. The controlling idea is the word or group of words in a topic sentence that contains the specific idea or opinion to be developed in the paragraph. All of the information chosen to develop the topic sentence must be clearly related to the paragraph's controlling idea. We have italicized the controlling idea in each of our sample topic sentences:

The experiment yielded two findings that were *surprising*.

The interactions observed in matter *can be grouped* into four distinct categories.

Brakes and clutches serve many different functions, but their *principles of operation* are the same.

We decided to investigate *the effects on the employment* situation here of the rapid growth in the use of computers.

The ring-wound armature is *seldom used* in modern generators.

The molecules of a gas are in *a perpetual state of motion*, constantly colliding with one another.

A topic sentence consists of at least two basic elements, both of which are essential to paragraph unity. First, you must identify and limit the subject of the paragraph: the experiment, brakes and clutches, the rapid growth, the ring-wound armature, and so on. Second, you must clearly state through a controlling idea precisely what it is you want to say about that subject.

The controlling idea is extremely important in the development of a paragraph. Development of a paragraph simply means adding the supporting information you include to illustrate, to explain, or to justify your topic sentence. But this is not just any information about a subject; every detail you bring into a paragraph must relate to the controlling idea, and that relationship should be immediately apparent to your reader. If this is not the case, your paragraph does not possess the essential quality of unity.

A controlling idea operates in a paragraph in much the same way a distributor functions in an automobile engine. The distributor supplies the tiny sparks that ignite the explosions in the engine's combustion chambers. Without this spark, the engine cannot function, and if these sparks do not occur in the proper firing order, the engine will run erratically or not at all. Take, for example, the topic sentence dealing with the effects of computers on the employment situation in a given region. The supporting information must have a direct relationship to these effects. Information about the various types of computers being used or the costs of these computers or their various methods of operation has no place in this paragraph, unless, of course, these facts contribute to unemployment in a direct and meaningful way. It is, in fact, your job as writer to make clear the relationship between the facts you present and the paragraph's controlling idea.

Repeating the controlling idea throughout a paragraph strengthens its relationship to the facts and creates unity in the paragraph. Key words or synonyms (words with similar meanings) that echo the controlling idea can tie your paragraph together, as in the following example:

Why is man a worker? First of all, of course, man *works* to sustain physical life—to provide food, clothing, and shelter. But clearly *work* is central to our lives for other reasons as well. According to Freud, *work* provides us with a sense of reality; to Elton Mayo, *work* is a bind to community; to Marx, *its* function is primarily economic. Theologians are interested in *work's* moral dimensions; sociologists see *it* as a determinant of status, and some contemporary critics say that *it* is simply the best way of filling up a lot of time. To the ancient Greeks, who had slaves to do *it*, *work* was a curse. The Hebrews saw *work* as punishment. The early Christians found *work* for profit offensive, but by the time of St. Thomas Aquinas, *work* was being praised as a natural right and a duty—a source of grace along with learning and contemplation. During the Reformation, *work* became the only way of serving God. Luther pronounced that conscientious performance of one's *labor* was man's highest duty. Later interpretations of Calvinistic doctrine gave religious sanction to worldly wealth and *achievement*. This belief, when wedded to Social Darwinism and laissiz-faire liberalism, became the foundation for what we call the Protestant ethic. Marx, however, took the concept of *work* and put it in an even more central position in life: freed from capitalist exploitation, *work* would become a joy as workers improved the material environment around them.[1]

We have italicized all the words in this passage that refer directly to the controlling idea, here expressed as a question. Repetition gives this paragraph unity as the writer tries to offer some answers to an important question. Repeating key words and phrases relates the factual information to the controlling idea. These repeated words and phrases resemble the wires linking each cylinder in an automobile with the unifying source of power—the distributor.

If we use our analogy once again, the distributor on each engine has a definite firing order that determines the sequence or order in which combustion will occur. The engine will often run if the firing order is confused, but its operation will be neither very smooth nor very efficient. The same is true for paragraphs. The

---

[1] James O'Toole et al., *Work in America* (Cambridge, Mass.: M.I.T. Press, 1974), pp. 1–2. Italics ours.

information that develops and explains the topic sentence must be presented in a logical order for the paragraph to achieve the utmost in smoothness and clarity. To accomplish this, the writer must arrange individual sentences in such a way that the paragraph doesn't wander about, but flows smoothly from point to point. We will discuss techniques of order in some detail in the next unit of this book, but a few general hints are helpful here.

The order in which you present the information in a paragraph depends largely on simple common sense. There are, however, some common patterns on which many writers frequently rely. The order of chronology or time order is very useful in some types of writing, especially those that explain how something happened, how a thing works, or how something is done. When there is no time sequence pertinent to your subject, you might rely on the order of space. This ordering technique simply means moving from outside to inside as you describe an object or from top to bottom or from right to left. Related to the technique of spatial order are various methods of development that begin with something large and then gradually focus down to the smallest features (sometimes called moving from general to specific). The same order is sometimes reversed as a writer begins with the smallest details and moves gradually to the largest (sometimes called specific to general order). Finally, many writers follow a general rule that says one should leave the most important facts until the last position in the paragraph. In other words, arrange your facts in an increasing order of importance, giving the least important information early in the paragraph and the most important toward the end. The decision as to which information is most important depends, of course, on your controlling idea. Decisions regarding the order in which you present information involve three factors: (1) the nature of your subject, (2) common sense, and (3) the purpose for which you are writing the paragraph.

Transitions

Transitions are a means of achieving unity and order in a paragraph. The word *transition* means to carry something across or to make a bridge between one sentence and another. For our purposes, transitions are those devices that help each sentence in your paragraph fit smoothly into the whole. Transitions help the "flow" of your writing, so that one sentence seems to follow naturally from another. A transition supplies a bridge between sentences, enabling your reader to move smoothly from one idea or one detail to the next with a minimum of confusion. There are a variety of methods for accomplishing smooth transitions.

Numerical Transitions

The first type of transitional device is *numerical transition,* which simply means using numbers in your paragraph. Much of the writing in business and industry is characterized by the listing of procedures to be followed or steps in a process already completed. Job descriptions and laboratory reports are two examples of writing that many times includes a list of steps or procedures.

Numerical transition simply requires numbering the steps in a procedure as *first, second, third,* and so on. This transitional device works well in situations that demand listing the reasons for an opinion or the causes of a certain event or the effects of a certain course of action, and it is also helpful in writing that divides information into classes or categories. The example that follows relies on the technique of numerical transition to gain unity and illustrates how useful this technique can be to a writer.

These cases dramatize the sort of conditions workers must endure as a result of the LSB's [the Bureau of Labor Standards] casual enforcement process. [Each] of them involved major threats to worker safety. In one of them, the air workmen breathed in a marble plant contained such high concentrations of free silica that at least two men were coughing blood and another was required to curtail heavy physical labor due to lung ailments apparently caused by inhalation of dust over a long period of time. A second case concerned twenty-seven unsafe and unsanitary conditions in a small manufacturing establishment. Among them were unguarded machinery, ungrounded motors and tools, electrical wiring lying in water, exposed electrical contacts, excessive noise levels, unprotected elevator openings, and inadequate ventilation for the removal of flammable vapors. The third case involved twenty-nine serious violations. The worst two were sanitation and dust. The employee bathroom—which also served as a lunchroom and locker area—was described as slippery and filthy ("slimy water covered the floor"). The entire plant was covered with a measurable layer of dust, which was the result of a cotton-shredding operation. According to the industrial hygienist assigned to the case, airborne dust was so thick that it was impossible to see from one side of the plant to the other. "Frankly," he added, "I don't know why they didn't have a dust explosion before we got there." (Considering the seven-month delay between the first inspection and the initiation of legal action, it is also surprising they didn't have a dust explosion *after* the LSB inspectors got there.) The plant employed unskilled minimum-wage laborers, nearly all of whom were black. Management's attitude toward them was described as extremely callous. In the words of one LSB inspector assigned to the case, "They were getting the work for peanuts, so they treated the employees like animals."[2]

The simple device of numerical transition helps unify this paragraph. Every sentence in this paragraph is linked to the one before it, and every sentence clearly relates to the controlling idea. With this example as a basis, we can list some of the most common terms signaling numerical transition:

first, second, third, and so on
in addition
further
the first (second, third, . . .) step is
then
next
after this
one, two, three, and so on
finally

Transitional Words and Phrases

The English language has a large number of words that express relationships between sentences (of results, of contrast, of addition, of exception, and others) and, in clarifying the relationship between ideas, also manage a smooth transition between sentences. These words should be used with care, however, because the wrong word can create a great deal of confusion for your reader. Most of these *transitional words and phrases* are movable; that is, they can appear at the beginning of a sentence followed by a comma, or they can be inserted within the sentence and enclosed in commas. There follows a list of some commonly used transitional words and phrases, most of which you will readily

---

[2] Joseph A. Page and Mary-Win O'Brien, *Bitter Wages* (New York: Grossman Publishers, 1973), pp. 102–03.

recognize. Be sure, however, that you know the exact meaning carried by each word or phrase before using it in a sentence.

therefore	conversely
consequently	however
furthermore	on the contrary
on the other hand	in fact
of course	in other words
moreover	yet
similarly	and
likewise	but
by contrast	too
for instance	also
as a result	for example
nevertheless	

An important group of transitional phrases worth mentioning here is associated with the words *this, these,* and *those.* Many times sentences can be linked through the use of phrases like the following:

because of this
for this reason
in this way
on account of this
as a result of this
contrary to this
the effect of this

The various forms of *this, these,* and *those* perform a valuable transitional or linking function in a paragraph. These words by their very nature point backward to a preceding sentence and so build a bridge to the next stage in the paragraph's development. Writers rely a great deal on this group of words to create smooth transitions. Many of the techniques we have discussed are illustrated in the following paragraphs:

Although none of these studies is proof positive that noise alone caused the observed higher incidence of illness, it seems reasonable to conclude that noise and the concurrent stress contributed significantly. In addition, much of the controversy may be without value, because in fact one can almost always expect anxiety and physical stress in a noisy shop. And it is most important to remember that the object of industrial hygiene research should not be to supply absolute proofs, but to uncover *potential* dangers and see to it that they are eliminated. Absolute proof requires that workers become sick or die so that scientists can then determine what it was that injured or killed them.

Noise also interferes with communication between workers. This can create safety hazards when one worker cannot warn another of danger. In addition, not being able to speak to each other deprives workers of the normal personal relationships that all people need. It also limits their ability to discuss mutual work problems, and may even be considered a barrier to concerted activities, which are a right of all workers. Finally, since some speech communication is necessary even in noisy shops, many workers in noisy industries develop throat disorders and voice problems from having to shout to one another to be heard.[3]

Transition by Repetition

Still another effective method for making transitions is to link sentences by *repeating key words or phrases* from the previous sentence. Repeating a word or a phrase used in one sentence near the beginning of the next establishes a natural link between two ideas. Consider this series of sentences:

First, we know something more about PBB than the argument suggests. We know that it is harmful to animals. And if a substance is harmful to animals, it is likely to be harmful to us. That is, we ordinarily "presume" of a substance harmful to animals that it is harmful to us until proven otherwise. If someone were now to suggest that PBB be introduced into our food supply as, say, a food filler for hot dogs, we would assume a tasteless hoax. Why? Not because we know that PBB is harmful to animals. But because it is reasonable to suppose that what is bad for anything as biologically complex as a cow is likely to be bad for us. We are thus presumed at risk in eating PBB.[4]

The key word, *harmful,* is repeated throughout the passage and provides links between key ideas. This technique of repetition can be combined with other transitional devices; in fact, it is a good rule of thumb to look back at the preceding sentence before be-

---

[3] Jeanne M. Stellman and Susan M. Daum, *Work Is Dangerous to Your Health* (New York: Pantheon Books, 1973), p. 106.
[4] Wade Robinson, "Philosophy and Public Policy: A Look at PBB," *The Michigan Connection* (Spring, 1977), p. 7.

ginning a new one to see if any opportunity for effective repetition exists. If it does exist, you may be able to build a bridge between two ideas by using the device of repetition, as we have done at the beginning of this sentence. Introducing a new sentence with word groups beginning with *if, when, after, since, because, while,* and other subordinating conjunctions provides many opportunities for repeating a key word from the previous sentence in a subordinate clause or an introductory phrase ("beginners").

Closely related to the transitional device of repeating key words or phrases is *the use of pronouns* to refer to a thing or a person mentioned in a previous sentence. Pronouns replace nouns and, as a result, are effective linking devices between sentences. The most common pronouns are *he, his, him, she, her, they, them,* and *it.* The paragraph that follows makes extensive use of pronouns as linking devices.

> The phone company is especially interesting, then, because it fore-shadows, however dimly, coming events. Its customer service workers are oppressed and exploited, though in subtle ways compared with the old industrial system. They recognize this somewhat, but most apparently accept both the company's rules and the ideology which justifies them. This willingness to identify with the system is a peculiarly middle-class trait. Life makes working-class people cynical about their jobs. They have few illusions, but few are required of them. What they do does not commonly demand conviction. But where service is the chief product, as with the phone company, belief is required. So the phone company recruits lower-middle-class women who have the bourgeois need to identify with their employers, yet are not sufficiently educated or experienced to be critical of them. In the future more and more jobs will be like this, and, as the working class keeps declining, there will be more and more properly conditioned people to fill them.[5]

Development

In getting acquainted with the raw materials of writing, you need to know something about the various shapes a paragraph can assume. The next unit will present in detail specialized techniques for developing paragraphs, but there are three primary structural

[5] William L. O'Neill, ed., *Women at Work* (New York: The New York Times Book Co., 1975), pp. xiii–xiv.

devices for assembling a paragraph that can be adapted for use in many situations.

Detail

The first method of building a paragraph from the raw materials of sentences and words is through detail. *Detail* can be numerical facts, statistics, or a physical description of an object or person. Building a paragraph from detail simply means listing (cataloging) bits and pieces of information in some reasonable order.

Each of the paragraphs that follow uses facts to develop the topic sentence. In each case, the topic sentence with its controlling idea gives shape and meaning to the facts presented. The same facts, in each case, could be used to support a different topic sentence with only slight changes in wording. By themselves, facts are merely unstructured information; it is your job as writer to turn this raw information into an act of communication, shaping and forming the facts to give them relevance and meaning in terms of the whole paragraph.

The American people are wasting billions of dollars each year to feed and support their pet population. Americans throw away $2.5 billion per year to feed pets and another $165 million on pet food advertising, not to mention $100 million to exterminate unwanted pets. Another $100 million is squandered on such items for animals as clothes, jewelry, grooming, dentures, wristwatches, contact lenses, and perfume. Business has cashed in by offering toothpaste for animals and people crackers for dogs, while some butcher shops deal only in pet meats. And while affluent Americans buy "pet" boa constrictors, tigers, and elephants; transport them in special limousines; and bury them in expensive gravesites, one third of the world's population goes hungry. It is time the American people stop wasting money and food on needless pets and start to show some responsibility toward the world's hungry.

To this list of working problems are added observations I made as a worker and as a chief steward of the motor line at the Chrysler East Jefferson Plant in Detroit (1949–53). The roofs frequently leaked when it rained, soaking the workers on the assembly line below; overhead pipes sweated in the winter and rained down on the workers. In the summer the sun shone through the skylights causing vision problems. During lunchtime or on a break there was always difficulty finding a place to sit or to rest. In other departments, I remember that the air was frequently saturated with dust, a derivative of spraying or of metal buffing, which provoked more walkouts than the speed of the line.[6]

In each case, the writer has built the paragraph from factual detail that develops and supports a definite point. Although each paragraph resembles a simple listing of information, the writers transform the lists of facts into a meaningful act of communication (a paragraph) by means of a clear topic sentence with a definite controlling idea. Each writer has evaluated the facts and passed judgment on them. Paragraph development by detail does not require firm statements of opinion but does demand some unifying perspective, a controlling idea, that can transform a list of facts into a paragraph.

Reason

Naturally, every paragraph is based on reason; we employ the term *reason* here to describe a particular type of paragraph structure. This structural method closely resembles the techniques discussed in Unit II (under "Classification"), but it is suitable for a wide variety of purposes besides classification. A "reason" paragraph employs a structural method in which the writer adopts a definite stance and clearly states his or her reasons for believing or thinking as he or she does. This type of paragraph structure also is built from details (as all writing is), but the details are presented in a slightly different form. They are arranged into distinct categories that support the reasons the writer thinks or believes the way he or she does. In this structure, the topic sentence not only introduces the subject and the controlling idea but also supplies the "because," the reasons for adopting a particular point of view or for holding a certain opinion. This structural method is the basis of the following student paragraph:

I think comic books are a good investment because they are interesting to read, they have a certain amount of educational content, and they provide a good hobby. If you are between the ages of six and ninety-six, comic books have something for you. You can open the

---

[6] Al Nash, "Job Satisfaction: A Critique," in B. J. Widick, ed., *Auto Work and Its Discontents* (Baltimore: The Johns Hopkins University Press, 1976), pp. 78–79.

book to the first page and immediately feel as though you are a part of the adventure. One minute you can be aboard a spaceship headed for Mars, and the next you can become involved in a war between the planets. If you are more interested in a heroic episode, just pick up a Superman comic book and read about the good deeds he performs for mankind. If you would rather read about feats accomplished in the sea world, thumb through an Aquaman story, and you'll be amazed at his astounding adventures. Comic books also have an educational value. A small boy will be able to increase his vocabulary and improve his spelling by spending a few minutes a day reading about his favorite hero. A young woman who is just starting a career in writing can improve her creativity and imagination by reading a comic book while she is under a hair dryer in a beauty salon. Teen-agers can also improve their writing skills and maybe even better their grades in English classes by gazing at comic books when they have nothing else to do. If you don't have a hobby, start a comic book collection. The next time you happen to be in a drugstore look over the different kinds of comics, and choose one according to your interests. You can collect them and keep up with each story from month to month. A comic book collection always makes a good conversation piece. You'd be amazed at how many people collect them! If these aren't good enough reasons to start this entertaining hobby, then just think about it this way: you can collect comic books and be the only person in your city with an authentic, twenty-year-old comic book. You may become a millionaire!

This very simple yet extremely effective structural technique can be relied on in a great variety of writing situations. It begins by stating what the writer thinks or believes and supplies the principal reasons why he or she takes that particular position. Each reason is then developed individually in the body of the paragraph, supported and clarified through details and examples. This structure can be diagrammed to highlight its orderly pattern, as in Figure 1.

A reason paragraph lends itself well to the unifying devices of repetition and numerical transition. To manage this structure effectively, you need to develop the ability to sort your information and details into groups or classes that share common features.

Example

An effective structural technique for building paragraphs centers on a single example—or, in some cases, two or three examples

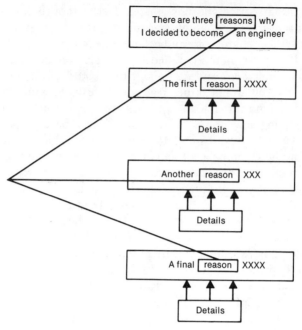

FIGURE 1.

—to illustrate and support a general point. This structure imitates a habit of speech we all share. In the midst of a discussion, it is common to hear someone say, "Let me give you an example" and then go on to describe a specific circumstance that clarifies the point. Presenting a specific example in some detail helps explain a complex idea to the listener or to the reader. It is important to remember, however, that an example will be an effective explanatory device only if the reader can see clearly how it relates to the topic sentence.

Developing an idea through example demands care on the part of the writer. You must always assume that your reader will not necessarily see your example in the same way you do (a point commonly known to policemen, who find that witnesses to the same accident give directly conflicting accounts of what they saw). You must provide the proper angle of vision. To do this, arrange your paragraph in a way that guarantees that the reader will see your point. In describing the example, select only the most directly relevant features; focus on those details that most directly illustrate and support your point.

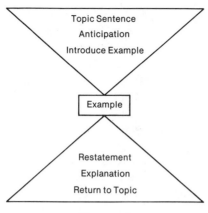

FIGURE 2.

This type of paragraph structure can also be diagrammed (see Figure 2). The diagram shows a step-by-step process leading your reader to see what you want him or her to see. A writer may not include all the steps shown in our diagram; but if he or she doesn't, there is usually a good reason for omitting any one of the steps. The major steps in constructing an example paragraph are, first, to state your generalization (topic sentence). Second, tell the reader that you are going to present a specific example demonstrating the truth of that generalization and tell him or her precisely what you expect him or her to see in the example. Then present the example, arranged and described in a manner that highlights the features relevant to your main point. After describing the example, tell the reader clearly the main point of the example. You might even repeat some of the example's key words in your explanation. Finally, relate the main point of the example to your generalization. Figure 2 resembles an hourglass as you focus the reader's attention on the example and then broaden the perspective once again to return to your topic sentence.

This writer's strategy follows the diagram in Figure 2; here the introduction to the example and the conclusion are set off in separate paragraphs. This technique highlights the example:

One way you can combat the prejudice against the housewife is by writing your résumé as if this prejudice doesn't exist. You have control of what goes on those résumé pages. Your ability—what you have done and can do—is what is important.

Suppose, for example, that you've been an active member of League of Women Voters for the past twenty years. That has been unpaid work, sometimes forty hours a week of it. The League has provided women with continuing educations and practical experience for more than half a century. Suppose you were in a League government workshop that had studied the pros and cons of a city-manager form of government for your town. Then suppose you later became the workshop chairperson and finally the chapter president or vice-president. You have had management experience, and don't let anybody tell you that you haven't. You have paced the floor worrying about real—not make-believe—problems. You have accomplished a lot on a limited budget. You have juggled and set priorities, and you have chaired countless board meetings while babies crawled under the table.

In short, you have worked under circumstances as trying as those faced by the corporation president. Put your experience up front on your résumé, not down in the extracurricular activities with your hobbies.[7]

The example paragraph is only as effective as the frame you build around the example. An apt analogy is the process of "cropping" a photograph. All the extraneous details of the photograph are cut away to focus attention on the most important features. By using a similar framing technique to focus your reader's attention, you are able to support and explain a general statement with one specific example. Writers faced with the task of explaining tables or graphs find this paragraph structure essential to a clear explanation of the significance of their facts. The table or graph is framed in the same way we have framed an example:

Information on acceptance of "voluntary" risk by individuals as a function of income benefits is not easily available, although we know that such a relationship must exist. Of particular interest, therefore, is the special case of miners exposed to high occupational risks. In Fig. 1, the accident rate and the severity rate of mining injuries are plotted against the hourly wage (2, 3). The acceptance of individual risk is an exponential function of the wage, and can be roughly approximated by a third-power relationship in this range. If this relationship has validity, it may mean that several "quality of life" parameters (perhaps health, living essentials, and recreation) are each partly influenced by

[7] Karin Abarbanel and Connie McClung Siegel, *Woman's Work Book* (New York: Information House Books, Inc., 1975), p. 139.

any increase in available personal resources, and that thus the increased acceptance of risk is exponentially motivated. The extent to which this relationship is "voluntary" for the miners is not obvious, but the subject is interesting nevertheless.[8]

EXERCISES

1. Write five topic sentences on subjects related to your field of study. Underline the controlling idea in each. Make a list of details that develop each controlling idea.

2. Supply appropriate transitions between the sentences in the following paragraph:

> I am going to trade in my car this weekend. My girl does not like its color. She says that an orange and blue finish just does not go with her hair. The top is in bad condition. A bad hailstorm left the convertible top in shreds. I need a new tail pipe. The old one fell off and nearly caused a ten-car pileup. I guess the thing that convinced me that old Bertha was ready for the junkyard was the transmission. I can't shift from second to third any more. I have to go chugging along the highway at 45 in second gear.

3. Assemble the following information into a paragraph. Leave out irrelevant details. Add details if you wish.

   a. The city worker has moved to the suburbs.
   b. Americans have some $95 billion invested in 100 million passenger cars.
   c. The car has become a commuter conveyance.
   d. The average car costs 14 cents per mile to operate.
   e. The automobile business accounts for 13 per cent of the GNP.
   f. As much as two thirds of the land in urban areas is devoted to freeways, parking, gas stations, and auto-related uses.
   g. The automobile business accounts for one out of six jobs.
   h. The automobile may cost more than 50,000 lives each year in road accidents.
   i. The car provides privacy and prevents the annoyances caused by others.
   j. In 1973, 12 million vehicles were produced by the auto industry.
   k. The automobile has changed the shape of our cities.

[8] Chauncey Starr, "Social Benefit Versus Technological Risk," *Science,* **165** (September 19, 1969), p. 1235.

U N I T II

The Tools of the Trade

DESCRIPTION

THE techniques of descriptive writing are already quite familiar to you; you have been using description since you first began to distinguish between big and little and learned how to distinguish one color from another. Any attempt to tell someone else about something you have seen or experienced uses description. Description adds interest and color to conversation—all of us enjoy listening to someone who can tell a story or describe an experience in a way that helps us see the characters or feel that we are sharing the experience. Clear, accurate description often provides information that can entertain as well as provide a basis for making decisions.

For many of us the decision whether or not to spend money to see a particular movie can be a fairly serious one, particularly if the week's budget is running low. Some people read movie reviews, but the opinion of a friend who has already seen the film often helps make the decision. Consider the following conversation:

"It was great."
"It was?"
"Yes, it really was. You should see it."

(This judgment may be enough, but some of us might demand a little more information.)

"What was great about it?"
"Oh, I don't know. The whole thing. The way it was done."
"What do you mean?"
"The acting was fantastic. A great cast."
"Who was in it?"
"I don't really remember the names. But the story was terrific. You should go see it."

Such enthusiasm from a good friend who generally has good taste would probably assure us our money will be well spent. But if you look carefully at the conversation, you can see that we learn nothing about the movie itself; what we get is an expression of our friend's feelings. This is valuable information, of course, but our friend's reaction does not provide us with any real facts about the movie. Basing a decision on this type of information is very chancy. What do we need? A little more detail would help:

> "Well, it was about a child possessed by a devil and all the tragedy this caused his family. One scene shows the father being thrown out of a window and splattering his brains all over a car. The mother hangs herself. Lots of really gory scenes. The kid was a good actor; you really think he is a devil or something."

You may still go to see the movie, but at least you'll know what to expect and will avoid taking your six-year-old sister with you. The difference between these two passages illustrates an important characteristic of description: descriptive writing relies on facts and details.

Many people immediately associate descriptive writing with flowery passages of purple prose or poetry. Poets and fiction writers do use description, and some of the finest writing in our language occurs in descriptions of fictional characters or fictional events. But the descriptive passages in a poem or novel—as beautiful and powerful as they often are—have little practical value in a world of real events and real decisions. Imagine, for example, a police officer providing the following description to fellow police officers so that they can apprehend a car thief or mugger:

> Pacing back and forth the length of the hatchway, and savagely chewing the end of a cigar, was the man whose casual glance had rescued me from the sea. His height was probably five feet ten inches, or ten and a half; but my first impression, or feel of the man, was not of this, but of his strength. And yet, while he was of massive build, with broad shoulders and deep chest, I could not characterize his strength as massive. It was what might be termed a sinewy, knotty strength, of the kind we ascribe to lean and wiry men, but which, in him, because of his heavy build, partook more of the enlarged gorilla order. Not that in appearance he seemed in the least gorilla-like. What I am striving to express is this strength itself, more as a thing apart from his physical semblance. It was a strength we are wont to associate with things primitive, with wild animals, and the creatures we imagine our tree-dwelling prototypes to have been—a strength savage, ferocious, alive in itself, the essence of life in that it is the potency of motion, the elemental stuff itself out of which the many forms of life have been molded; in short, that which writhes in the body of a snake

when the head is cut off, and the snake, as a snake, is dead, or which lingers in a shapeless lump of turtle-meat and recoils and quivers from the prod of a finger.[1]

It would be nice if all of us could write like Jack London. But even Jack London would not make this description part of a police report. A novelist or poet writes to stimulate a reader's emotions and imagination, whereas descriptive writing appropriate to most professions engages the reader's understanding and reason.

Nevertheless, creative writing can teach us a great deal about writing principles fundamental to all types of writing in a variety of situations for a variety of audiences. Much of our knowledge about the world around us comes through our five senses; and descriptive writing—in both real and fictional worlds—helps our readers understand by telling them how an object looks, smells, sounds, tastes, and feels.

The ability to write clear, accurate descriptions is an important professional skill. People in every profession write or read daily some form of description. Describing a piece of equipment, telling someone how to operate a device or repair it, or issuing a simple order depend on the techniques of description. In many jobs, communication skills go hand in hand with professional skills. A policeman must write an accurate description of an arrest or accident to ensure that justice is done. A materials handling specialist once remarked that his entire livelihood depended on the ability to describe the appearance, function, and quality of his products to a potential customer. Clear descriptions of problem areas, jobs to be done, operating procedures, and new equipment become more important and more frequent with increasing professional responsibility.

This section discusses the components of clear, accurate description. Of all the communication strategies, description is perhaps the most important because descriptive writing deals most directly with facts. Well-written descriptions share the following characteristics:

1. The writer has a definite purpose in mind. When you write, you must know why you are describing the object and who is likely to read the description.

---

[1] Jack London, *The Sea Wolf* (New York: Airmont Publishing Co., 1965), p. 19.

2. Details and facts must be relevant to the purpose of the description.
3. The description has a controlling sentence that identifies the object and specifies its unique quality or qualities.
4. The description "pictures" the object by appealing to the reader's senses.
5. The words chosen to describe the object have clear meanings. The reader should feel you have used a camera instead of a pen.
6. The details of the description must be presented in a logical sequence.

Purpose

Writing without knowing the reason why you are writing resembles weeding a garden without knowing the difference between flowers and weeds. For example, imagine the difference between a report describing O. J. Simpson written by a professional football scout and one written by a Hollywood talent scout. Both descriptions would concern the same man, but the facts included in each would differ considerably. The football scout would take little notice of Simpson's good looks or effective speaking style—these qualities don't help a running back break tackles—whereas the talent scout would emphasize these qualities, omitting any mention of Simpson's speed in the 100-yard dash or his pass-catching ability. In the same way, a description designed to sell someone a product—an automobile, for example—will differ markedly from the service specifications written for the mechanic who is expected to repair the same automobile. Before writing the first word, you must know *why* you are writing the description.

In 1897, H. G. Wells published *War of the Worlds*, a description of a Martian invasion of the earth. One passage in the novel describes an incredibly powerful weapon possessed by the Martians. Wells's purpose was to describe the most terrifying weapon he could. Amazingly, his description of this weapon anticipates the invention of the laser in 1960. Some of Wells's details are extremely accurate:

The invasion was backed by an immensely powerful weapon—a mysterious sword of heat. This intense heat they project in a parallel beam against any object they choose by means of a polished parabolic mirror of unknown composition, much as the parabolic mirror of a lighthouse projects a beam of light. . . . Whatever is combustible flashes into flame at its touch, lead runs like water, it softens iron, cracks and melts glass and when it falls upon water, incontinently that explodes into steam.

All good descriptive writing must have the qualities of clarity and accuracy. But a writer strives for clarity and accuracy to accomplish a purpose. When one realizes how much it is possible to say about any given subject, the question arises why the writer chose to present some details and not others. The first example describes an industrial cleaning agent, muriatic acid. The description could appear in a chemical company's brochure announcing the availability of the product for industrial use. The brochure does not have a picture of the product, so the description must show the product to the reader.

Muriatic acid is a highly corrosive solution which in higher concentrations exhibits the sharp, pungent odor of hydrogen chloride and strongly fumes in moist air. The pure solution is colorless, but traces of iron, chlorine, or organic matter impart a yellowish color.

Concentrated muriatic acid is one of the strongest acids known. It readily attacks all of the common metals to yield hydrogen, which in certain concentrations in air may be highly explosive. Concentrated solutions are capable of causing severe flesh burns, and its vapors are irritating to the skin, eyes, and mucous membranes.

Notice how the writer appeals to our basic senses: seeing, smelling, touching, and, indirectly, hearing. Muriatic acid has a "pungent" smell, and assuming we know a little about chemistry (as most of the brochure's audience probably does), the writer helps us by mentioning the smell of hydrogen chloride (like rotten eggs). After appealing to our sense of smell, this writer engages our sense of sight by mentioning the yellowish color of muriatic acid, and emphasizing the strongly irritating effects of this acid on the skin, eyes, and nose stimulates our sense of touch. Even here, in a technical brochure, the writer's tools are those of creative and technical writer alike. A good description, whether of a sunset or of muriatic acid, appeals to the senses of the reader.

A clearly defined purpose determines the details and key words in the description. There are many things, for example, the description of muriatic acid *does not* tell us about the product. Muriatic acid has been in use for nearly four hundred years under different names and in a variety of forms, but these historic details, however interesting, are not included because they do not suit the purpose of the description. In addition, the precautions necessary for safely handling and transporting muriatic acid are not mentioned. From a different source a reference to muriatic acid emphasizes different details because the writer's purpose is different:

> A solution of muriatic acid will often do the job. Its cleansing action is actually one of dissolving a thin section of the front of stone or brick so as to present a clean face. To use, first mix one part muriatic acid to ten parts water in a plastic or glass container. Precautionary note: always add the acid to the water—never add the water to the acid. If you don't understand the reason for this it means you are not experienced in handling acids and it is best to forget this method.[2]

The homeowner looking for an effective way to clean a fireplace needs different information about muriatic acid.

What, then, is the controlling purpose that determines the choice of certain details and not others? Effective descriptions begin by clearly identifying the most important quality of the object: "Muriatic acid is a highly corrosive solution . . . ." Throughout the description the writer chooses key words to emphasize this corrosive quality of the acid, keeping the major point of the description constantly in the reader's mind: "sharp," "attacks," "explosive," "irritating." The purpose of this description is to show clearly and emphatically the main physical properties of the acid. The selection of words supports and identifies the corrosive properties of this product, which is a cleaning agent for boilers, heat exchangers, and other industrial equipment.

The example illustrates one principle of good descriptive writing —know your purpose. With a definite purpose in mind, you can choose from among all the facts you know about an object those details most directly related to that purpose. It is your job as writer to separate the important details from the trivial or irrelevant—no matter how interesting some of the information you

---

[2] Warren Donnelly, "Cleaning the Chimney," *Wood Burning Quarterly*, 1 (Summer 1976), p. 24.

leave out might be. Seldom will a reader have any patience with writing that does not immediately and concisely present the object. How would a busy executive react to this rewritten version of the muriatic acid description?

> Muriatic acid is a very dangerous chemical. Its name comes from a Latin word that means "pickled." Muriatic acid also has a strong smell. It looks slightly yellow and sometimes foams. You have to wear special protective clothing when you handle muriatic acid because it can cause injury. Sometimes it can also explode. The ingredients of muriatic acid are hydrogen and chlorine.

The description that follows appears in an unpublished technical article describing a device developed for the Alaska pipeline project. A controversy over the potentially damaging effects of hot oil on Alaska's delicate permafrost surrounded the construction of the pipeline. In reading the passage, see if you can recognize how the writer's purpose to convince the reader that the "heat sink" device will protect Alaska's ecology influences the selection of details and choice of words.

> Heat sinks are constructed of high density polyethylene. They are of double-walled construction, "C" shaped in cross section, and 8 feet long. The units are installed in pairs around the circumference of the pipe outside the insulation, forming a circular tank. Figure 2 shows a typical heat sink unit. Units are internally supported by a core structure that maintains their concentricity and symmetry, whether the contained fluid is in a frozen or thawed state. The core structure results in a double unit which will help the pipe to withstand any shocks and stresses it might be subjected to. If a unit is damaged it is easily replaced or repaired. Only a small amount of fluid mixture is lost, pipeline operation is not interrupted, and no ecological damage occurs.

This description leaves a dominant impression of strength and solidity. The solid construction of the heat sink protects the permafrost from ecological damage. This is the device's most significant characteristic. The opening sentence focuses our attention on the "high density" material from which heat sinks are constructed. We are given a clear picture of the heat sink's physical shape and are shown its solidity through terms such as "double-walled construction," "internally supported," "double unit," and "withstand shocks and stresses."

Like many technical descriptions, this one is accompanied by a diagram (referred to as Figure 2). But the reader's image of the heat sink does not depend on the diagram alone. The writer selects details that emphasize the significant qualities of the device (strength and solidity). Referring to the diagram after the description of physical appearance compels the reader to notice the details of the diagram most relevant to the writer's purpose. In organizing this description, the writer first shows us the external features of the heat sink, then moves to details of internal construction, and finally specifies the function of this construction. The writer has organized the description to leave one piece of information in the reader's mind. This is not the polyethylene material from which the device is made, but that "no ecological damage occurs" if a unit of pipe is damaged.

Organization

A description with a clearly defined purpose and relevant details may still fail as effective communication if the details lack arrangement and order. Whatever the purpose of a description, the details must be shaped into a logical, natural form before the reader can perceive the object clearly. The writer resembles a carpenter who has cut all the pieces of wood needed to build a chair. The individual pieces may be perfectly formed from the best wood available, but they must be assembled in a precise order before the chair can fulfill its purpose or, for that matter, even look like a chair. A writer is much like a skilled carpenter, "gluing and nailing" into shape the materials of observation and thought.

Effective organization of a description is usually a matter of common sense. In general, though, an effective organizational pattern for a description will include the following information in this order:

1. Identification of the object. The reader must know what the object is and, in many cases, what it does or what its purpose is.

    The 4010 Computer Display Terminal is a communication link and display device for use with a wide range of computer systems.

2. Dimensions. Especially in cases where pictures or diagrams are not available, the reader should know the size and shape

of the object as well as the materials from which it is constructed.

The units consist of a stainless steel belt of fine mesh passing through and over five-foot-long steam chambers that surround the material with hot steam.

3. Component parts. The movement from whole to parts is a common organizational device in description. Following a picture of size, shape, and construction comes a description of component parts. This technique resembles a movie camera zooming in on a scene. A description of component parts relies on the general organization of the object itself; or, put another way, you describe the parts in the order in which you would remove them to disassemble the device.

In an exploded view, with the conical cap at the left, the pen has five parts: from the right end, one, the top of the casing; two, the metal band or sleeve; three, the ink container or refill; four, the spring; and five, the bottom of the casing.

4. Function. After telling the reader what the object is and what it looks like as a whole and in its parts, you can then describe the operating principles of the object. Some mention of the object's function might appear earlier, but a detailed description of function is best given after you are sure the reader has a clear picture of the object's physical appearance and construction.

An extruder cylinder in plastic fabrication contains the plastics as they are being heated, pressurized, homogenized, and plasticated prior to extruding.

When describing an object, the writer is more often concerned with what the object looks like and how it is constructed than with how it operates or functions. Many examples of this are found in service manuals. Of course, this is mainly a matter of emphasis because it would be awkward not to mention at least the general principles of operation of a device or of its parts while describing them. Some notion of how a device works often helps the reader visualize it more clearly. In fact, one effective organization for a description mirrors the function of the object. The organizing principle is supplied by the structure of the object itself. The following description of a common household tool, a wood bit, illustrates the characteristics of this kind of organization.

Drills for wood or metal differ slightly in shape, but their mode of action is almost identical, whether operated by hand or electrically powered. The wood drill (or bit) has a screwlike part at its center, which drives into the wood and pulls the cutting edges after it. The cutting section approaches the wood with two sharply pointed knife edges that spear straight down into the wood and cut through the fibers in the cross grains so that they won't splinter. The cutting edges proper, two knives that turn and slant down into the wood, clean out all the wood between the spearing blades and carry it up along the twisted path on the body of the drill.

This description demonstrates an important principle—a description must have a logical order. Most descriptions of objects rely on the *order of space*. In other words, when describing an object that is sitting still, you can give the clearest picture of that object by following its physical shape. The decision where to begin depends a great deal on the function of the object and your purpose in describing it. In describing a stereo console to a prospective buyer, a salesman would probably begin with the outside appearance of the stereo (its shape, its size, the quality of the cabinet), then move inside to describe some of the components that make this a high-quality stereo. On the other hand, a description of the same product in a service manual would probably begin with the internal components of the stereo and only incidentally mention the external appearance, perhaps to indicate access points or to locate controls.

The major decision the writer must make when describing an object is where to begin. In some cases this decision is quite simple. If the object is linear (a screwdriver, for example), the choice is simply whether to begin at one end or the other. Most of the time, however, an object will have three dimensions, so the decision regarding what to mention first becomes a little more complicated. A description can move from one side of an object to the other or from bottom to top or from top to bottom; the movement can be from outside to inside or vice versa. The most important guideline in making this choice is to follow a consistent pattern: Don't start at one point and then suddenly jump to another. The shape and function of the object as well as your purpose in writing the description will be determining factors in choosing a method of organization.

The description of the wood bit begins with the screwlike part of the drill that first touches the wood, then moves outward to the cutting edges and upward along the twisted path characteristic of drills. Here the description follows very closely the actual function of the drill. Think how confusing this description would be if it began at the other end, describing the squared-off section of the bit that is clasped by the brace or drill and then moving down along the twisted track. The description of an object's shape should relate directly to its function.

Techniques for ordering descriptive details are not limited to spatial arrangement, although this is the most common and most useful strategy. Sometimes an effective description seems to have no definite system for ordering details, yet makes perfect sense. Countless examples of descriptive writing seem to be little more than lists or catalogs of information set down in no particular order whatsoever. This haphazardness is only an appearance, however. All effective descriptive writing has some principle of order. Can you discover a principle of order in the following passage?

The famous 99-cubic-inch Perkins Four 99, developing 43 brake horsepower at 4,000 revolutions per minute, is available for vehicle, agricultural, marine, and industrial applications. Believed to be the smallest water-cooled diesel engine in production, it weighs only 361 pounds with starting equipment and is extremely compact. The distributor-type fuel pump can be fitted with either a mechanical or hydraulic governor. The Four 99 has wet liners, a three-bearing crankshaft and gear-driven auxiliaries. All bearings are of the prefinished, steel-backed copper lead type. The Four 99 combustion system has been designed specifically for small diesel engines.

This description quickly sketches the distinguishing characteristics of the diesel engine. The writing is as efficient as the engine it describes, presenting many details in very few words. The writer's purpose is to communicate the smallness and compactness of this engine, qualities that make it suitable for specific uses; but the passage must be examined very carefully to detect the ordering technique at work. The movement in this passage is from general (the horsepower, the weight, the uses of the engine) to specific (the fuel pump, the bearings, the combustion system). In other words, the writer first surveys the most general characteristics, then moves in with a microscope, as it were, to emphasize specific features and parts that best exemplify the compactness and efficiency of the engine. The whole is divided into its parts. In the final sentence, this writer once again reminds the reader of the unique quality of the engine ("the small diesel engine"). The passage is typical of descriptions that catalog or list the component parts of an object.

In an earlier chapter we introduced you to the use of transitions in writing effective paragraphs. Transitions are extremely important in writing clear descriptions. Take advantage of the opportunities for transition supplied by the structure of the object itself. The description that follows of another diesel engine modifies the "whole to part" organizational pattern. In this case, the writer begins with the parts (the internal components of the engine) and then logically moves to a description of the whole. Here the purpose influences organization. Those reading this description already know a great deal about diesel engines, and the writer's purpose is to stress the quality of this particular engine's internal construction:

> The crankshaft for the new engines is fully counterweighted and is statically and dynamically balanced. It has seven main bearings with 3¾ in. connecting rod journals. Connecting rods are precision balanced with an "I" section and are rifle-drilled. The piston pin is of the full-floating type and is held in place by a snap retainer. The pistons are heavy-duty, lightweight, aluminum alloy, cam-ground to insure perfect fit in the cylinder at operating temperatures. Each is fitted with five rings, three compression and two oil. The chrome faced top ring fits in a groove protected from wear by an iron insert cast into the piston. The pistons travel in alloy iron cylinder liners of the wet type built with "O" rings seals at the bottom. The cylinder block, produced from high tensile alloy iron, is internally ribbed so that the stress is carried on the inside of the block through a column of iron.

This description uses logical, spatial organization. An inside-to-outside movement unifies the description by following the structure of the engine. Beginning with the crankshaft, the movement is then to the connecting rods attached to the crankshaft, then up the rod to the pin attaching the piston to the rod. After the pistons are described, the writer moves to the rings that encircle the piston, then to the cylinders in which the pistons travel. Finally, the cylinder block is described by details emphasizing its strength. The transitions from one part to the next are smooth, following the structure of the engine itself. When this engine is operating, it is impossible to decide what happens first, for the engine's components all, in effect, function simultaneously. The writer has "frozen" the engine, then organized the description in accord with the operating principles of the engine. What we get, really, is an "exploded" view of the engine, showing each part in some detail. After we read this description, we could draw a fairly accurate picture of the engine's structure—one of the best tests of a good description.

One technique used in the preceding helps the reader picture the shape of an object. The writer uses the shapes of letters ("I" and "O") to illustrate the shape of certain components. The shapes of other letters can also help the reader see. We have all heard of an A-frame house, an S curve, and a U-turn. Anything that can help the reader visualize the object or its parts adds to the clarity and accuracy of a description.

When a picture or a diagram is not available to the reader, comparing an object or device to something familiar can clarify its appearance or highlight its distinctive characteristics. Even a picture may not accurately indicate size, so comparing an unfamiliar object with one more familiar can be extremely helpful to your reader in forming a mental picture of the object.

> A television picture tube looks like a large glass funnel.
> That table lamp looks like a fat man wearing a hat.
> A carburetor resembles a paper cylinder pinched in the middle.

Although it is becoming popular in some parts of the country, the game of jai alai is relatively unknown to most Americans. One writer describing this sport makes effective use of comparisons to give us a picture of jai alai:

> Jai alai is played on an immense court 176 feet long, 50 feet wide and 39 feet high, about five times the area of a tennis court. It has only one side wall; spectators sit along the open side to view the action. In his right arm, the player wears the cesta, a curved basket three feet long, which he wields like a scimitar. The ball, a little smaller than a baseball, but harder and heavier, is made of tightly wound rubber covered with goatskin. Between the cesta and the ball there exists a sinister relationship—like that between a rifle and a bullet. Jai alai's numero uno, known as Churruca (jai alai players often use only one

name), can whip the ball out of the basket at speeds in excess of 150 miles per hour. Tom Seaver's fast ball travels at about 90 miles per hour and Jimmy Connors' first serve at about 100. The high walls only seem to enhance the sense of speed. A floor-to-ceiling net protects the spectators from the action—and, on occasion, the players from spectators.[3]

You may never be called on to write about a subject like jai alai, but the principles used by this writer can be of use in a writing task you will certainly have to perform at some point. Soon you will be writing letters of application in search of a job, and in these letters you will find it necessary to describe effectively your own qualifications and experience. The section in this book on persuasion, as well as the letters of application discussed in Unit IV, will be of great help in this regard, but good description can help a potential employer see you as the best candidate for the job. In the example that follows, we have isolated the descriptive portion of a letter of application to illustrate how the techniques we have discussed apply to this important first step in your career.

I will receive my BBA in marketing from Adelphi University in June. Most of my education was financed by a part-time job, but, despite this drain on my time and energy, I will graduate in the upper third of my class. My course work at Adelphi has given me a wide theoretical background in salesmanship, retailing, and advertising. I also worked extensively with computers while in college.

To finance my education, I worked as a salesman for the J. P. Thompson Department Store in Garden City, New York. Most of my sales experience was in the clothing department of that store. Selling on a salary and commission, I earned enough money to finance 80 per cent of my college education. During the past year I have been responsible for buying stock for the clothing department. I have learned a great deal about fashion trends and have grown in my ability to handle responsibility. My experience has taught me that there is much more to selling than knowing the cut of a piece of clothing, having a good sense of color coordination, and being able to fill out a sales slip. I learned how to appeal to the customer and how to make the customer feel happy with a purchase. I feel this experience will make me a valuable member of the sales staff at Warston's Clothing Store.

---

[3] Hubert Saul, "The Basques of Bridgeport," *New York Times Magazine* (September 19, 1976), p. 43.

The formal letter of application, of course, has more to it than a description of education and experience. But the basic techniques of description used here give the potential employer a clear picture of this applicant's unique qualities. The description moves from the general to the particular, from the whole to the parts.

One strategy of effective description—especially when it also has a persuasive purpose—orders the details to leave a definite, single impression in the reader's mind. The organization moves from the least important details to the most important. In writing this letter of application, the writer knew that many other applicants would have education and experience equal or superior to his; so he reserved the details that describe the strongest qualification for a sales position—the ability to please and serve customers —until the last position in the description. If this information were buried in the middle of the passage, the prospective employer could easily skim over it and certainly would not be as likely to remember it.

Conclusion

In this section we have offered some suggestions on clear, accurate, and effective description. Most of those suggestions are based on common sense, and there certainly are good writers who use techniques that we have not even mentioned. But these are the basic tools, tried and proved effective over a long period of time by writers working in a variety of fields. You will find that the manner in which you communicate with employees, employers, colleagues, and people in other fields will have as much to do with your success at your job as the skills required to perform that job.

Clear, accurate description is vital to precise communication in all professions. A congressman's speech describing the potential benefits of a piece of legislation could improve the lives of millions; a paramedic's report of a patient's symptoms may well help save a life. The effects of both accurate and inaccurate descriptions can be dramatic. Some years ago Orson Welles made a radio broadcast describing an invasion from Mars. The account was fictitious, of course, but the description was so effective that the broadcast caused widespread panic among thousands of people who believed it. The "Invasion from Mars" description produced no lasting effects, but a more recent example of inaccurate and misleading description resulted in a major catastrophe. On June

5, 1976, the Teton Dam in Idaho collapsed: "Rushing like a 10-foot tidal wave, it took the lives of 11 people, ripped topsoil from 100,000 acres of fertile farm land, drowned 13,000 head of cattle and destroyed thousands of homes. In all, it caused a billion dollars' worth of damage."[4]

Congress's authorization to build the dam was based in large part on a document describing the proposed project supplied by the U.S. Bureau of Reclamation, a document that one reporter claims contained misleading and inaccurate descriptions of the circumstances involved.

> Finally, in addition to the Congress and the executive agency involved, one must fault a legal system that permits substantive evidence to remain unheard. The bureau claimed irrigation benefits for lands, much of which did not need water; it claimed flood-control benefits the dam could not provide; it claimed benefits for creating a recreation area while it was destroying one; it used an interest rate to justify the cost of its project which bore no relation to the actual cost of borrowing money.[5]

But neither case necessarily represents "bad" writing or "bad" speaking, does it? In fact, Orson Welles's broadcast is full of magnificent descriptions; and if the Bureau of Reclamation's proposal had been poorly written, the project might never have been funded. The issue here is the manner in which the tools of writing, particularly of description, are used.

EXERCISES

1. Imagine that you are a visitor from outer space. Write to the officials of your home planet, describing what you have seen. For example, you might perceive the automobiles as constituting the "earthling" population.

2. Write a selection for a children's book, describing a piece of equipment familiar to you.

3. Rewrite the description from Sea Wolf as if it were a description of the man who just stole your car.

---

[4] Dorothy Gallagher, "The Collapse of the Great Teton Dam," *The New York Times Magazine* (September 19, 1976), p. 16.
[5] Ibid., p. 108.

4. Become another H. G. Wells and describe a device likely to become a reality in the future.

5. Write a description of your background, experience, and other relevant qualifications that could be part of a letter of application for the type of job you would really like.

CLASSIFICATION

CLASSIFICATION helps us find order in the world. Human beings spend a great deal of time classifying persons, places, and events. We separate people into classes. A relatively small class consists of those we can call our friends, a much larger class contains our acquaintances, another group—small, one hopes—is made up of those we dislike, and there is a huge, faceless class of people we don't know. Classification means to put people, places, and events into classes or categories. Usually, we group things together because they have something in common. We often classify things unconsciously, as a matter of habit, to make life a little more orderly. Even simple acts like getting dressed in the morning are simplified by the human habit of classification. One trunk or one drawer seldom holds an entire wardrobe stuffed in at random. Rather, one drawer holds underwear, another might contain socks, and another is reserved for sweaters or shirts. People may even arrange their clothes according to the season: summer clothes, fall clothes, winter clothes, and spring clothes. Without some kind of organization (at least a clean pile and a dirty pile), getting dressed in the morning could be a time-consuming and frustrating effort.

A familiar example of how useful classification can be is the library. Without a system of classification, all the books in a library would be useless to us because we could never find one book among thousands randomly scattered on the shelves. Libraries classify books according to their subject matter: history, education, mathematics, business, and so on. Each large category is itself divided into smaller classes: histories of the United States, histories of Japan, histories of Russia. As a result, the great store of information in a library becomes readily available to us after a glance into the card catalogue. Classification offers us a systematic, orderly way of communicating information.

Classification demands a system of some kind. The choice of system depends on your purpose for writing and the type of information you are trying to organize. Consider the following list of foods:

soybeans	milk	lettuce
lentils	beer	tomatoes
yogurt	wine	spinach
rice	soda pop	ham
hamburger	corned beef	roast beef
potatoes	squash	bread
salami	cornflakes	onions
bologna	apple pie	cucumbers
spaghetti	ice cream	pork chops
pizza	fried chicken	oatmeal
eggs	broccoli	

Classification can impose a meaningful order on apparently disordered information. For example, these various foods could be broken into two categories: one consisting of foods you like, the other, of foods you don't like. This would show something about you, namely, your taste in food. A nutritionist looking at the same list might sort the foods into the four basic food groups: meats, dairy products, cereals, and vegetables. Someone concerned about being overweight might classify the foods according to their caloric content or as sources of carbohydrates and sources of proteins. Various other categories come to mind: food to eat while watching TV, foods for main courses, desserts, foods for making sandwiches, and meat substitutes.

Classification arranges ideas or things according to some principle of similarity. It is a method of putting facts into a clear, recognizable order for the purpose of better understanding. Classification breaks down a more complex object or group into parts. Classification arranges the materials of existence into significant patterns discovered through careful observation and analysis. Even an apparently simple classification like the one that follows is a results of years of observation by biologists and wildlife experts.

The true rabbit family is divided into five groups: The Eastern cottontail (the name is misleading) is found from the Atlantic coast to Wyoming and Arizona, even Central America; the Rocky Mountain cottontail, grayer than the Eastern, ranges from North Dakota and New Mexico west to Sierra Nevada. Larger and browner, the Audobon cottontail flourishes in the Southwest and northwestern Mexico—from Oklahoma and Texas to California. The marsh rabbit and the swamp rabbit (one group) have shorter, darker fur, and inhabit mainly marshy places in the Atlantic and Gulf areas, from Virginia to Florida, from Alabama to Texas. The brush rabbit is the smallest and darkest, and is common in the western United States.[6]

This passage illustrates an important feature of classification. Classification assumes a principle of similarity that can place certain things in one group and exclude them from another. On what basis did biologists separate rabbits into five groups? There are at least three possibilities. The rabbits could be classified according to where they are found (the Rocky Mountain cottontail, for example). After all, we do this with people, classifying them as English or Russian or Dutch or Nigerian on the basis of where they were born or live. But this does not seem to be true of the rabbits— an Eastern cottontail can be found in either Central America or Wyoming. Perhaps the characteristic that distinguishes one group of rabbits from another is size (the brush rabbit is described as the smallest). But in some cases the relative size of the rabbits receives no mention. The principle of classification determining into which category a rabbit falls seems to be the color of the rabbit's fur—the most easily recognizable characteristic for most non-experts. Classification divides a thing, an idea, or a group into component parts according to a consistent system.

Classification involves seeing relationships among the things of the world, perceiving pattern and order in the objects and events around us. Without the human ability to classify, all our knowledge and experience would remain a jumbled, disordered mass. Notice how your textbooks are arranged into chapters and sections of chapters and how you can find the sports news in one section of a newspaper and the movie listings in another. Most information can be ordered and classified in a variety of different ways, and some ways are much more useful and meaningful than others. As we develop experience and knowledge, our ability to classify governs many of our personal and professional decisions. Consider a child growing up in a world of plastics and synthetics:

To a small child, food is nearly anything that can be put in the mouth and swallowed, be it a crunchy sweet carrot pulled from the

---

[6] Jack Denton Scott, "The Amazing Cottontail," *National Wildlife,* **9** (December–January 1971), p. 22.

summer soil or a bottle of soda pop flavored, sweetened, carbonated, and of course preserved by chemicals. Does not a sausage grow on a sausage tree as does a peach on a peach tree? Some children will grow up never knowing why a carrot is different from soda pop, some will learn directly by not being able to plant soda pop in their gardens, and others will learn through their own ability to read and question what they have been eating all their lives.[7]

We have already referred to the human tendency to classify other people. The possible number of principles by which people can be classified is limitless: you could classify people by the shape of their noses, by the structure of their teeth, or by the color of their hair. The following example classifies people according to body types, but, as you can see, the writer uses this system of classification for a definite purpose:

William Sheldon of Yale divides body types into mesomorphs, ectomorphs, and endomorphs. Mesomorphs are the heavily muscled, heavy-boned, square, stocky individuals. They love strenuous physical activity and body contact. They like to perspire and they don't mind bleeding. They thrive on hard competition. The best time of their lives is when they've finished a workout and get into the shower. They probably finish off with a cold shower. This is the type of individual who usually becomes a physical-training director. They have no sympathy for ectomorphs and endomorphs.

Ectomorphs are the thin, frail, nervous type. By nature, they can't stand still. By the time they come to a gym class, they may already have had enough physical activity for the day. Nonetheless, they'll cooperate with the physical director because they're active by nature. They're easily driven to exhaustion.

Endomorphs hate exercise and leaders of exercise. They're the round, soft, flabby people who love ease and comfort. They resist the physical director's superenergy. They hide in dark corners when it's time to choose up for foot races. They're the physical director's favorite target. The director wants to change the endomorph into his own image. He wants his softness to be hardness, his love of Athenian comfort to transfer to affection for Spartan discomfort.

Most of the books on exercise are written by mesomorphs with endomorphs as their targets.[8]

---

[7] Ellen Buchman Ewald, *Recipes for a Small Planet* (New York: Ballantine Books, 1973), p. 23.

[8] Laurence E. Morehouse and Leonard Gross, *Total Fitness in 30 Minutes a Week* (New York: Simon and Schuster, 1975), p. 47.

This classification places people in categories according to their body structure; in addition, the members of each class, theoretically, share a similar attitude toward exercise. By examining each category in terms of the same yardstick—here, physical exercise—the writer can give us a reasonably accurate summary of common attitudes toward exercise and physical fitness.

Classification provides a useful strategy for effective, organized exposition. It can also be an essential tool in analyzing situations, solving problems, and making decisions. Most of us approach a problem by trying to break it into its component parts. Suppose, for instance, you want to attend a concert in a distant city, but find yourself short of money. A small financial difficulty keeps few of us from doing something we really want to do. You would probably work out a solution to your problem by mentally breaking it into its various categories. Some people actually sit down with a piece of paper and make lists like the following:

1. Transportation.

2. Food.

3. Money for Ticket.

4. Place to Stay.

The problem of how to finance the trip divides into four categories that require funds. The list also happens to be arranged in order of importance. If you cannot get transportation to the concert, there is not much sense in buying a ticket. Moreover, you won't enjoy the concert very much on an empty stomach. Money for an admission ticket becomes necessary only after you figure out how to get there and how to feed yourself. Even if you can't find a place to stay, you will probably go anyhow, because a good concert is more important than a little comfort. By classifying the different aspects of the problem and attacking them systematically, one at a time, you will probably find a reasonable solution. Your final list might look like this:

1. Transportation.
   a. Hitchhike.
   b. Find someone else who is going and bum a ride.
   c. Bike (too far?).
   d. Borrow bus fare from folks.
2. Food.
   a. Pack some sandwiches.
   b. Go hungry.
   c. Borrow food money from folks.
3. Money for Ticket.
   a. Take out an emergency loan.
   b. Borrow money from folks.
4. Place to Stay.
   a. Take a sleeping bag.
   b. Find someone who knows someone there.
   c. Borrow money from folks for a motel room.

The solution becomes obvious.

Many people seek efficient and relatively inexpensive ways to heat their homes, both to help preserve natural resources and to cut high fuel costs. Fireplaces and wood-burning stoves or furnaces offer an alternative to gas, electricity, or oil heat. But before wood can be an efficient fuel, certain problems must be overcome. The following passage uses classification to offer advice on using wood efficiently to heat a home.

> First of all, mentally separate the problem into its two basic components, vertical and horizontal. Getting heat up out of your cellar is a different matter than getting it from room to room. Everyone knows that warm air rises by itself. Unfortunately, it won't move sideways without help.[9]

Unless the homeowner can see both parts of the problem of circulating heat, a wood-burning system will not be very effective. Particularly if a home is fairly large, heat must circulate from room to room, as well as rise to heat the upper floors. Classifica-

---

[9] John Cadwallader in *Wood Burning Quarterly*, 1 (Summer 1976), p. 14.

tion, then, can be used both to communicate information and to analyze and solve problems.

Using classification to organize your writing requires that you tell the reader immediately what principle of classification determines the pattern you impose on the information. Selecting a principle of classification depends on your purpose for presenting the information. The American poet Wallace Stevens wrote a poem entitled "Thirteen Ways of Looking at a Blackbird," and indeed there are many ways of looking at even the most familiar object. The following sentences could introduce a piece of writing organized by classification; they give us several different views of a familiar tool—the chisel.

> Chisels come in three sizes: the butt chisel, the pocket chisel, and the mill chisel.[10]
>
> Chisels are designed for mortising, paring, or gouging.[11]
>
> Basic chisel construction is of four types: the traditional socket chisel, the traditional wooden-handled tang chisel, the modern plastic-handled tang chisel, and the metal-core handled chisel.[12]
>
> The chisel is the subject of various theories concerning its development.[13]

Each of these statements introduces a piece of writing organized on the principle of classification. An effective opening sentence has these characteristics:

1. It identifies the subject: rabbits, blackbirds, chisels.
2. It indicates the principle of classification: size, purposes, construction.
3. The opening sentence usually mentions the major classes or categories into which the information will be organized.

Here is a paragraph classifying chisels by size:

> Chisels come in three sizes: the butt chisel, the pocket chisel, and the mill chisel. The butt chisel is the shortest with a blade 2½″ to 3¼″

---

[10] Robert Campbell, ed., *How to Work with Tools and Wood* (New York: Simon & Schuster, 1975), p. 28.
[11] Ibid.
[12] Ibid., p. 29.
[13] Ibid., p. 30.

long, and an overall length from around 7¾" to 9", in widths from
⅛" to 2". This is the type for work in limited space. The pocket chisel,
now the most popular size, is larger, with a blade length of 4" to 5",
overall length from 9" to 10¼". This is the handiest size for general
use. Widths usually run from ¼" to 2". The mill chisel is the largest,
with a blade length of 8" to 10" and an overall length of around 16"
or more. Widths are usually in the 1" to 2" range. This one isn't likely
to figure in average shop work.[14]

Classification is an invaluable tool for organizing your ideas and
observations. Just as sorting the various aspects of a problem into
classes or categories can help you reach a solution in an orderly
way, so writing organized on the basis of this same principle can
help your reader understand the information being presented.

EXERCISES

1. Classify television commercials in terms of the techniques used to
   sell products. You might also classify the different types of television shows currently on the air.
2. Make a list of the career preferences of everyone in your class.
   Classify these job preferences in some meaningful way.
3. Observe people performing some activity (eating at McDonald's,
   walking, driving a car, playing tennis). Classify them into types
   (the nervous walker, the scurrier, the strider, the determined
   walker).
4. How can the United States solve its energy problems? Use techniques of classification to reach some possible answers to this question.

---

[14] Ibid., pp. 30–31.

PROCESS

EXPLAINING how to do a job or how to operate equipment involves a writing technique called *process*. Process is a close relative of description and shares some features with narration, but process writing appears so often and is required so frequently in all sorts of jobs that it needs to be discussed separately. The word *process* implies activity and movement, and process writing breaks an action or operation into a sequence of individual steps.

Those of us who have tried to master the art of hitting a decent serve in tennis are familiar with process. Before we can attain the graceful, smooth form that results in a sizzling ace, we must regard the act of serving as a sequence of steps. First, we learn how to grip the racket. Then we practice tossing the ball. Then the racket and the ball are brought up together. We work hard on where and when to hit the ball after it is tossed. Finally, we concentrate on following through properly. If all the pieces fit together into a smooth sequence, we are ready to serve some aces.

Writing that explains a process uses the order of time as its organizing principle. A process occurs when one event or procedure follows another in chronological order. Process writing can be divided into two general types. One type of process writing tells someone how to do something. Every set of assembly instructions or directions you have ever read—telling you how to cook oatmeal or how to register for a class—illustrates writing that explains a process. Anyone who has purchased an unassembled ten-speed bicycle can attest to the importance of accuracy and clarity in writing about a process. Unclear assembly instructions cause hours of frustration and confusion. The second type of process writing describes how something works or operates (a piece of machinery, a management system, the human brain). The first type assumes that a person or group of persons is going to carry out a procedure; the second leaves out the people and concentrates on the "inner" workings of the object or system.

Explaining how to do something or how to perform a certain task demands care because people are expected to follow the instructions or carry out the procedures, and human beings are capable of misunderstanding or making serious errors that can result in damage to sensitive equipment or in serious injury. Presenting the steps in a procedure requires a form that reduces the chances for human error. In fact, you can sometimes recognize an explanation of a procedure by the way it appears on the page. The sequence of steps in performing a complex process often appears as a list, one step following another, and the list is frequently numbered.

Red, Blue and Green Screens—These three controls balance the three colors that make up a color TV picture. They affect mostly the background, or low brightness, colors in your picture. The drive controls, which we will talk about next, affect the balance of brighter areas. Readjust screen and drive controls when the whole picture develops an off-color cast. The condition will be particularly noticeable between stations or on black-and-white programs. The red, blue, or green cast will even be noticeable with the color control turned all the way down if screens and drives are seriously out of whack. To adjust screen controls, follow this procedure exactly.

1. Turn contrast all the way down and set brightness for a slightly dim picture.
2. Turn color down and tune to an unused channel.
3. Turn all 3 screen controls all the way down.
4. Turn up red screen slowly, stopping as soon as the screen begins to turn slightly reddish.
5. Turn up green screen until the screen turns lemon yellow.
6. Turn up blue screen until the screen looks white or gray. You may have to touch up the other controls to get a perfectly neutral-color screen. Don't get discouraged if you end up starting over a few times. Judging color nuances is tricky.[15]

The color television set is an expensive and complicated product. Most people have no idea that the controls described in the preceding selection even exist and pay expensive repair bills to have a professional make adjustments that they could make themselves. When a procedure must be carried out in an exact order, the listing method helps cut down the chances for error. This technique is treated later in the section on writing instructions, but the listing method does illustrate some important features of ex-

[15] *Consumer Guide, 1974* (New York: New American Library, 1974), p. 233.

plaining a process. The steps in the process are arranged in the order of time. The listing method emphasizes that one step or procedure follows the other. This is important here because the procedures must be followed exactly to get the desired result. No unnecessary words mar the clarity of these instructions. The sentences are short and direct. Note the use of commands in the present tense; these contribute a tone of crispness and clarity. The listing method stresses the time sequence of the procedure and contributes to the clarity of the instructions or explanation.

The following example of a process also tells someone how to perform a task. In this case, however, the explanation takes the form of a conventional paragraph. This paragraph explains how to adjust the bearings in a bicycle axle.

> Adjusting these bearings takes a little time. You must tighten the cup or cone involved, adjust it, and lock it. First, tighten the cup or cone a little, say from twelve o'clock to nine o'clock (one-quarter turn). Then, tighten the lock nut. If the component still binds, it is too tight and you must start over. If the axle moves back and forth along its axis, it is too loose. Again, you must start over. Keep adjusting until the axle rotates firmly and smoothly in its bearing without binding and without wobbling. Make sure the lock nut is on tightly, but not so tightly that you are forced to ruin it in order to remove it. Finally, if you want to practice bearing adjustment, get an old adjustable pedal, and put it together a few times. The pedal mechanism is roughly the same as all the bearings on the bike.[16]

Some important characteristics of the listing method are incorporated into this paragraph. Time order supplies the organizing principle. The paragraph describes a step-by-step process in terms of what happens first, second, third, and so on. In a process explanation, the reader often needs to know something about a device's principles of operation before being given directions on tinkering with it. The bicycle owner willing to work on his or her own bicycle should know why adjusting the bearings is important. Once the principles are understood, a general description of procedure can be adapted to individual cases. Directions on adjusting bearings must allow some leeway for individual judgment and experimentation, so the listing format would be a little too rigid in

---

[16] Ibid., p. 282.

this case. Many people now repair and maintain their own homes and vehicles; more and more there will be a demand for clearly written, step-by-step instructions on how to perform both simple and complex jobs.

Without numbers to indicate which step follows which, the order or sequence of steps can be signaled by using words such as *next, then, later,* and *finally.* You can also rely on *first, second,* and *third* to show the movement from one step to the next. Sometimes, though, as in the case of serving a tennis ball, several actions must take place at the same time (tossing the ball and raising the racket). The following paragraph explains how to cast with a spinning reel:

> To make a cast with a spinning reel, you must open a "bail," secure the line on the tip of your index finger, and flex the rod back, then forward. During the forward movement the line is released from the finger tip and the lure pulls the line off the stationary spool. To slow or halt progress of the lure, you merely drop the tip of your index finger to the edge of the spool, thus contacting the line. With most spinning reels the bail automatically picks up the line to be rewound onto the spool as soon as the reel handle is turned forward.[17]

A definite sequence of events takes place in casting a lure, but some things occur simultaneously. The line, for example, is released at the same time the rod flexes forward. The common time signals give way to more sophisticated transitions that show the simultaneity of some of the steps in the process.

Process explanations are most familiar to us as sets of instructions or directions, but process writing can serve other purposes as well. It may be necessary, for example, to explain an unfamiliar procedure to your readers without expecting them to perform that procedure. A writer trying to convince readers that strip-mining for coal creates terrible ugliness must at some point explain the process of strip-mining:

> Typically a strip-mine operator needed only a tiny crew of men. He required two bulldozers, one of which could be substantially smaller than the other. He required an air compressor and drill for the boring of holes into the rock overlying the coal. He also required a power

---

17 Ibid., pp. 290–91.

shovel for use in loading the coal from the seam into the trucks. These four machines could be operated by as many men. To their wages were added those of a night watchman and two or three laborers, and the crew was complete. With these men and machines the operator first built a road from the nearest highway up the hillside to the coal seam. The bulldozers pursued the seam around the hillside, uprooting the timber and removing all the soil until the coal was reached. Then the dirt was scraped from the sloping mountainside above to expose the crumbling rock. This cut proceeded along the contours of the ridge for half a mile. Then rows of holes were drilled in the rock strata and were tamped with explosives. When the explosives were set off, most of the dirt and rock was blown violently down the mountainside. The remainder lay, soft and crumbly, on top of the coal. The "dozers" then bestrode the shattered "overburden," and with their steel snouts shoved it down the steep slopes. This process left the outer edge of the outcrop exposed. A sheet of coal eight feet thick, fifty feet wide and a half mile long could thus be bared within a few days.[18]

People use and operate equipment every day without ever understanding its principles of operation. Many people cannot explain how an automobile's engine works, much less explain the operation of a television set, a microwave oven, or even the telephone. Making it clear how a complex technical device works depends a great deal on the ability of those who know to communicate lucidly with those who don't know. Process writing is used to explain the inner workings of complex machinery. The example that follows explains how a movie projector produces sound:

In the projector, a light shines through the pictures on the film, projecting them on the screen. At the same time, another light shines through the dark bands of the sound track and falls upon a phototube. Because the film is moving, the light entering the tube will be interrupted at a frequency corresponding to the number of bands on the film, which corresponds to the frequency of the original sound. The intensity of the light reaching the tube will vary with the density of the bands, which corresponds to the loudness and pitch of the original sound. Consequently, a varying beam of light, whose variations correspond to the frequency and to the loudness of the original sound, enters the phototube. As a result, a varying current will flow in the

---

[18] Harry M. Caudill, "The Rape of the Appalachians," *Night Comes to the Cumberlands* (Boston: Little, Brown, 1963), p. 310.

tube. The current is amplified and passed into a loudspeaker, which reproduces the original sound that entered the microphone.

Sometimes reality has to be modified slightly to show the steps in a system. When a movie projector is working, for example, the steps in the process described earlier occur, in effect, simultaneously. There is no real starting point and no real ending point, except for starting and shutting off the projector; so for the purpose of explanation the writer has to "stop" the machine and reconstruct each step in the process. The explanation does not rely on the common time signals (first, second, third) to mark development; instead, another set of words provide transitions—"at the same time," "because," "consequently," "as a result." These words reinforce the point that we can't really see this sequence of events happening except in our mind's eye. This "stop action" technique explains the inner workings of a piece of equipment that, to all outward appearances, is performing several operations simultaneously. In general, an explanation of a process can be used for the following purposes:

1. To record a procedure so that someone else can use it in the future.
2. To describe for your company the methods of operation or equipment used by some other organization.
3. To describe how you handled an investigation or an assignment so that your findings and conclusions will be accepted as valid.
4. To describe how a product is made so that people will have confidence in it.

Process explanations share some general characteristics. Usually, an introductory section defines the process. This introduction also indicates why, when, where, or by whom the process is performed. Any materials or apparatus needed in the process are also described here, as are any special requirements of space, time, or personnel for carrying out the process. Some processes, especially those conducted in a laboratory setting, require certain preparations; these preparations are also mentioned in the introduction.

The main body of the explanation generally falls into two parts.

The first part explains the theory on which the process is based, if that theory is important to understand the process. The second part presents the steps in the process. Try to restrict the main steps to five or six; too many make it difficult for the reader to grasp and retain the overall picture of the process. The steps should follow a chronological order as far as possible. As a rule of thumb, the steps in your process should be numbered if there are more than three. Our final example in this section illustrates this organizational pattern.

After a visual check of the engine, looking for oil, fuel, water or exhaust leaks, you can begin checking out the electrical system, since most tune-ups are concerned with the areas of ignition and carburetion. You can check your plug wires (bad carbon-core resistance wires are often a source of misfire) easily with a screwdriver and jumper wire. With the engine running, disconnect one plug wire at a time and keep the terminal from grounding. Clip the jumper wire to the screwdriver blade (use a plastic-handled tool) and connect the other end to a good ground on the engine.

By running the screwdriver blade along the disconnected wire, any parts of the wire that are leaking voltage will show up as jumped sparks to the screwdriver. If one wire is bad, it's generally best and easiest to replace the set. Check the terminals at each end of the wires, then pull the spark plugs and clean the threaded plug holes. If this is your annual tune-up, then you'll be replacing the plugs with new ones, but if you tune your car twice a year, then you can *clean* the plugs at the mid-year tune-up.

There are a number of things that need periodic checking and maintenance, and the manifold heat control valve and the exhaust gas floor jet are two that you may not have thought of. The manifold heat control valve, or "flapper" valve, is in your exhaust manifold and should be sprayed with solvent once or twice a year to keep it . . . .[19]

EXERCISES

1. Write a letter to a friend—real or imaginary—giving directions for getting to your residence.
2. Invent a gadget. Explain how the gadget works.

[19] Spence Murray, ed., *Petersen's Complete Book of Plymouth, Dodge, Chrysler* (Los Angeles: Petersen Publishing Co., 1973), p. 98.

3. Explain how to do something that you do especially well (how to make the best spaghetti, how to fly an airplane, how to stay awake for two nights in a row).
4. Pick out some device or piece of equipment that is a "mystery" to you. Write your own explanation of how it does what it does.

CAUSE AND EFFECT

SEARCHING for the reasons why things are the way they are and speculating about the future effects of present action consume much human energy. Entire professions exist to study the relationship between causes and effects: Economists tell us why things cost so much, doctors diagnose why we feel so terrible, and psychologists argue about why we act the way we do. It is virtually impossible to open a newspaper or turn on a television set without encountering a discussion of causes and effects. Rising prices might be caused by oil and food shortages. Pollsters measure the effects of debates on voter preferences. The causes of inner-city crime provide the subject for constant analysis. The maxim that we have to understand the disease before finding the cure seems to hold true. Much of your professional and personal life will be spent diagnosing causes or speculating about the future effects of decisions made by yourself or others.

The ability to discover causes characterizes the true professional in every field. The mechanic who tells you why your car makes that funny noise was trained to understand the cause of certain effects. Our lives are no longer threatened by dread diseases such as polio, typhus, diphtheria, or smallpox because scientists sought out the causes of these diseases and found ways to eliminate or prevent those causes. For centuries men have argued over the origin of the universe: what caused it to be? One theory maintains a First Cause (God) created the universe from nothing. On the other hand, some scientists have proposed the "Big Bang" theory that finds the cause of the universe as we know it in a huge explosion billions of years ago. The curiosity that impels us to search out causes is balanced by our absorption with effects.

We have come to recognize, for example, that our desire for the good life and for progress at any cost can result in profoundly damaging effects on our environment. One controversy affecting all of us in the near future concerns the construction of nuclear power plants. Dwindling natural resources created the need for new, economical sources of power. Nuclear power plants can provide the power necessary to light our cities and heat our homes for centuries to come. But many citizens are convinced that the environmental effects and potential hazards to human life posed by nuclear power plants outweigh the good effects of an adequate power supply. The controversy over nuclear power plants illustrates how causes and effects can react with each other in such a way that what from one view is considered a cause can from another point of view be considered an effect. Nuclear power plants require large bodies of cold water as a coolant; the discharge from the plants raises the temperature of surrounding bodies of water. One effect of nuclear power plants is higher water temperature in lakes and rivers. The water temperature of the Columbia River, for example, has been rising gradually for the past few years, in part because of a nuclear power plant's discharge. *This effect* (higher water temperature), in turn, causes a variety of changes in aquatic life. Excessively high temperatures are lethal to the fish population, and a body of warm water in a river can prevent fish from reaching spawning grounds, in this way endangering the entire species. If this occurs, a decrease in the fish population will become the cause of other effects: a decrease in food supply and a loss of recreational opportunity among them. Effects and causes are very closely related to one another, and at some point in time an effect can itself become a cause. This implies, of course, that one wrong decision can set off a chain reaction of effects influencing life on our planet for generations.

Understanding causes and anticipating effects provide valuable information on which to base decisions in both personal and professional life. Communicating this information to others effectively requires a knowledge of some strategies useful in cause-and-effect writing. Cause-and-effect writing can simply explain how an event happened—this cause (an earthquake) had these effects (destruction of life and property). Information can also be provided through either analysis or speculation. Analytic writing examines effects to determine a cause or causes. After studying the symptoms of lung cancer for many years, scientists found cigarette smoking to be a major cause of the disease. Speculative writing, on the other hand, projects or forecasts the effects a certain decision or set of circumstances might have in the future. The decision to vote for one political candidate rather than another rests on speculation about the future. Referendum issues on the ballot often require careful speculation about future effects before a conscientious voter casts a yes or no vote.

The statements that follow come from an ad urging conservation of America's forests and telling us that one industry, at least, is doing something to avoid depletion of a valuable natural resource:

> Nature needs help. For two centuries she has been supplying America—and other parts of the world—with all the trees we needed. Now the demand is increasing faster than nature alone can replenish the supply.
>
> America uses more than half a ton of wood each year, for every man, woman and child. (That's the equivalent of a 55-foot tall southern pine tree with a 12-inch diameter for each of us.)
>
> And, the demand will double by the year 2000 if we are to meet our needs for housing, protective packaging, communications, and other critical demands of a modern economy.
>
> So America must grow more trees—and trees with a lot more usable wood fiber. That's where International Paper is helping.[20]

Once we can establish the cause of a problem, it becomes possible to avoid that problem in the future. Many people feel that our society is changing so rapidly that serious efforts must be made to anticipate the future effects and present actions. No longer can we rely on crystal balls and guesswork to give us reliable information about the future; we must turn to scientists of the future (futurists) for guidance and rational speculation about what we can expect in the near and distant future. This passage asks some pertinent questions:

> At present, one third of all the electric power generated in the U.S. comes from strip-mined coal. But rising oil prices have revived interest in the vast coalfields of Montana, Wyoming and North Dakota, which contains an estimated 1.3 trillion tons, or 40% of domestic coal reserves, only part of which can be strip-mined. Already the price per ton for steam coal has risen from a mid-'50s low of $2 to $3 to $16 to $20. Bumper stickers in Pennsylvania, reading COAL—NO FUEL LIKE AN OLD FUEL, reflect the optimism of the eastern industry.
>
> But the question plaguing farmers, cattle and sheep ranchers, environmentalists and sportsmen is whether the earth can be put back to its useful and/or natural state after the coal is extracted. Where does wildlife go during the strip mining? Does it return to its former

---

[20] International Paper Company Advertisement, *Ms.*, 5 (March 1977), p. 39.

habitats after mining? What happens to water quality in streams and wells? Will reclaimed farmland be as productive as it was before being mined? These questions vex experts and concerned laymen.[21]

A variety of relationships can exist between causes and effects. Some possibilities:

1. One cause ⟶ multiple effects.
2. Multiple causes ⟶ one effect.
3. One cause ⟶ one effect.
4. Multiple causes ⟶ multiple effects.

Although it is true that causes always happen before effects, writers do not always follow this order in presenting their information. Should you present the causes first, or should you describe effects and then specify causes? The answer to these questions will vary with the circumstances and the purpose of your writing task. As a general rule, if your purpose is analytic (to examine certain effects to discover a cause), then you will probably describe the effects first. On the other hand, purely explanatory or speculative writing (anticipating the effects of certain causes) will probably present the cause or causes first and then describe the effects.

One Cause ⟶ Multiple Effects

The following example explains how a single cause (a relatively mild earthquake) had devastating effects. The writer records his observations after visiting the scene of the disaster:

At 5:11 P.M. on December 28, 1974, an earthquake of magnitude 5.5 on the Richter scale shook the mountains of Indus Kahistan, in the north of Pakistan. Great devastation occurred over an area of some 300 square miles. Thousands of people were killed and several times as many injured. Whole villages were razed and the economic base of the region badly dislocated. Homes, bazaars, and recently built schools, uncounted tiers of terraced fields and irrigation systems were shaken apart by the tremors or crushed by the rockfalls and landslides that followed. Large numbers of cattle, buffalo, and goats died, often buried, as were so many of the human casualties, in buildings that had

---

[21] J. D. Reed, "Healing the Wounded Earth," *Sports Illustrated*, 45 (September 20, 1976), p. 66.

been their shelter against the hazards of winter. The Karakoram Highway, Pakistan's costly and prestigious new trade route to China, was
blocked or swept away by hundreds of landslides for a distance of some
forty miles.[22]

The format is simple. The earthquake described in the first sentence brought about the effects listed in the paragraph. The author
gives us a detailed picture of the earthquake's effects. But this
writer has another purpose in mind, too. He wants to know why
this earthquake and earthquakes elsewhere have had such terrible
effects. In other words, could this frightful devastation have been
avoided? The article goes on to examine the effects more closely
and finds reasons for the excessive damage in circumstances other
than the earthquake itself. The writer describes effects, observing
that nearly all types of buildings in the region fared badly in the
disaster:

> Again and again during the earthquake, the roofs fell in single,
> crushing masses, while walls merely crumbled away in the tremors. At
> Palas, . . . the massive roof of an old mosque collapsed while the
> entire adult male population was at prayer. Only one survived, and he
> sustained serious head injuries. The collapse of this otherwise solidly
> built structure was due to the old, rotten timber in the walls. The sad
> fate of all buildings at Palas seemed to reflect the wide treeless slopes
> or poor scrub in that area, forcing builders to make do with inferior
> or old timber.[23]

After specific effects of the earthquake have been carefully looked
into, the severity of the damage can be linked to an environmental
factor: an inadequate supply of lumber. Examination of many
buildings that collapsed during the earthquake provides the evidence for specifying poor construction as one major cause of their
collapse. In turn, poor construction is linked to a lack of wood, and
this lack results from poor forest management. In Pakistan and in
other regions of the world, government officials and citizens alike
have not looked ahead to anticipate the effects of such an ap-

---

[22] Kenneth Hewitt, "Earthquake Hazards in the Mountains," *Natural History*, **85**
(May 1976), p. 31.
[23] Ibid., p. 32.

parently trivial matter as cutting down all the trees without taking steps to replace them. In Pakistan, this shortsightedness helped intensify the tragic effects of the earthquake. Besides the collapse of buildings, landslides and other effects of the earthquake were intensified by the denuded landscape. This writer engaged in an analysis of effects to find a cause, and one hopes that this analysis will help people prevent such disasters in the future.

Multiple Causes ⟶ *One Effect*

Sometimes a single effect can be linked to several causes. An effective strategy in this case describes the effect first, then presents the possible causes. We have all had the frustrating experience of paying an "expert" to do a job only to discover that the job was not done correctly. One writer describes taking his motorcycle to a shop for expensive repairs and having the machine butchered:

> I got out of there as fast as possible, noisy tappets, shot tappet covers, greasy machine, down the road, and then felt a bad vibration at speeds over twenty. At the curb I discovered two of the four engine mounting bolts were missing and a nut was missing from the third. The whole engine was hanging on by only one bolt. . . .
>
> Why did they butcher it so? These were not people running away from technology, like John and Sylvia. These were the technologists themselves. They sat down to do a job and they performed it like chimpanzees. Nothing personal in it. There was no obvious reason for it. And I tried to think back into that shop, that nightmare place, to try to remember anything that could have been the cause.
>
> The radio was a clue. You can't really think hard about what you're doing and listen to the radio at the same time. Maybe they didn't see their job as having anything to do with hard thought, just wrench twiddling. If you can twiddle wrenches while listening to the radio that's more enjoyable.
>
> Their speed was another clue. They were really slopping things around in a hurry and not looking where they slopped them. More money that way—if you don't stop to think that it usually takes longer or comes out worse.
>
> But the biggest clue seemed to be their expressions. They were hard to explain. Good-natured, friendly, easygoing—and uninvolved. They were like spectators. You had the feeling they had just wandered in there themselves and somebody had handed them a wrench. There was no identification with the job. No saying, "I am a mechanic." At

5 P.M. or whenever their eight hours were in, you knew they would cut it off and not have another thought about their work. They were already trying not to have any thoughts about their work *on* the job.[24]

This example traces a single effect—incompetent work—to a number of causes. Notice that the causes themselves (the radio, the mechanics' haste and their attitudes) must be explained to show their direct connection with the effect. This is what is meant by analysis. Often the relationship between causes and effects must be explained in some detail before the reader can see the connection.

One Cause ⟶ One Effect

The assertion that cigarettes cause lung cancer links cause and effect, but we know that cigarettes are not the only cause of lung cancer, nor does smoking cigarettes necessarily guarantee the onset of cancer. It is difficult to find a circumstance in which one cause can be considered the only cause of a certain effect, with the exception of a highly controlled scientific experiment. But in writing we often find examples linking a single cause to a single effect for purposes of both explanation and persuasion. This type of writing characterizes many of the articles and books written about our social and physical environment.

Sophisticated technology has given humanity the power to produce new substances that never existed before in nature. Anticipating and controlling the effects of these substances has become a serious problem for scientist and citizen alike.

Modern industry, agriculture, and medicine float on a sea of synthetic chemical compounds. Every year thousands of such new products are devised. Each purports to solve some human problem or satisfy some human need better than its predecessors. Some are uneconomic to make and never reach the production line or sales counter. Others are weeded out between the testing laboratory and the production line because they are obviously dangerous or toxic to human life. But even those that get through the screens imposed by private companies and the various local, state, and federal agencies cannot automatically be

---

[24] Robert M. Pirsig, *Zen and the Art of Motorcycle Maintenance* (New York: William Morrow & Co., 1974), pp. 33–34.

considered safe. In fact, an alarming number of compounds and processes, long accepted and used, have recently been found to have unexpected and deleterious effects on biological systems. Thus it has become imperative to inquire closely into the criteria that are, and ought to be, employed to safeguard the public health and well-being: continually to explore the question, How safe should safe be?[25]

Ralph Nader devotes his life to eliminating potential causes of tragic effects from our lives. His book *Unsafe at Any Speed* was itself the cause of many improvements in automobile safety. One section of that book describes how certain stylistic features of cars (hood ornaments, tail fins) cause injuries that could be avoided. In one startling passage, Mr. Nader shows the cause and effect relationship between Cadillac tail fins of the late fifties and early sixties and personal injuries:

In the year of its greatest height, the Cadillac fin bore an uncanny resemblance to the tail of the stegosaurus, a dinosaur that had two sharp rearward-projecting horns on each side of the tail. In 1964 a California motorcycle driver learned the dangers of the Cadillac tail fin. The cyclist was following a heavy line of traffic on the freeway going toward Newport Harbor in Santa Ana. As the four-lane road narrowed to two lanes, the confusion of highway construction and the swerving of vehicles in the merging traffic led to the Cadillac's sudden stop. The motorcyclist was boxed in and was unable to turn aside. He hit the rear bumper of the car at a speed of about twenty miles per hour, and was hurled into the tail fin, which pierced his body below the heart and cut him all the way down to the thigh bone in a large circular gash. Both fin and man survived this encounter.

The same was not true in the case of nine-year-old Peggy Swan. On September 29, 1963, she was riding her bicycle near her home in Kensington, Maryland. Coming down Kensington Blvd. she bumped into a parked car in a typical childhood accident. But the car was a 1962 Cadillac, and she hit the tail fin, which ripped into her body below the throat. She died at Holy Cross Hospital a few hours later of thoracic hemorrhage.[26]

---

[25] Arthur W. Galston, "How Safe Should Safe Be?" *Natural History*, **85** (April 1976), p. 32.
[26] Ralph Nader, *Unsafe at Any Speed* (New York: Grossman & Co., 1972), pp. 223–24.

Mr. Nader helps make his point by using specific examples that show direct cause-effect relationship between the design of the car and personal injury. Of course, the ultimate responsibility for this tragic accident falls on the car's designers and their refusal to consider safety more important than tail fins.

Speculative thinking considers the potential effects of a certain action or decision. As a general rule, when you speculate about future effects, the most natural organizational pattern is first to describe the cause (some circumstance or action in the present), then speculate on the effects. This is basically the "if-then" thinking people do all the time. If you jog two miles every day, then you'll be healthy. If you eat Goop for breakfast, you'll get all the vitamins you need. If you put more insulation in the attic, you'll save heat and gas. If you drink, don't drive. Here is an interesting piece of speculation on the effects of the way we dress on professional success:

> This research is based on the very reasonable premise that the two great behaviorists Pavlov and Skinner are right: We are preconditioned by our environment, and the clothing we wear is an integral part of that environment. The way we dress has remarkable impact on the people we meet professionally or socially and greatly (sometimes crucially) affects how they treat us.
>
> It is possible, through the skillful manipulation of dress in any particular situation, to evoke a favorable response to your personality and your needs.
>
> And it is possible for me, based on the research I have done, to teach you to dress for success.
>
> I do not ask you to accept these conclusions immediately; I do hope that you will accept them when you have finished this book.
>
> I will never ask you to concede that it is fair or just or moral for a man's success or failure to depend, to a large extent, on how he dresses. But that is very much the way the money-oriented sectors of our culture work; and it is my contention that in matters of individual striving, it is far more rewarding to let reality be your guide, to use the system rather than ignore or flout it.
>
> Many critics may charge that my approach to successful dress is snobbish, conservative, bland, and conformist. They may further charge that I am encouraging the executive herd-instinct. To these charges, I must plead guilty, for my research documents that, in matters of clothing, conservative, class-conscious conformity is absolutely essential to the individual success of the American business and professional man.

Executives in particular do constitute a herd, and those who understand how to cope rather than fight are much more likely to emerge as leaders than as casualties.[27]

Another example is the speculation that the continued use of aerosol sprays for dispensing deodorants, shaving cream, hair spray, and other products will eventually destroy the ozone layer in the earth's atmosphere. The projected results of the disappearance of the ozone layer to filter the direct rays of the sun have compelled many people to stop using aerosol sprays. In many ways, speculating from present causes to future effects is essential to human survival.

Multiple Causes ⎯⎯⎯⎯⟶ *Multiple Effects*

The term *preventive maintenance* describes the efforts of consumers to avoid high repair bills and to maintain the quality of products they purchase. Most automobile owners receive an owner's manual with their new automobile to help them maintain the car in good running condition. Preventive maintenance guidelines combine the analysis of previous equipment failure in order to discover causes and the speculation that, if these causes are avoided, chances of malfunction will decrease.

The following passage explores the reasons why the economic situation of women is not improving. In a way, this is an analysis of a social "malfunction":

> A major reason for this uncomfortable truth is that the great majority of women workers are ghettoized in traditionally female occupations. In those areas, "equal pay for comparable work" and "equal chance for advancement" have very little meaning. Equal to whom? Advancement to where? These giant pools of cheap female labor—whether they are sales work or food service; typing for corporations or for government agencies—share many characteristics. First, they are paid according to the social value of the worker, not the intrinsic nature of the work. (A barber, for instance, performs less complicated tasks than a beautician, just as an assembly-line worker usually needs fewer skills than a secretary; yet the first two groups are paid and honored more, simply because they are men.) Second, the work areas traditionally occupied by women are usually nonunionized. Even existing unions that should

[27] John T. Molloy, *Dress for Success* (New York: Warner Books, Inc., 1975), pp. 11–12.

or could organize such workers are rarely helpful. Third, the female work force is encouraged to be temporary by lack of advancement, pension, and sometimes even full-time opportunities. (Though women are said to be less employable because of family responsibilities, the subterranean truth seems to be that employers encourage the part-time worker, the young woman who leaves to care for children, and the older woman coming back into the labor force in an entry-level job.)

Fourth, even the few men who are in traditionally female work areas are at the high end of the pyramid, leaving women workers still ghettoized at the bottom. (Here, too, there's no logic to job divisions. High-tip restaurants employ white males, while women, as well as minority men, are confined to cheaper restaurants, though the trays are just as heavy. Women sales personnel sell men's underwear while men sell kitchen ranges: the crucial difference is the higher commission, not who uses the product.)[28]

Some Cautions

We have assumed that the cause-and-effect relationships presented through these patterns will be logical. You can look very foolish—almost as foolish as a doctor who decides to remove the appendix of a patient suffering from indigestion—if the cause-effect relationship is not a valid one. Remember the story of the rooster who thought his crowing caused the sun to rise every morning? You can derive a cause-and-effect relationship only if all the following conditions are present, unless some natural law, such as the law of gravity, definitely establishes a cause-effect relationship.

1. Every time one condition is present, the same result happens. You must examine enough different circumstances to verify the relationship. Suppose, for example, a baseball pitcher has an outstanding record with a particular team that won a pennant during every year he played. It would be foolish to maintain that this pitcher was the sole cause of the team's winning ways. There are too many other factors involved, including twenty-five or so other players.

2. When this condition is removed, the result does not happen.

[28] Gloria Steinem, "The Rise of the Pink Collar Ghetto—Where Women Workers Are," *Ms.*, 5 (March 1977), pp. 51–52.

When the pitcher is traded, the previously winning team may start losing. However, even if situations 1 and 2 suggest a conclusion, they are insufficient to establish a valid cause-and-effect relationship. Perhaps the other players are getting old, or one of the other key players suffered an injury.

3. If all the other factors remain equal when the condition is removed, the result does not happen without the condition. In other words, if you can establish that our theoretical baseball team has not changed in any way except for losing the star pitcher and that it loses without him, then you have reason to believe there is a valid causal relationship.

EXERCISES

1. Choose a song or album that is high on the best-seller charts. Listen to it. Explain the reasons why this song or album has gained such popularity.
2. What would be the effects of a law banning the use of automobiles in major cities? What would be the effects of the legalization of marijuana?
3. Is there a valid causal relationship between going to college and getting a good job?
4. Some scientists speculate that we are entering a new ice age and that climactic conditions are changing throughout the world. Have you observed any changes in climate that could support this speculation?
5. Has any one person or one decision or one action had an effect on your life?

COMPARISON

B Y NOW you realize that most writing strategies reflect processes of reasoning and selecting that we use every day of our lives. Every choice we make, from selecting a dog food to choosing a career, relies on the methods of comparison discussed in this section. Most composition books use two terms—*comparison* and *contrast*—to explain the strategies introduced here. Comparison explains significant similarities between two or more objects, persons, or events. Contrast, on the other hand, shows important differences between two or more objects, persons, or events. Seldom do we compare two things without also contrasting them. In general, whether we concentrate on likenesses (comparison) or differences (contrast), the same writing strategies apply in each case. We use the term *comparison* here to include both likenesses and differences simply to avoid awkwardness in our explanation.

1. To explain something unfamiliar by comparing it with something familiar.
2. To examine two or more things or ideas to show likenesses and differences between them.

The first of these purposes is purely expository in helping someone else understand something unfamiliar or unknown. This happens often in daily conversation. Before you try an unfamiliar food (rattlesnake meat, for example), a friend might assure you that "it tastes like chicken" and so help overcome your reluctance to eat snake. A comparison of this type uses the reader's knowledge and experience as points of reference.

Man, tumbling about in his thin, metal-skinned spacecraft, simply cannot perform the complex mathematical functions needed to bring his vehicle alongside another object in space. It would be like trying to drive your car into the garage while the garage moves away from you and the road that usually leads to it has vanished and you yourself have no more idea of which end of the car is the front than if you were seated in a closed, black box.[29]

The second purpose often merges with persuasion when two things are compared to prompt a choice of one over the other; at least the reader gains information that contributes to a choice between two things or a decision to pursue one course of action rather than another. Rarely are any two things exactly the same in every respect (if they are, you won't need to compare them), and very seldom will you have to write a comparison that does not lead to some sort of choice or decision. You probably used comparison in choosing what college to attend, and every significant purchase you make is more than likely preceded by careful evaluation of the good points and bad points of similar products. *Consumer Reports* magazine is devoted to supplying data to guide in the selection of automobiles, stereo sets, bicycles, boats, and a multitude of other products.

In the writing of any kind of comparison, certain principles hold true. First, the things compared should belong to the same general class; they should have something in common. Shakespeare did write "all the world's a stage," but the creative imagination that can find similarities in things that appear totally unlike each other is not of much use in a more practical world. Between which items in the following list could you make a useful comparison? Which comparisons would be of little value?

camera	soldier
bicycle	airplane
ant	bee
human eye	mule
motorcycle	automobile
bird	train
horse	

Second, all comparisons must have a definite set of principles that provide the organizing structure. This means that you must measure things with the same yardstick. If your boss asked you to com-

---

[29] Fred Warshofsky, *The 21st Century: The New Age of Exploration* (New York: Viking Press, 1969), p. 96.

pare two applicants for the same job, you would not help make the decision by organizing your report in the following way:

APPLICANT A	APPLICANT B
experience	age
technical skills	drinking habits
communication skills	athletic ability
ability to get along with others	race
	religious beliefs

A comparison based on data like these has no value and cannot provide a basis on which to choose one candidate over the other. For a comparison to be effective and organized, the same set of principles must be applied to each of the things compared. Third, it is possible to distort a comparison and provide inaccurate and misleading information if only the similarities between two things are mentioned. Comparing rugby and football by describing only similar features would not offer your reader a very clear picture of either sport.

Organization

Organizing a comparison is simplified by knowing some of the alternatives available to you. The most important step in organizing a comparison has already been mentioned: apply a definite and consistent set of principles to each thing being compared.

For tread life, all tires will be tested against a standard tire, a two-ply rayon test model specially designed by the government. . . . The standard tire's tread life will be determined over a 16,000 mile run, at the end of which between 65 and 90 per cent of its original tread depth is expected to be worn away. Commercially available tires will be run over the same course and compared with the standard tire on a percentage basis. The tires will be scored from "less than 60" on up. A score of 85 will mean a tire gave 85 per cent of the tread life of the standard tire. A score of 150 will mean it gave 1½ times the tread life of the standard tire. The higher the number, the better the tire's tread life.[30]

The task of organizing a comparison is simplified by following or modifying to your own needs some basic patterns used effectively by many writers. Suppose you are comparing two things

---

[30] "Radial Tires," *Consumer Reports*, **38** (October 1973), p. 607.

FIGURE 3.

(*A* and *B*). The simplest organization for the information may be pictured as in Figure 3.

Here is an example in which two similar situations, case studies really, are presented next to each other to make a point. In this case, the similarities between the two circumstances are important to the writer's point.

> Like arsine, arsenic compounds in general present health hazards. So deadly are some arsenic compounds that minimal exposures may cause severe reactions. In Los Angeles, a laborer on an asphalt-paving crew came down with an inexplicable case of arsenic poisoning. Investigators uncovered this sequence of events: On hot days, the laborer was in the habit of carrying a canvas water bag, placing the bag near him on the ground and swigging from it as the day wore on. On one job, he was helping to pave ground that had recently been sprayed with the weed killer sodium arsenite. The chemical penetrated the canvas and was absorbed into the water, where the laborer drank it.
>
> In Kansas, the source of the arsenic poisoning of a twenty-three-year-old secretary was even more elusive. At last it was realized that the girl worked in the office of a feed mill that used arsenic compounds in one step of a process. While the girl worked exclusively in the office and seldom entered the mill, she handled operational sheets from the processing area. The arsenic she accumulated from these sheets slowly built up in her body to a poisonous level.[31]

The similarities between the two incidents support the writer's point. In both cases minimal contact with arsenic resulted in poisoning. In this selection, the similarities are emphasized by the introductory sentences, and we have no trouble seeing the writer's point.

The block organizational pattern can also show differences effectively. The search for new sources of energy has led scientists to consider energy sources once common centuries ago. The follow-

---

[31] Howard R. Lewis, "With Every Breath You Take," in David L. Wheeler, ed., *The Human Habitat* (New York: Van Nostrand Reinhold, 1971), p. 93.

96 WRITING IN AN AGE OF TECHNOLOGY

ing comparison lays out some of the differences between two
different sources of energy:

> Fossil fuels, as we have been using them so far, are very inefficient.
> Five-sixths of the energy used in transportation, two-thirds of the fuel
> burned to create electricity, and almost one-third of all the remaining
> energy is discarded as waste heat. . . . Furthermore, a good part of
> these fuels that isn't converted into power or waste heat is emitted as
> polluting compounds [such as] carbon and sulfur dioxide and nitrous
> oxide. Yet, despite the many problems inherent in their use, we have
> become dependent on fossil fuels over the decades. . . . And, until
> recently, most of us assumed they were in plentiful supply. Now, after
> some dramatic brownouts and blackouts, gasoline and heating oil short-
> ages, and skyrocketing fuel prices, we know that coal, oil, and gas aren't
> going to last forever.
>
> Fortunately, we are now realizing that there are other huge reserves
> of energy that aren't many decades out of our reach. At long last, we are
> taking a long look at the other sources nature makes available to us
> every day—wind, water, organic matter, and the sun. And we're finding
> these sources to be very attractive. Unlike fossil and nuclear fuels, we
> can tap and use them while doing minimum damage to the environ-
> ment. Solar, wind, and water power emit no solid or gaseous pollutants.
> Methane gas production actually rids our environment of wastes, since
> it converts farm waste and garbage to fuel and valuable fertilizer.
> Methane, with an octane rating of 120, is a very clean fuel; it burns
> completely. Moreover, all these energy supplies are renewable and avail-
> able in plentiful amounts in most parts of the world.[32]

The most important consideration in comparison is to measure
each item by the same yardstick, to look at all the things or ideas
being compared from the same perspective. What are the principles here? We can list them:

1. Fossil Fuels.
   a. Inefficiency.
   b. Pollutants.
   c. Exhaustible.
2. Alternative Sources.
   a. No pollutants.
   b. Efficiency; no waste.
   c. Renewable.

---

[32] Carol Hupping Stoner, ed., *Producing Your Own Power* (Emmaus, Pa.: Emmaus Press, 1974), p. vii.

The order of discussion changes slightly, but both sources of energy are presented in terms of the same ideas. The essential points of differences are clarified, and the differences are emphasized by referring to the discussion of fossil fuels ("Unlike fossil and nuclear fuels . . ."). This writer wants us to make a choice in favor of renewable resources; so these sources are presented *second* in the comparison—a technique used effectively by many writers.

The block structure often explains before-and-after situations, much like the ads for weight-reducing aids in popular magazines. A before-and-after comparison describes two aspects of the same thing; the difference is one of time. This comparison involves a record of change, so similar features to those described in the "before" section must be described in the "after" section. William O. Douglas uses the before-and-after pattern to describe changes in a once beautiful natural setting:

> Recently, I revisited Houston, Texas, and the Buffalo Bayou, as fascinating a waterway as God ever made, which skirts the San Jacinto Battleground, famous in Texas history. Once it sparkled with myriads of life. The alligator was there and many species of fish. Birds without number frequented it, including great white pelicans and the water turkey that swims under water in pursuit of fish and has so little oil on its wings and body that it must spend long hours each day on the sunny side of a tree, drying its feathers. Then men dug out Buffalo Bayou, making it wider than a football field, deep enough for ocean liners and 50 miles long. As a result, Houston today is the nation's third largest port, supporting the largest industrial complex in the Southwest. But Buffalo Bayou today is a stinking open sewer and a disgrace to any area. It carries to the Gulf the sewage of about 2,000,000 people and 200 industries. One need not be an expert to detect both its chemical and its fecal odor. Buffalo Bayou is now a dead river, supporting only the gar, a symbol of ugliness. A red-brown scum covers the surface and occasionally streaks of white detergent foam. Fascinating Buffalo Bayou is now a smelly corpse.[33]

It is interesting, perhaps, to speculate on how the engineers who designed the waterway and the industrialists who benefit finan-

---

[33] William O. Douglas, "An Inquest on Our Lakes and Rivers," in David L. Wheeler, ed., *The Human Habitat* (New York: Van Nostrand Reinhold, 1971), p. 109.

cially from it would describe the same changes. Very likely we would receive a much different type of comparison arranged around a set of principles other than Justice Douglas's alive-dead, beautiful-ugly set of contrasts.

An industrialist who also experienced the changes in the Buffalo Bayou could perhaps justify those changes in terms of advantages and disadvantages. The advantages of giving Houston access to the sea, thus enabling the city to become a thriving industrial center, would outweigh the aesthetic disadvantages described by Justice Douglas. The block pattern effectively shows the advantages and disadvantages of a situation or course of action. Some striking examples of how government leaders weigh advantages and disadvantages before making decisions with long-lasting effects on government policy and public well-being appear in the *Pentagon Papers*.

Important decisions are made every day by balancing advantage against disadvantage and risk against benefit:

> Developing these criteria is not entirely an exercise in rational dispassionate analysis. More and more, the process involves reconciling the often conflicting interests of business, agriculture, and the environmentalists. Known benefits are carefully weighed against demonstrated or possible side effects. The final choices are both subjective and evaluative. DDT is an example. The fact that it can wipe out malaria-bearing mosquitoes must be balanced against its inadvertent destruction of useful insects, such as bees and others serving as sources of food for birds. Similarly, the drop in crop productivity and loss of income that result from the banning of DDT must be balanced against the possibility that its slow biodegradability may ultimately produce new dangers to man. There are still unanswered questions concerning DDT, but while they are being worked out, countries where insect-borne human diseases are still a major problem cannot be expected to ban the compound.[34]

Careful weighing of the advantages (benefits) and disadvantages (risks) of a given situation can help society's leaders make crucial decisions, but the ordinary citizen must also realize the truth of the saying that "there are no simple solutions, only intelligent choices."

---

[34] Arthur W. Galston, "How Safe Should Safe Be?" *Natural History*, **85** (April 1976), p. 32.

Our final example of the block method uses comparison to show the disadvantages the average working person faces at income tax time.

> We learned, after Watergate, that the Administration leaned on IRS to audit its enemies and, according to some reports, not audit its friends —but of course that has nothing to do with the average man, who makes no governmental list of enemies or friends. The average man loses out not because someone has fingered him by name but by the impersonal workings of the system. What matters here is that the IRS man, again like any cop fishing for his quota, catches more easy ones than hard ones, and the average man with his earned income is the easiest fish in the stream. He wears his earnings on his sleeve: a copy of his W-2 form is already in his file at IRS. It takes no effort for the IRS man to catch a working person underreporting his income: all he has to do is compare the return with the IRS copy of the man's W-2.
>
> By contrast, capital gains transactions—the main source of income of the very rich—are not reported to IRS. There is no piece of paper comparable to the W-2 available to the IRS man studying a capital-gainer's return; as Diogenes observes, finding the income of the rich is "hunting in the dark." The result, according to Diogenes, is that it is "safe to say that every weekday Wall Streeters make at least a million dollars that IRS will never discover." The comparable figures for income earned by salaried work is roughly zero. Similarly, the physician who knows IRS doesn't have the manpower to check all his patients' returns against his own return has a much better chance of understating his income than the unfortunate working man, nailed to his fiscal cross by that W-2 form. Certainly doctors try harder, for they are convicted of tax evasion at four times the rate that prevails in the general population, and that statistic of course measures only the ones that got caught.[35]

Although the block method provides an efficient pattern for organizing a comparison, it does have one important disadvantage. If the subject matter is fairly complex and involves a large amount of detail, the reader may have difficulty keeping all the facts about the first topic in mind while examining details about the second. In many cases, an alternating organizational pattern makes a comparison more effectively. This method separates the data into

---

[35] David Hapgood, *The Screwing of the Average Man* (New York: Bantam Books, 1975), pp. 252–53.

topics, then discusses both items in terms of each topic. A diagram like Figure 4 is helpful:

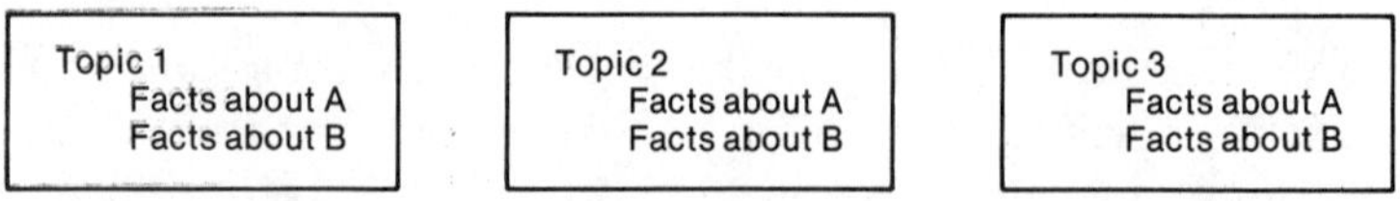

```
┌─────────────────┐   ┌─────────────────┐   ┌─────────────────┐
│ Topic 1         │   │ Topic 2         │   │ Topic 3         │
│   Facts about A │   │   Facts about A │   │   Facts about A │
│   Facts about B │   │   Facts about B │   │   Facts about B │
└─────────────────┘   └─────────────────┘   └─────────────────┘
```

FIGURE 4.

The comparison that follows uses alternating structure to show how motorcycles can actually be considered safer to operate than automobiles:

Motorcycles have built-in safety factors not found in automobiles. For example, a motorcycle has unequaled ease of handling. The relatively small size and remarkable maneuverability of a motorcycle can keep the rider out of a good many situations that would be disastrous for an automobile. Escaping when squeezed toward the guard rails due to a passing motorist judging the speed of an oncoming car too closely would be one instance. The response to controls is almost instantaneous on a motorcycle. A surprisingly light twist of the throttle accelerates a motorcycle like a jackrabbit; full power can involve less than a half-twist of the hand. Simply leaning away from impending trouble turns the bike from danger as quickly as it is seen, far faster than anybody could turn a steering wheel. The brake and throttle on a motorcycle can be used at the same time for fullest command of the controls. The gearshift can also be used at the same time. There's no switching of a foot from one control pedal to another. According to the National Safety Council, the average driver in a car going 50 mph will travel more than 80 feet before he can get his foot from the gas pedal to the brake. The bike rider, however, has a foot poised over his brake pedal for instant use at any time, and his left hand is only a fraction of a second's reflex away from the front-brake lever.[36]

The automobile is a known quantity to most people, so extensive detail concerning an automobile's operation is not really necessary. The familiarity of the automobile also makes it awkward and cumbersome to list all the details about an automobile first and

[36] Al Griffin, *Motorcycles: Buyer's and Rider's Guide* (Chicago: H. Regnery & Co., 1972), p. 35.

then present the contrasting facts about the motorcycle. Instead, the writer has divided the subject into topics: ease of handling, response to controls, command of controls. Under each of these topics the motorcycle's features are compared with those of the automobile. In this comparison the emphasis falls on the qualities of the motorcycle because a larger amount of detail is devoted to the motorcycle. Frequently, it is necessary to give fuller information about each of the subjects being compared, especially when the comparison is intended to help someone else make a choice.

The alternating technique balances one feature against another:

Many of the internal workings of electric typewriters are similar to those of manuals; the real difference is that they are performed by an electric motor instead of by hand. Many people are under the impression that the advantage of an electric is that it works faster than a manual. This is not true. Any modern office manual is capable of operating faster than the fastest typist, and this has been true of almost all standard office machines since just after the turn of the century. The true advantages of the electric include the fact that the motorized mechanism produces a more uniform impression of type on the paper—although a skillful typist can do nearly as well with a manual.

The other advantage is that, during the course of a full day's work, typing can, surprisingly enough, be tremendously fatiguing. Tapping the keys, shifting for capitals, and returning the carriage for the beginning of a new line have been proven to be major consumers of the typist's energy, resulting in tiredness and lack of efficiency. Since the keys of an electric do not have to be tapped quite so hard—they really only have to be touched—and since shifting and carriage return are performed by motor, an electric is less tiring for the operator.[37]

This resembles the advantage-disadvantage structure discussed earlier, but here the alternating method first shows similarities— there is no difference in speed—then discusses the advantages of the electric typewriter in producing a more uniform type and in lessening fatigue. This comparison could save someone time and money in purchasing a typewriter. For infrequent, personal use, the manual is obviously the best choice; but a busy office manager would be justified in buying electric typewriters for the secretaries.

---

[37] *Consumer Guide, 1974* (New York: New American Library, 1974), pp. 327–28.

Notice that this example presents both similarities and differences between the electric and the manual typewriter. The similarities are important, for many people do not realize that an electric typewriter is not necessarily faster than a manual. But the differences are more significant with regard to choosing between the two typewriters, so they are discussed after the likenesses. This organizational strategy generally holds true: present whatever is most important (likenesses or differences) in the second section of the comparison.

As consumers, we are not always fortunate enough to have only two items or products to compare. Even choosing a toothpaste requires comparing a multitude of brands for relative price, fluoride content, taste, abrasive qualities, and so on. Products of every type have proliferated, and the consumer welcomes someone who will take the time and trouble to make comparisons among many apparently similar products. The same principles underlying a comparison of two objects or ideas hold for comparing a number of objects or ideas. The most fundamental rule of all requires a definite principle of measurement. Imported cars, for example, could be compared in terms of the quality and availability of authorized dealers who can service them. This principle of measurement allows the comparison of many makes of important cars and provides useful information to a prospective buyer.

Some foreign-car distributors have a reputation for expanding too quickly in the U.S. market—for adding new dealers to their rosters faster than they can train their mechanics. Also, in some cases, even a competent and cooperative dealer may not be able to get the necessary parts quickly. Some imports have only a few hundred dealers in this country, and most of those may be concentrated in coastal and metropolitan areas. Thus, if your car breaks down on a long trip, you may find yourself hundreds of miles from the nearest authorized dealer. To add to your woes, you may discover that many independent repair shops are unwilling or unable to repair imports. As of mid 1974, there were 675 Fiat dealers in the entire country, only about one-tenth the number of Chevrolet dealers, for example. And in a recent CU survey (details on page 423), *Fiat* owners reported that the service they had been receiving was below par. The *Opel* (a line of General Motors "captive" imports), *Volkswagen*, and BMW are German cars. GM boasts that more than 2000 Buick dealers also sell and service *Opels*. But many of those dealers apparently have shown little interest in the *Opels*. In our survey, *Opel* owners reported that the service they had been receiving was below par. *Volkswagen* has about 1000 dealers in this country— half as many as the *Opel*. And yet, *Volkswagen* owners reported that service was about average—decidedly better than the *Opel's*. And BMW, with only 240 dealers, came out among the best when it came to service. If you often take long trips in your car, the number and distribution of authorized dealers become an important consideration.[38]

For the layman, the large number of prescription and non-prescription drugs available for a variety of purposes can cause confusion and needless expense. Knowing similarities and differences in this case can enable us to ask for drugs by their generic names rather than by a brand name that may cost a great deal more. The following passage compares some of the pain-killers available on the market.

The most potent of all analgesics is the derivative of opium known as heroin. Ironically, heroin was first introduced as a substitute for another pain-killing opium derivative, morphine, on the premise that it would not cause addiction. It is not legally available for the treatment of patients in the United States for any purpose, and the street price can run as high as $100,000 a pound. Luckily, other less effective chemical derivatives of opium are legal, and they comprise the only remotely satisfactory weapons in the treatment of severe pain.

The drawbacks of opium derivatives are obvious. All create physical and psychological dependence; all require increasing dosages to sustain pain relief; all cause some degree of drowsiness and respiratory depression. Which is best depends upon which side effects are least obnoxious to the patient. For intense pain after surgery, physical and emotional dependence are unimportant—the need for the analgesic will rapidly disappear. Morphine and Dilaudid, both of which are exceedingly addictive, are often used. But for the chronically ill, the trade-offs between side effects and analgesia can become very important. Demerol produces only mild withdrawal symptoms, but generates enough of a high to create substantial emotional dependence. Methadone, still another opium derivative, produces almost no withdrawal symptoms at all (hence its standard use), but seems to be as psychologically addictive as morphine. Percodan, a combination of opiates and other drugs, is only

---

38 "Buying a New Car," *Consumer Reports*, 39 (December 1974), p. 395.

moderately addictive, but is much less effective than morphine or Dilaudid.[39]

EXERCISES

1. Write a consumer guide comparing "fast food" establishments. Where can you get the best hamburger? The best pizza?

2. Technology has developed many devices that make daily life more pleasant. Write a before-and-after description about such a device (the microwave oven, for example).

3. Write a comparison in which you summarize the advantages and disadvantages of going to college.

4. If you had to choose between living in a rural area or in an urban environment, which would you prefer? Write a comparison showing the reasons for your choice.

---

[39] Peter Russell and Leonard Ross, *The Best* (New York: Farrar, Straus, and Giroux, 1974), pp. 85–86.

NARRATION

R EDUCED to its simplest terms, narration is the telling of a
story. Narration is dynamic because it deals with events
and actions that occur in time. As we have suggested,
description may be limited to inanimate objects, and in business
and technical writing this will most often be the case. Narration,
on the other hand, requires characters or people acting out events
in some orderly sequence of time; the organizing principle of narration, then, is a sequence of time or a chronology.

Narration is commonly thought of as the exclusive province of
fiction writing; it can be used to tell about real events as well. History, biography, autobiography, and news stories all deal with
people and with events as they take place in time. In the sort of
writing we are interested in here, narration contributes to both
persuasion and exposition. In persuasion, for example, a narrative
may be used to introduce evidence, support a judgment, or sub-
stantiate a thesis. And in certain forms of exposition, most notably
the process, narration can be an indispensable tool.

A good share of your writing will fall in the category of process
writing, and, in fact, a common sort of process writing is nothing
more than simple narration. Most formal reports and progress
reports include narratives that relate the steps by which a job was
accomplished or the current status of a job in progress. Narratives
of this type are ordinarily written in chronological order, beginning at the time the job started and progressing either to its present state or its completion point. The following example comes
from a narrative explaining the installation of a bio-gas plant
designed to extract methane fuel from cow manure:

> The site choice on our farm posed some problems. We figured the
> natural place for a cow manure digester was near the source of the raw
> material; however, . . . many visitors would be arriving to see this un-
> usual installation and . . . they shouldn't be expected to muck their
> way through the barnyard. The only possible spot near the house was
> on the north side. If you can arrange it, a southern exposure would pro-
> vide more heat for cool weather operation. In a small set-up like ours,
> it is not practical to get involved in compressing gas, so the generator

has to be near the point of use or you will end up with miles of copper tubing. The manure is the more movable commodity at this point!

We hired a backhoe to excavate the site and make a pit for the digester to rest in. At 10 feet, water began to ooze into the hole, so we stopped digging. We poured a 3-inch pad of cement into the bottom of our hole, smoothed it, and let it harden. Over this we placed a sheet of black plastic . . . , and over that, a second sheet of plastic. We carefully lowered the tank into position and sealed the whole business in place with a second layer of cement. We threaded the agitator cable through the center pipe and settled the dome over the center guide. Then we were ready to start making methane.[40]

This narrative follows a chronological order, from choosing the site for the tank to the installation of the tank and the site. Narration explains how something was done or how a job was accomplished. This passage reports the sequence of events leading up to the actual operation of the plant. While reading this narrative, we recognize that someone who participated in the project is talking to us. The voice speaking in the passage belongs to someone who took part in this project and, in fact, is one of the owners of the farm (this is clear from the "we" and "our" pronouns used throughout). A report on the same project written by an outside observer —who, perhaps, happened to drop by during the project—would have a different voice and would probably present slightly different details (for example, the reason for choosing the site might escape the outside observer). The operator of the backhoe would also report a significantly different version of the project. In narration the identity or voice of the writer must be clearly established.

There are many voices available to a writer, but only two need concern us here—those using the first and third person. *Person* refers simply to the choice of pronoun. In the first person the writer uses the pronoun *I* and relates the events as though he or she were the principal actor in them. This point of view has the advantage of immediacy and authenticity. The "I" narrator gives an impression of authenticity because the speaker takes part in the events described. The story is told from the "inside," as it were. As you know, a first-hand account by a participant is more effective than

[40] Sharon and James Whitehurst, "Our Four-Cow Bio-Gas Plant," *Producing Your Own Power*, ed. Carol Hupping Stoner (Emmaus, Pa.: Emmaus Press, 1974), pp. 183–84.

the same story told by someone who remained outside the action. The first-person narrative, however, can only report those incidents actually observed by the speaker, and (like the center on a football team) someone engaged in a series of events or circumstances can only see a limited part of the whole scene. The "I" narrator is, in other words, limited to reporting his or her own experiences, observations, and perceptions.

In the sort of practical writing situations we are dealing with, this limitation may not be a severe handicap. Suppose, for example, you are employed by a management consulting firm. Your supervisor has instructed you to go to a prospective client (a printing company), study its operations, and write a report on your experiences for the ultimate purpose of preparing a job analysis. Because the subject is *your* experiences, narration will predominate in your report on the visit; and that account will fall naturally into a chronological sequence, from your departure to your return, with the significant steps between. Such a report might read as follows:

On January 18, 1974, I flew to the home office of the Speedee Printing Company in La Grange, Illinois, for the purpose of a preanalysis interview. I arrived at O'Hare Airport late in the evening and took a room at the Hyatt House in Oak Brook, Illinois.

The following morning, January 19, I met with the senior vice-president for production, Mr. George Kendall. I spent approximately two hours with Mr. Kendall, explaining our consulting service and some of our methods. I explained further what I would require in the way of company documents, records, plant layout diagrams, in-house forms, and procedures manuals, in order to complete my initial evaluation. Mr. Kendall appeared to be very receptive to the idea of an analysis, and he implied indirectly that there was a considerable problem of inefficiency in the present operation. On terminating our discussion, he assigned his assistant, Mr. Arlen Trout, to work with me for the day.

I spent the remainder of the morning with Mr. Trout. He supplied me with copies of all the requisite documents (see attachments) and briefed me on the current patterns of work flow. In the afternoon we toured the plant and business office and walked through the steps of a typical printing order.

Later in the afternoon I met again briefly with Mr. Kendall. I outlined our analysis procedure and informed him we could have a team on site within two weeks. He agreed to this and promised the full cooperation of his staff. That night I began a preliminary review of the documents, and in the morning, January 20, I returned to our Los Angeles office.

From my initial review of Speedee Company's operation, I estimate that a detailed analysis would require a minimum of three consultants working on site for one week. Ten working days after that visit should be ample time to prepare the presentation.

A report of this type is nothing more than a narrative or "story" of the writer's activities during his visit to the prospective client. Although it is a generalized or summary report, it nonetheless follows a strict chronological sequence, and it is obviously best told in the first person. The limitations of the "I" narrator pose no problems here; indeed, that point of view allows for the writer's interpretation of certain events ("Mr. Kendall appeared to be . . ."; "he implied . . .") and his perception of the task ahead ("From my initial review . . . I estimate . . .").

In our preceding example, the focus falls naturally, as it should, on the writer and his activities, interpretations, and perceptions. The first person narrative point of view is the logical choice for reports of this nature. But there are certain occasions on which a writer should exclude himself or herself from the center of attention to focus instead either on the actions of other people or simply on actions and events themselves. In such instances, the *third person* pronoun is appropriate and certainly far more flexible as a narrative tool, for it removes the "I" from the account and replaces it with the pronouns *he, she,* or *it* or with pertinent proper nouns.

Let us consider another example—or rather an extension of our previous one. Assume your consulting firm got the job at Speedee Printing Company, and on its completion you were required to prepare the usual job summary report. Your introduction to that report might read something like this:

Corporate Introduction

During most of its years of existence Speedee Printing Company received most of its work from the telephone company and was largely dependent upon telephone directory work for its profit. For a long time business prospered, but in recent years competition and the increasing loss of directory business caused profit margins to deteriorate rapidly.

In February 1974, an analysis of the company was performed, and the following corporate weaknesses were identified:

1. Lines of authority were vague and unclear.
2. No overall or master corporate plan existed.
3. Management was neither directing nor controlling the activities of its employees. Employees established their own priorities, and productivity was abysmally low.
4. Coordination and communication between departments and different areas of the company were virtually nonexistent. There was no sense of teamwork.
5. Responsibility was not clearly defined, and managers were not held responsible for their performance.
6. Reporting was neither timely nor meaningful. There was uncertainty about true costs and actual profit and loss positions— and little credibility in the proliferation of reports that were employed.
7. Company morale, from labor to top management, was very low.

In order to reverse the downward course of the company, management must regain control of its operations, upgrade its ability to compete, redirect its energies and resources into commercial business, and instill a sense of urgency and desire for improvement within its whole corporate structure.

Initial efforts were directed at focusing management on its responsibilities and on the task ahead. A series of weekly communications meetings were implemented to define lines of authority and zones of responsibility and to educate all managers on the necessity for planning and timely reporting at each level.

Aids were developed, and early in the project a new reporting system was designed and put into effect. Management began to evaluate performance objectively and to know what the major recurrent problems were. With aids and a reporting system in place, planning tools were next introduced. Top management began to use a master schedule. Overall objectives were defined, capacities established and thinking begun on how to balance and coordinate these capacities. An integrated system of planning, executing, excepting, and reporting was designed and installed to help implement and control the master schedule. At the same time, untimely and less meaningful reports and documents were purged. Finally, a total management report was implemented that locked all mechanics of the system together and provided top management with a concise and meaningful single-page, weekly report on the entire operation and status of the company.

Speedee Printing is not yet out of its profit dilemma, but there are sparks of change showing everywhere: improved production performance, improved communications between departments, and glimmers of a renewed company élan among younger managers and most employees. The key to further improvement remains in the will of management to maintain the current momentum and aggressively use the tools at its disposal.

You will notice that the emphasis here is not on you or the members of your consulting team. It has shifted now to your activities and accomplishments, to what you *did* during your stay at Speedee. With this change in perspective comes a modification in style, particularly in the choice of verb forms. Rather than say, "We implemented a series of weekly communications meetings" the report states that "a series of weekly communications meetings were implemented." As you can see, this report is still a narrative. It still follows a chronological sequence, though precise dates are clearly less significant to its purpose. But the fact that it is cast in the third person lends it a tone of objectivity, and objectivity is one of the principal virtues of this voice.

Narration can serve many purposes. Scientists often record their discoveries in narrative form, and the result makes fascinating reading (John C. Lilly's *The Mind of the Dolphin*, John Nance's *The Gentle Tasaday*, and the works of Loren Eiseley are notable examples). Narrative also finds its way into expository writing (it resembles process a great deal) to illustrate a point or idea by reporting a personal experience or actual incident. Ralph Nader makes extensive use of narration in his book *Unsafe at Any Speed*, and in the following example an astronaut reports a personal experience to illustrate the importance of "keeping cool" under stress.

I had another pretty good test of my nerves after Korea when I was helping start out the Sidewinder missile program at the Navy Ordinance Station at China Lake, California. The Sidewinder is an extremely clever antiaircraft missile which one airplane fires at an enemy airplane to blow it out of the skies. The missile seeks out the engine of the enemy plane, just from the heat of it, and then flies right up the enemy's tail pipe before it explodes. I got to fire the first Sidewinder at a drone target to see what would happen. I was in an F3D night-fighter, and right after I let the Sidewinder loose it went a little haywire and started a loop which would cause it to chase me instead of the drone. Here was something trying to kill me, and I wasn't even mad at it. I was trying to help it along. All I could think of at the time was that I could not let this little jerk climb up *my* tail pipe. So I made a fast loop trying to stay behind it. I simply wanted to keep its front end from ever seeing my back end. Obviously, I succeeded, although the test engineer who was with me suffered slightly from the "clanks," which is pilot talk for the shakes.[41]

Let's review the major principles of narration as it applies to the kinds of writing we can expect to encounter in business and industry:

1. Narration is essentially the telling of a story, in which the events follow chronological order. In a few cases chronology may have to be modified. If, for instance, you report on several different activities performed by several different people, you may arrange your material in a number of separate chronological narratives. Or if two or more projects have been carried on simultaneously, it may be necessary to apply separate chronologies to each. But in almost every other case, exact chronological order is appropriate.

2. Use such signal words as *next, following this, later, subsequently,* and *after this* to provide clear transitions where necessary.

3. Keep your verb tenses consistent. You will ordinarily use the past tense, for you will be reporting events after the fact. When your narrative includes present events, switch to the present tense to report *is* for *was, do* for *did,* or *go* for *went.* If you conclude a narrative report with projections for events or activities in the future, shift to the future tense: *will be, will do,* or *will go.*

4. Select your narrative point of view carefully and always in accordance with the focus of your report. If that focus is primarily on your actions and impressions, use the first person pronoun *I.* If it is on other people or on events and activities, use the third person pronouns *he, she,* or *it* or proper nouns.

5. Finally, as in all practical writing situations, keep your narrative brief and to the point. The proper choice of point of view will help diminish problems of detail selection, but always take pains to use only those details that are pertinent.

---

[41] Walter M. Schirra, Jr., et al., *We Seven* (New York: Simon & Schuster, 1962), p. 78.

Never "pad" your narrative or clutter it with needless detail. Keep in mind your audience and the purpose of your writing.

EXERCISES

1. Write a narrative telling about a "first" experience (your first date, your first airplane trip, your first visit to the dentist). Write one version in the first person ("I") and another in the third person, as if you were observing your own actions through someone else's eyes.
2. Summarize the plot of a novel, story, movie, or television show.
3. Pretend that you are an undercover agent assigned to investigate the educational process. Write a narrative report to your superiors on your experiences thus far.
4. Nearly everyone has had a mysterious "supernatural" experience that seems to defy rational explanation. Write a narrative about such an experience. If you have not had one, maybe you have known or heard about someone who has.
5. Do you know any legends or folktales that you may have heard from parents, friends, or neighbors? American soldiers in Vietnam, for example, often told a story about a huge cannon hidden inside a hollowed-out mountain. Teen-agers of the fifties and sixties all knew the legend of the mysterious figure with a hook for a hand who prowled lovers' lanes.

PERSUASION

E VERY strategy for arranging and presenting information presented so far influences the thoughts and actions of others. This influence is called *persuasion*. Persuasion influences others to share your opinion or belief or convinces them to act in a certain way. When persuasion becomes the purpose for writing, your approach to the observations and facts at your disposal undergoes significant changes. Your primary concerns remain, enlightening the reader and supplying information in a clear and accurate way; but you also want to convince the reader that the facts and observations support a definite opinion or judgment.

All the forms of exposition, as well as of description and narration, are tools in the effort to persuade. Careful study of the advertising in almost any magazine provides an intensive course in persuasion. Advertisers use many different writing strategies to convince us that a certain product is the best available and, perhaps, essential to our health and happiness. Every ad implicitly tries to persuade us to take action—to buy the product. Here are some examples, with the dominant writing strategy indicated:

DESCRIPTION

Stop perspiration stains forever; *No-Stain* is soft and flexible. It looks like natural flesh. Once placed in your armpits it emits a pleasant odor, like the scent of a spring morning. And lasts for weeks.

NARRATION

When you were a kid, your parents couldn't get you to eat green beans. Now your kids won't eat them either.
You managed to grow up without beans. But life was simpler then. Give your kids a little help. Give them vitamins.

CAUSE AND EFFECT

These underwater photographs prove that Shark-Go really works. It takes the worry out of swimming.

CLASSIFICATION

So, spend your next vacation in Siberia. You can save money, avoid the crowds, and see some famous people.

COMPARISON

Old Goose is the best bourbon on the market.
Take the taste test. You'll switch to Puppy-Grow.

DESCRIPTION

Through Supracolor you'll see deep reds. And natural flesh tones.
So you'll get incredibly sharp, lifelike pictures from your Quasar,
right from the carton.

NARRATION

When you were a kid, your parents couldn't get you to listen to long-
haired music.

Sixty years ago, you didn't need a college education. In fact, you
didn't need much of anything except a willingness to work sixteen hours
a day. For 8 cents an hour. Under brutal conditions.

Persuasion relies on the techniques of written expression to influence someone else's thinking or action.

Audience

Persuading someone to accept your ideas as true and to take
action in accord with them demands some knowledge of the person or group you are trying to influence. Advertisers rely on psychological research to understand their audience, but in most cases
a little common sense can figure out the characteristics of your
intended audience. If you know the opinions a group of people
already share, you won't have to waste your time proving those
opinions are correct. Speaking against amnesty for Vietnam deserters to an American Legion convention demands much less
rigorous preparation than convincing them the deserters should be
granted amnesty. The same holds true for writing. The concerns
and values of the audience reading your work will determine your
strategy, as will educational backgrounds, social backgrounds, and
political attitudes.

A car salesman will use one approach to sell an eighteen-year-
old a car and another to sell the same car to a middle-aged businessman. Once again, effective advertising depends on a thorough
knowledge of audience: What type of people are likely to read a
certain magazine? What are their concerns and values? The following ad copy comes from a single issue of one magazine. Can
you describe the audience the advertisers are appealing to?

High Fidelity for the Price of Mediocre Fidelity.
The Cricketeer Difference: Spending less than you'd expect, for a change. Executive taste doesn't have to cost you chairman of the board prices.
Why a Boulton Stereo is the *Finest* you can own.
Never underestimate the value of art.
The fountain pen that never went out of style.
Own an original Thonet for $40.
No thanks, no substitute . . . I WANT THE BEST!

The Proposition

Common sense dictates that it is necessary to tell the reader what you are trying to prove. This statement of judgment or opinion is called a *proposition*. A proposition is a statement that can be affirmed or denied. A proposition has two sides; it can be accepted or rejected. Once you make a proposition, you have placed yourself on one side or the other. Because the proposition asks the reader to accept or act upon a point of view, it must be expressed in a complete statement, a sentence complete with subject and verb. The following statements are propositions:

Consumers are wasting $8 billion to $10 billion on auto repairs yearly.

(This statement makes a judgment expressed by the word *wasting*.)

An increase in India's food supply could occur without additional destruction of forest lands.

(Propositions often carry a sense of *could* or *ought* with them. The use of *could* here implies there is another possible opinion.)

Developing countries need technical assistance to solve economic problems.

(Congress is not going to allocate funds for this assistance until persuaded of the need.)

The king can do no wrong.

(Circumstances of recent history suggest that there may be another side to this proposition.)

Richard Nixon is guilty of impeachable offenses.

(The lawyer who made this proposition did a fair job of getting others to agree with him.)

These propositions have common features:

1. They are judgments and/or expressions of opinion.
2. They imply an alternative position could be held (Mr. Nixon is *not* guilty).
3. They all require the support of concrete evidence and examples. Even the most sympathetic audience is going to ask, "Why? What are your reasons?"

Evidence

Once the issue has been stated in a proposition, you have to support it with evidence. After the 1976 World Series, many observers maintained that the Cincinnati Reds had the greatest baseball team in history. Even a proposition like this made over a friendly beer demands evidence to support it. If a newspaper, for example, quoted Joe DiMaggio as raving about how great the Reds were, his statement would offer an expert opinion lending weight to a judgment on the Reds' greatness. Describing the abilities of Bench or Perez or Rose also would support this opinion. Or you could compare each member of the Reds' team with greats of the past at the same position. Batting statistics provide hard facts, as would facts about speed and base-stealing ability. In other words, you would use what you have seen, read, or heard to support your opinion. All of this supporting material is evidence.

Observation

One source of supporting evidence for a proposition is your own observations. Whatever caused you to state the proposition is probably linked to personal observation. Scientists depend on observation to formulate their propositions:

At 3:00 A.M. I sat alone on the concrete floor of the grain godown (warehouse), amused by the group of seventeen rats that had just walked across my lap. As long as I remained quiet, the wild rats investigated me as they would any object—by sniffing, licking, and walking over me. That they would attack when threatened or cornered was evidenced by the stories of several laborers with telltale scars on their ankles and feet. For most of my observations I sat atop a 10-foot-high platform against one wall of the godown, but for detailed observations of behavior, I found it necessary to sit on the floor and "become a rat."[42]

Firsthand observation provides valuable evidence, but let's hope none of us have to "become a rat" to collect evidence. Incidentally, the observations made among the rats led to the discovery that in one warehouse in one year the rats ate enough grain to feed an average Indian for eleven years. Firsthand observation, then, can lend support to an opinion or judgment.

Henry David Thoreau was an accurate and sensitive observer of nature and society. The personal observations he recorded in *Walden* influenced many readers to change life-styles and reconsider their goals in life. One famous passage from *Walden* illustrates how persuasive personal observations can be:

Our life is frittered away by detail. An honest man has hardly need to count more than his ten fingers, or in extreme cases he may add his ten toes, and lump the rest. Simplicity, simplicity, simplicity! I say, let your affairs be as two or three, and not a hundred or a thousand; instead of a million count half a dozen, and keep your accounts on your thumbnail. In the midst of this chopping sea of civilized life, such are the clouds and storms and quicksands and thousand-and-one items to be allowed for, that a man has to live, if he would not founder and go to the bottom and not make his port at all, by dead reckoning, and he must be a great calculator indeed who succeeds. Simplify, simplify. Instead of three meals a day, if it be necessary eat but one; instead of a hundred dishes, five; and reduce other things in proportion. Our life is like a German Confederacy, made up of petty states, with its boundary forever fluctuating, so that even a German cannot tell you how it is bounded at any moment. The nation itself, with all its so-called internal improvements, which, by the way are all external and superficial, is just such an unwieldy and overgrown establishment, cluttered with furniture and tripped up by its own traps, ruined by luxury and heedless expense, by want of calculation and a worthy aim, as the million households in the land; and the only cure for it, as for them, is in a

---

[42] Stephen C. Frantz, "The Web of Hunger," *Natural History*, 85 (February 1976), p. 10.

rigid economy, a stern and more than Spartan simplicity of life and elevation of purpose.[43]

Authority

Your own trained and accurate observations provide a solid basis for judgment and opinion, but your own observations may not carry enough weight to be truly persuasive. It is helpful to call in expert help. Referring to an expert or to an authority's opinion strengthens your proposition. All of us tend to respect the judgment of people who have demonstrated knowledge and experience in a given field. Ralph Nader calls on the experts to support his famous attack on the Chevrolet Corvair:

> It is well established that cornering stability can be improved with any weight distribution, front or rear, by manipulating tire inflation pressures. (Equally inflated tire pressures, front and rear, says Professor Eugene Larrabee of the Massachusetts Institute of Technology, make the Corvair dangerous to drive.) But any policy which throws the burden of such stability on the driver by requiring him to monitor closely and persistently tire pressure differentials cannot be described as sound or sane engineering practice. The prominent automotive engineer Robert Janeway expressed a deeply rooted technical opinion in engineering circles when he evaluated the use of this human expedient: "Instead of stability being inherent in the vehicle design, the operator is relied upon to maintain a required pressure differential in front and rear tires. This responsibility, in turn, is passed along to service station attendants, who are notoriously unreliable in abiding by requested tire pressures. There is also serious doubt whether the owner or service man is fully aware of the importance of maintaining the recommended pressures."[44]

Nader not only refers to expert authorities to support his opinion, but also establishes the credentials of the authorities. These two experts hold positions that lend credibility to their opinions. If Nader had asked a General Motors engineer for an opinion, the response would likely have differed considerably from that of an outside, objective observer.

In the letter that follows, a consumer tries to persuade a businessman to refund excess charges for repair work on her car:

---

[43] Henry David Thoreau, *Walden* (New York: W. W. Norton, 1951), pp. 106–108.
[44] Ralph Nader, *Unsafe at Any Speed* (New York: Grossman & Co., 1972), pp. 23–24.

February 26, 1977

Mr. Paul Rayburn
Lovell Toyota, Inc.
787 Rogers Street
Portland, Maine

Dear Paul,

After some reflection on the amount of the labor charges for repairing my automobile, I decided to contact Mr. Adler, the Toyota regional service representative, to obtain his opinion on the fairness of the charges involved. I have also consulted the district attorney's office here and have spoken at some length with the consumer advocate in his office and am now fully informed with regard to Chapter 93A of the Maine General Law concerning the Consumer Protection Act. Following these conversations, I am now substantially convinced that there definitely is an overcharge for the labor indicated on your repair invoice #C 0143 and on my copy of the same. Furthermore, there is no indication of the number of hours involved in the labor or of the hourly rate for which I was billed.

Although my first reaction was to stop payment on one or both of the checks I left with your charming cashier, I do not feel that in all fairness I should do that, but that I should let you take the initiative and offer me a refund in an amount that represents a more equitable settlement for the repairs. I have no doubts or misgivings at this time about the quality of the work, and I very much appreciate the courtesy you have shown me in this matter. However, I do expect to receive a refund from your company, and Mr. Adler has indicated to me that this should at the very least be $30/$40. Although I do not wish to bring the district attorney's office any further into this matter or to take the matter to Small Claims Court, these are clearly options that remain open to me. All too frequently, the consumer is courted in the automobile showroom, but treated with disdain in the service department. I, for one, expect equal and fair treatment in both instances, and will not settle for less.

Sincerely,

Katherine Battle

Factual Evidence

The most convincing evidence in support of an opinion or judgment consists of facts. You've heard the expression "Just give me the facts" and have probably asserted in the course of an argument, "And that's a fact!" Facts are real. A fact is an event or incident that actually happened or a circumstance that really exists.

Commercial, nuclear power plants have caused no injury to the public.
All steam electrical plants, both nuclear and fossil-fueled, must return
    waste heat to the environment. . . .
All radiation is harmful to living things.

Facts can also be translated into numbers that are a result of observation and measurement. You might observe, for example,
several accidents occurring at an intersection without a stop sign
or traffic light. A letter to local government officials requesting the
installation of a traffic signal would carry much more weight and
produce more immediate action if you counted the number of accidents in a given period and used these facts to support your request. The following example uses facts to support the author's
proposition:

> In New York City, welfare recipients demonstrated to get credit
> cards from Sears and Korvette's (a discount chain), and these demon-
> strations met with some success, which, in a perverse way, they should
> have. At this time, in particular, welfare recipients have a steadier
> source of income than many highly skilled, highly paid people who
> work for their money. Also, believe it or not, many welfare families en-
> joy better real incomes than some blue-collar working families. The
> Joint Subcommittee on Fiscal Policy of the House of Representatives
> Joint Economic Committee conducted a nationwide sampling of 1,059
> poverty families in six low-income areas in representative parts of the
> country and found that many so-called poverty families were receiving
> cash and in-kind benefits from a wide variety of welfare programs (food
> stamps, day care, medicaid, etc.), and that after computing the cash
> value of in-kind welfare, the income levels of a sizable percentage ex-
> ceeded the take-home pay of people who work for a living. About 20
> percent of the welfare families were enrolled in five or more federal aid
> programs, and their monthly incomes ranged from $306 to $676 (this
> works out to $3,672 to $8,112 per year, *before taxes*). "These tax-free
> benefits," the Subcommittee reported, "exceed the median wage levels
> for full-time workingmen, which range from $303 to $502 [per month]
> in the five urban areas. . . . The sizable average benefits going to these
> [welfare] households indicate that many of them are better off now than
> they would be if they derived all of their income from wages, given the
> wage level at which their members would find employment and the
> social security and income taxes that would have to be paid from those
> wages."[45]

What course of action do you think this writer would recommend
on the basis of these facts? Could it be argued that the economic

---

[45] Bruce Goldman, Robert Franklin, Kenneth Pepper, *Your Check Is in the Mail*
(New York: Warner Books, Inc., 1976), p. 12.

THE TOOLS OF THE TRADE

benefits of spending by welfare households outweigh the damage
to other programs, such as cancer research, upon which the government could spend its tax revenues?

Although numerical facts provide convincing evidence, note
that the same facts can be used to support entirely different arguments. The facts about fluoride emissions in the preceding example could become part of an argument to keep fluoride out of a
city's water supply. Facts demand interpretation, and often two
experts examining the same body of facts arrive at different conclusions. The resolution of the controversy over nuclear power
plants, for example, could be vital to our personal and national
health and well-being. Two experts use similar facts in different
ways: one, to persuade us of the safety of nuclear plants, the other,
to convince us that these plants are extremely dangerous to human
health.

This limit allowable under Atomic Energy Commission standards is
equal to the amount of radiation we receive from nature.

This background radiation, which has always been with us, is produced by cosmic rays and natural radioactive isotopes in the human
body and in our surroundings. The level of radiation exposure to the
average U.S. citizen today as the result of nuclear power plant operation
is less than $\frac{1}{1000}$ of one per cent of that due to background radiation
to which everyone is exposed.[46]

The radiation exposure that a person might receive if nuclear reactors emitted the full amount of radiation allowable under present
Atomic Energy Commission standards would be about equal to the exposure from natural sources. Thus exposure at the allowable level would
increase the harmful effects on humans from background radiation
about 100 per cent.

Dr. K. Z. Morgan of the AEC's Oak Ridge National Laboratory estimates that radiation actually emitted from reactors now in operation
will probably increase the lethal effects of radiation-induced disease
among the population by about 1.2 to 7 per cent (that is, a 1.2 to 7 per
cent increase over the lethal effects of background radiation).[47]

---

[46] Glenn T. Seaborg, "Nuclear Power Plants: Boon or Blight?" *National Wildlife*,
9 (April 1971), p. 22.
[47] Barry Commoner, "Nuclear Power Plants: Boon or Blight?" *National Wildlife*,
9 (April 1971), p. 23.

Facts are indisputable, but the way someone interprets those facts often leads to serious disagreement. In the course of your professional career, you will inevitably be asked to recommend a course of action or a solution to a problem; this recommendation will grow out of your careful observation and study of the facts.

Suppose you have been called upon to recommend one of three employees under your supervision for promotion to a more responsible, demanding job. Your own boss wants you to assess the qualities of each employee and make a reasoned recommendation. In effect, he wants you to argue a case for one of the three.

Perhaps you know or can discreetly solicit the opinions of other members of your staff on the capabilities of each candidate. Furthermore, from working with the candidates you have personal experience of their talents and abilities. You have also had many opportunities to observe the results of their various job-related activities. Now all of this information can be used to create distinct profiles of the three candidates for promotion, and from these profiles there should emerge the facts that will support your recommendations. Candidate A, let's say, has initiated and brought to successful conclusion fourteen new projects that have resulted in profit for the company. On a dozen documented occasions you have asked him to work overtime, and he has cheerfully, willingly agreed. In your judgment, the quality of his work outshines that of the other candidates. On balance, then, this candidate performs his work more effectively and demonstrates greater initiative than either of his competitors. Your conclusions and, therefore, your recommendations are inescapable.

Recommendations, you must remember, are only conjectures for the future based on the historical evidence of the past. They combine the relevant features of many types of evidence to arrive at the facts as you, the recommender, perceive them. It is your task to interpret all of those types of evidence and translate them into factual data in support of your proposition. The following example summarizes the evidence that led the FDA to recommend precautions against exposure to microwave radiation.

Like many other tools of modern technology, microwaves themselves, which fall along the energy spectrum between ordinary radio waves and infra-red rays, have come under suspicion of late for bearing possibly unhealthy and uncontrolled side-effects. The long-term effects of low-level radiation that might leak from microwave ovens are not yet known and are probably not serious. Microwaves do not—unlike high-energy X-rays —break apart the complex molecules of biological tissue into their component parts. Very high levels of microwaves, however, are dangerous in other ways.

By interacting with water molecules as they do in food, microwaves at very high power levels can burn areas of the human body. Two especially heat-sensitive human organs, the eye and the male testis, are particularly vulnerable to microwave radiation. Because it lacks a blood supply, the lens of the eye is unable to cool itself, and excessive heat can literally cook the lens protein the same way it coagulates egg white. Over-exposure to microwaves can thus produce cataracts, or cloudiness in the lens, and can lead to blindness. In the testis, sperm can form only at temperatures lower than that of the body itself, and microwave heating could lead to temporary sterility. No one knows the extent to which people have accidentally been injured by microwave heat over the years, but many such injuries have been demonstrated in experiments with laboratory animals.

In addition, microwaves, as well as other types of electromagnetic radiation, have on occasion interfered with the operation of pacemakers by distorting the electrical signals these life-sustaining instruments send to the heart muscle. Pacemaker users have been known to faint when exposed to high-level microwave emissions, although known incidences of such interferences are few and pacemaker manufacturers have recently improved their electrical shielding.

Because of these hazards, for a long time now, both industry and the Federal government have decreed safety standards that set a maximum permissible exposure for anyone working near microwave sources. The exposure limit has generally been fixed at 10 milliwatts (thousandths of a watt) per square centimeter. And the Food and Drug Administration has decreed that microwave ovens in the home may not leak more than five milliwatts per square centimeter (measured at five centimeters— about 2 inches—from the oven); the F.D.A. says the ovens are safe. Such precautions have minimized the dangers from high-level microwaves, but what about microwaves at lower power levels, such as the relatively low amounts that might leak from microwave ovens?[48]

[48] Marion Steinman, "The Waves of the Future," *The New York Times Magazine* (November 7, 1976), pp. 78–79.

CONCLUSION

PERSUASION uses every tool at the writer's command. Getting someone else to see things your way is no easy task and the success of that task depends on the validity of the evidence you use to support your proposition. The passage discussing microwave ovens gives us facts to support the author's claim that these ovens are "possibly unhealthy." In your career you will be called on to make decisions based on the kind of evidence this writer provides. Perhaps a good way to begin exercising the skills you have been practicing is to assume the roles of, first, a manufacturer of microwave ovens and defend their use by the public. Then assume the role of a concerned citizen who thinks the risks outweigh the benefits in this case and write a persuasive letter to the F.D.A.

EXERCISES

1. Think of an entirely "useless" product (bottled sunshine, a spoon made of sugar, a left-handed monkey wrench). Create an advertising campaign that will persuade the public to buy it.
2. Write a letter to a large corporation, convincing it to recompense you for the failure of one of its products. This can be an imaginary or a real exercise.
3. Reread the example given in this chapter on recommending one of three candidates for promotion. Write the recommendation you would send to your boss.

III

Writing for the "Real" World

LIFE ON THE LINE
Roger Rapoport

T HE Ford Motor Co. auto assembly line here is an impressive sight. Bare frames are put on a slowly moving conveyor. Wheels, engines, seats, body sections and hundreds of other components are added along the way. At the end of the quarter-mile, 90-minute trip, finished cars are driven off to be inspected and shipped to dealers.

It takes some 275 workers to put the cars together on the Wixom line. To hear a guide at Ford's big River Rouge plant, a popular tourist stop in nearby Dearborn, tell it, life on the line is a snap. "Each worker on an assembly line has one little job to do," he says. "It's simple. Anyone could learn it in two minutes."

That's bunk.

Working on the line is grueling and frustrating, and while it may be repetitive, it's not simple. I learned how tough it can be by working for six days at Ford's Wixom plant, which assembles Thunderbirds and Lincoln Continentals.

I learned first-hand why 250,000 auto workers are unhappy about working conditions. Ford calls Wixom the "most progressive automobile assembly plant on the North American continent." Facilities at the 10-year-old plant here are indeed better than those at many of the 46 other auto assembly plants scattered around the country. Wixom is clean and well-lighted by auto industry standards. It boasts adequate rest rooms, plenty of drinking fountains and an air-conditioned cafeteria. Even so, working conditions are less than ideal.

I also learned why quality control is a major problem for the industry and why so many Americans complain about poor workmanship in the cars they buy. I saw one blue fender installed on a white car and saw the steering column fall off another newly built car. Wixom's repair area, nearly the size of a football field, usually had a line-up of 500 cars waiting to have steering adjusted, scratches painted, brakes repaired and other faults fixed—but not all defects are caught before cars leave the plant. The four auto companies have recalled from customers more than a million 1967 model cars since last September because of suspected manufacturing defects.

Ford didn't know I was a reporter. Along with a handful of other young men, I was hired as a summer replacement, and to the personnel

F R O M *The Wall Street Journal* (July 24, 1967), pp. 14–16. Reprinted with permission of *The Wall Street Journal*, © Dow Jones & Company, Inc. (1967). All Rights Reserved.

department I was simply Social Security number 362–44–9616. The foreman on the line knew me as "9616" for short.

Names aren't necessary on the line. The conveyor moves at $\frac{1}{8}$ of a mile an hour, and while that may not sound terribly fast, it doesn't leave much time for conversation. Also, the cacophony of bells, whistles, buzzers, hammers, whining pneumatic wrenches and clanking, rumbling machinery drowns out voices, so most communicating is done by arm waving and hand gestures.

Only two of the dozens of men I worked beside at various points on the line ever learned my name, and I knew only the first names of two workmen. One was Clyde, a husky Negro who had been an assembler for about a year. My first day on the job, a foreman assigned Clyde to teach me the ropes at one work station.

Clyde, a 220-pound six-footer, showed me how to bolt the car body to the chassis in three pieces. It was fairly easy for me, a 160-pound six-footer. He showed me how to lean inside the trunk, tighten two bolts and make an electrical connection. I managed that task, too. He showed me how to maneuver a big V–8 engine dangling overhead down into a car's engine compartment. By this time, I considered myself fairly versatile.

Then Clyde showed me how to scramble from one car to the next, putting chassis and trunk bolts in the first two cars and helping with the engine in the third—all in less than five minutes. When I tried it, I got stuck in the trunk of one car, missed the chassis bolts on the next and was too late to help install the engine on the third car.

Gradually, I became more proficient. But, I didn't last long at any job. As a temporary worker, I was assigned to fill in for absent workmen at five different work stations at various times during my six days on the line. Except for Clyde, the men who showed me the jobs weren't very good teachers. One workman demonstrated the way to attach clamps to heater hoses, but he didn't mention that the clamps have tops and bottoms. A foreman caught my error after I had installed a dozen clamps upside down.

Nobody told me to put on steering wheels that match the color of the dashboard—I figured that out myself. But I made some mistakes because nobody warned me that tinted glass makes it difficult to distinguish the color of the dash by looking through the windshield. I installed some blue steering wheels on cars with aqua dashboards and mismatched a black wheel with a gray dashboard.

On experienced worker told me that a color-blind assembler recently installed the wrong color vent plates under the windshield wipers on cars for two hours before a foreman spotted the error and assigned the man to another job.

I wasn't checked for color blindness when I was hired. Rapid turnover and a major expansion at Wixom made getting a job easy, even though the plant was heading for a temporary shutdown to make the annual model change-over. I passed a three-hour physical exam and an 11-minute written test. (Sample questions: "Which of the following doesn't belong? spade, queen, king, ace; oak, maple, leaf, elm.") There was no interview. I was issued a free pair of safety glasses, given a five-minute lecture on safety and plant safety rules, and told to report to work.

Along with some 2,700 other employes on the third work turn, I arrived at the sprawling, suburban Detroit plant shortly after 3 P.M. and punched the time clock. Most of the men on the line were between 20 and 35 years old. Most wore sport shirts and slacks or green coveralls. About a third were Negroes.

The windowless assembly line area inside the two-story plant reminded me of a tunnel. Down the middle ran the assembly line. Overhead were fluorescent lights and conveyors carrying engines, fenders and other components. Tall racks and bins full of auto parts lined the sides. A narrow slit trench for underbody installations stretched the length of the line.

At 3:30 P.M. the conveyor began moving, and work started on the assembly line. For the next three hours until a relief man shouted at me to take a 20-minute break while he replaced me—I rarely spoke or was spoken to.

For a while, I concentrated hard to get each job done within the 90 seconds the moving car was in front of my work station without dropping the five-pound pneumatic wrench on my foot. Every third car on the line was a Continental, and required a slight variation from Thunderbird installation procedures.

Nevertheless, each task soon became a mind-deadening routine, and my thoughts turned to everything but cars. ("You just leave your brains at home and work out of habit," one experienced worker later advised me.) Sometimes, after many minutes of bending over and zeroing in on a moving target, I would step back, and the line would appear to be stationary while everything else seemed to be moving.

I'm in fairly good physical shape, but I ached all over after each day's work on the line. At one station, I had to bend down into the engine compartment to bolt on the steering column. To install carpeting, I sat on the door frame with one foot dragging and drilled holes, then stretched out on my side under the instrument panel to fasten the carpet to the floor. Attaching steering wheels meant stretching through the open car window to stick the wheel on the column and bolt it down.

Nobody seemed to take any particular pride in his work. Some workers considered some of the parts shoddy. The kick-pads that I installed under instrument panels, for example, were made of relatively brittle plastic and sometimes broke off during installation. One workman told me that "over 400 of them broke off one month last winter."

One day when I was helping two men bolt steering columns in place, the columns on a dozen cars were mounted improperly by someone up the line, so we couldn't bolt them down and men further down the line couldn't attach the steering wheels. Such chain reactions often result from a single slip-up, and regularly snarl the precision of the computer-controlled assembly line.

It was Clyde who first told me what to do if I made or discovered a mistake. "Get the next car and don't worry," he said. "They'll catch that one further down the line." When I spotted the white Thunderbird bearing a blue fender, another worker explained: "They'll paint over it in the repair shop. It's easier to catch it there than it is on the line."

About 10 repairmen stationed at various points along the way catch and fix some minor defects right on the assembly line. But it's up to the 15 or 20 inspectors along the line to check each car thoroughly and route those with improperly installed parts into the plant's 100-man repair shop. One inspector was an inexperienced college student. Some regular inspectors seemed far from dedicated.

I saw one standing with his eyes closed. When a workman pointed out a faulty engine, the inspector tagged the defect, then closed his eyes again. Once I spotted a loose steering wheel and told an inspector. He said he had just checked that wheel and "found it tight," but he double-checked and admitted, "You were right—it was loose."

I saw a loose steering column fall off a Thunderbird when an inspector checked it. Later he told me that . . . he had "only missed marking up three loose steering columns, which is pretty good since 80% of them were going through loose yesterday." Another inspector further down the line spotted the three loose columns.

An inspector who had five things to check on each car told me: "There isn't nearly enough time to do all the inspections. I'm supposed to check shock absorbers, but I haven't had a chance to look at one in a month." Another inspector jokingly said he inspects a car trunk just closely enough "to make sure there's no dead foreman in there."

Because Wixom builds luxury cars priced to sell from $4,600 to over $7,300, the assembly line moves at what, for the auto industry, is considered a slow production pace of about 40 cars an hour. Some other luxury cars are built at a faster rate. General Motors Corp.'s Cadillac assembly line rolls out 50 cars an hour, and Chrysler Corp. builds about 55 Chryslers and Imperials an hour. Lower priced cars such as Fords, Chevrolets and Plymouths usually come off the line at a rate of up to 65 cars an hour.

That can seem like breakneck speed to a weary worker on the assembly line. The speed of the line, in fact, has been a major cause of half a dozen local strikes by United Auto Workers Union members at other auto assembly plants in the past few years.

Even Wixom's pace seemed fast to me. When my 20-minute break started at 6:30 each night, I staggered to the pop machine to buy a cold drink. Then I looked for someplace to sit and rest. There aren't many places to sit in the plant. My favorite spot was atop a cart loaded with big white laundry sacks full of dirty coveralls, a place where I could stretch out.

Sometimes a few workers would talk and joke during their breaks. Foremen and other supervisors were the butt of many jokes—particularly one balding supervisor who was referred to as "Khrushchev." But the assemblers actually got along well with the foremen, who worked hard themselves and generally were patient and polite when correcting workmen's mistakes. Supervisors insisted on informality. When I called one "sir," he quickly told me: "That isn't necessary around here."

After my relief period, I spent another hour and 10 minutes on the line. Then, at 7:30 P.M., the conveyors stopped, and the scramble for lunch started. There wasn't time to wash the grease off my hands or pull the slivers of glass fiber insulation out of my arms before eating.

Usually lunch periods were staggered, but sometimes the day's production schedule was arranged so that all 2,700 workers in the plant ate at the same time. The first day that happened, I cut in near the front of the long line outside the air-conditioned company cafeteria. It took 15 minutes, half my lunch period, to reach the counter, pick up iced tea, milk, soup, roast beef, Jell-O, pie and pay the cashier $1.50. I ate in 11 minutes.

That left two minutes to go to the bathroom and another two minutes to get back to my place on the line. I had indigestion for an hour after lunch. Some workers had to wait 25 minutes to get served that day. I don't know how, or if, they ate and got back to work in five minutes.

Many workmen brought sack lunches and sat on stock ranks or in cars on the line eating sandwiches. Eating in the cars was against plant rules. Nevertheless, when I was installing carpets, I frequently had to throw out lunch sacks, cigaret butts and coffee cups along with the usual assortment of screws, fuses and bolts before laying a carpet. I picked an empty beer can out of a car, too—even though another plant rule prohibits drinking alcohol.

Safety rules frequently were violated, too. I saw foremen running and assemblers jumping across the assembly line trench, both supposedly forbidden. Occasionally there was horseplay on the line. But I didn't see any accidents. Indeed, when I was there, Wixom had gone two million man-hours without an accident.

Ennui set in during the second half of the work turn. To break the monotony, some workers played practical jokes, like detaching the air hose from an assembler's pneumatic wrench. Others performed timpani concerts on plant ventilation ducts with rubber mallets. They hooted and whistled whenever women office employes ventured into the production area.

My second relief break began at 10 P.M. and lasted 16 minutes. (In the UAW's contract negotiations with Ford and the three other auto companies, the Union is demanding two 30-minute paid relief breaks daily for assemblers. Auto workers aren't paid during their half hour lunch periods.) There was less bantering among workers during the second break. Some of them talked of quitting. One man groused about "too much pressure" and said: "When I was working in an auto parts plant, I could meet my quota in four hours and then goof off, but here there's no rest."

When the quitting whistle blew at midnight, smiles returned to most workers' faces. They washed up quickly and headed for the parking lot. I drove straight home and went to bed. But some of the men went out moonlighting. One young guy making about $3.30 an hour at Wixom worked several hours as a night pressman for a small morning newspaper. Another, earning about $3.50 an hour, went home and slept for five hours, then put in eight hours doing maintenance work at a nearby golf course. "I made $11,000 last year," he told me.

After the final whistle blew on my last work turn before the plant closed for model change-over, Clyde kidded me at the water cooler. "You should feel ashamed of yourself, taking all that good Ford money after the way you worked," he said.

Hiring me might not have been one of Ford's better ideas, but I think I earned my $110 take-home pay. Ford apparently thought so, too. The foreman told me to report for work again when Wixom resumes production next week.

But I don't intend to go back to the plant—except perhaps to pick up my pay check. Ford wouldn't mail it to me. "We've got 6,000 guys who would like to have their checks mailed to them," a personnel man told me. "What makes you think you're any different?"

EXERCISES

VOCABULARY

cacophony	precision	proficient
versatile	ennui	distinguish
grueling		

1. What was the author's purpose in writing this article?
2. This article relies heavily on one of the kinds of evidence discussed in the section on persuasion. What type of evidence does the writer use?
3. Rapoport says he learned three main things from working on the assembly line. What are they? Does the essay give each of these ideas adequate development later on?
4. Find an example of description. What techniques of description does Rapaport employ to present the details?
5. Why does Rapoport describe his lunch break in such detail—even down to the contents of his tray?
6. How does the personnel man's comment in the last paragraph tie in with the rest of the article? Is this an effective conclusion?

END OF THE LINE FOR JOB MECHANIZATION?

Do the Problems Have Solutions?

Theodore A. Jackson and A. A. Imberman

The steady clanking of the overhead conveyor chain and the staccato, whistling rattle of the pneumatic nut runners form a mind-numbing cacophony. Forty-two units per hour; seven bolts per unit; two thousand three hundred and fifty-two bolts to be tightened each day. Two eighteen-minute rest periods a day—just time enough for a cup of coffee, a quick smoke, and a trip to the toilet—then it's back to the line again. Today is just like yesterday and tomorrow will be the same . . . and the day after that . . . and the day after that. The boredom . . . the noise . . . and throughout it all, the unceasing, inexorable movement of the line as it carries unit after unit past the work-station . . . hour after hour after hour. Surely life holds more than this. Isn't there a better way?

This is the question that more and more industrial workers and their union spokesmen are raising these days. And in their demand for answers, they are forcing managers to review and re-evaluate the fundamental concepts and procedures upon which America's productive might has long been based. Being questioned is the concept of mechanized manufacturing, the wellspring from which the mass production of goods at low unit cost emanates.

This unrest or dissatisfaction with mechanized manufacturing methods that is being expressed by production workers today is manifesting itself in many ways. In some cases, it is merely vocal and is being placed on the agenda as a point of discussion for future negotiating sessions with management. In other cases, it is resulting in work stoppages, "wildcat" walkouts, and the like. In quite a few instances, this disenchantment on the part of the more militant workers is resulting in either sabotage of the production equipment itself or in a concerted effort to produce poor quality goods through shoddy workmanship, in the belief that this course of action enables the worker to "get even" with management.

In any event, irrespective of the form it takes, the frequency and extent of this worker dissatisfaction is increasing at an alarming rate. It is rapidly becoming, if it is not already, the primary headache of the managers whose responsibility is meeting production goals.

FROM *Automation* (June 1973), pp. 48–55. Reprinted from *Automation*, June 1973. Copyright 1973 by Penton, Inc., Cleveland, Ohio 44114. Reprinted by permission.

The mechanized production operation is segmented into a series of small, repetitive, and easily-learned tasks, each of which can be performed without expensive training. By thus deskilling the operation, better control over output can be maintained, since there is less dependence upon the availability of special skills. For instance, if an ordinary assembly line worker is absent, virtually anyone can substitute for him with a minimum of training. However, if a highly skilled worker is absent, it is unlikely that a replacement will be readily available and—as a consequence—productive output is curtailed.

From the standpoint of the engineers and the work simplification specialists, this concept was the key to increased production at low unit cost. For a considerable time it worked, too—particularly when the over-all economy was in a depressed state, jobs were scarce, and the general level of education, experience, and sophistication of the average industrial worker was at a considerably lower level than it is today.

But, tremendous change has taken place in recent years in education and the comparatively wide-ranging experience and exposure that most people have had via television, radio, motion pictures, travel, and printed media. As a result, the "expectation" level of the average worker is at an all-time high. He expects as his due a level of challenge, interest, and sense of accomplishment in his work that is commensurate with the general level of abilities he believes he brings to the job.

Today's industrial workers are rebelling against the boredom, the monotony, the mindless repetition, and the generally depressing environment that is so large a part of much, if not most, present-day mechanized production. This is particularly true of younger workers who have neither become locked-in with seniority and pension rights, nor have yet become resigned to the inevitability of continuing in this milieu.

To correct this state of affairs will require a considerable change in basic production methods and the abandonment of certain long-held beliefs. While the workers' expectations continue to rise, the level of skill required for mechanized production jobs continues to fall. Given our contemporary patterns of life, there seems to be no way that these expectations will diminish.

If any change is to occur, it will have to be made in the job itself. The work will have to be made more interesting and challenging. It will have to provide a great deal more psychological appeal than it currently has.

However, the biggest change will have to occur in the philosophy underlying the job itself. Recognition must be made of the fact that workers are people and not merely extensions of the machines they manipulate. A more enlightened approach is required so that a certain measure of dignity and pride can be restored to the workers.

Money alone isn't the answer. Merely increasing the number of dollars that are paid each week to the worker is not enough. As has been so effectively shown in the psychological studies by Herzberg, the basics of money, safe working conditions, health insurance programs, vacations, holiday periods, and all the other so-called fringe benefits are taken for granted by workers today. The presence of these factors no longer makes a job attractive and interesting.

What the worker wants today is an opportunity to use his abilities and to make some decisions in his work. He wants a feeling of recognition and a sense of fulfillment in his work. These items, unfortunately, are all too lacking in the highly mechanized milieu of present-day industry.

The average worker in a highly mechanized production operation does not have the opportunity to achieve any real sense of fulfillment in his work, nor does he receive any feedback from outside sources. By the very way his job is constituted, he is unable to either develop or exercise much responsibility or exercise any significant amount of decision making or judgment. In short, there is no feeling of worthwhile accomplishment engendered by the work itself, and there is no team or group spirit evident in the limited contact he has with his fellow workers. Even during his regimented rest periods there is little, if any, of the fun or relaxation element present. These periods are always subconsciously overshadowed by the authoritarian influence of the ever-present clock.

One approach to the problem of humanizing work has been made by Robert L. Kahn of the University of Michigan in his concept of "the work module." This concept allows a worker to change the type of work that he does after about a two-hour stint. (A module is the smallest allocation of time that is economically and psychologically meaningful to a worker.) A given worker has the freedom to arrange his modules— i.e., to construct his job—to suit himself. The idea is that "workers are happier when they can construct their jobs rather than when the jobs construct them."

Parent-Adult-Child at Work

The concept of mechanized production is actually a classic epitomization of the Parent-Adult-Child relationship in Transactional Analysis wherein the system itself is the Parent and the worker is the Child. (Transactional Analysis and the P-A-C concept have been popularized recently in the book I'm O.K., You're O.K. by Dr. T. A. Harris.) The system, by its very nature, is confining, with its Parent-like multiplicity of rules and regulations governing virtually every action of the worker during the time he is on the job. Under these circumstances, the worker has a tendency to revert to Child-like thought patterns and behavior. The

Parent influence inevitably fosters a Child response such as compliance, fear, rebellion, and the like.

Ideally, of course, the relationship between the system and the worker should be one that allows the worker to make use of his productive Adult and also the positive aspects of his Child—his creativity, etc. Such utilization would, of course, presuppose a drastic shift in prerogatives. The worker would assume added responsibility for such things as output, quality standards, time off the job, etc., with a concomitant relinquishing of the control of these factors by management.

There is movement in American industry to consider such developments. IBM, for one example, started a job enlargement program more than ten years ago. Texas Instruments has researched this problem and has made many changes. More recently, many corporations are getting into the act with serious attention being given to this aspect of production. The term that has come to be most generally used to describe these programs is "job enrichment." It seems that American industry is finally waking up to the fact that there is a serious problem. Obviously it will not be easy to introduce and effectively integrate this new awareness into

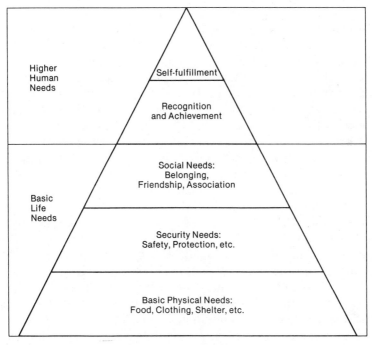

Hierarchy of Needs—Maslow

present methods because of the tremendous momentum of the current system.

A notable example of the introduction of this new work ethic that has been advertised recently is that of the Saab organization in Sweden. There, the assembly line has been replaced with assembly teams—groups of three or four people who are responsible for a particular assembly process from start to finish. Each team makes its own decisions as to who does what, and when. Each team member has been trained to do the entire assembly single-handedly, so that the various tasks can be interchanged if necessary and at their will. The results appear to be phenomenal. The people are more involved, they care more about quality, and there is less absenteeism and turnover of personnel. It is a good example of where a worker is more nearly able to utilize his whole self—Parent, Adult, and Child.

The situation that exists in most mechanized production facilities today is not necessarily the fault of the engineers, the time and motion experts, and the cost accountants who developed the current method of manufacturing. The system was based almost entirely on engineering and economic considerations. It was refined and improved over the years until it theoretically represented the most effective and efficient way to produce goods in the greatest quantity, in the quickest time, and at the lowest unit price. The one major drawback to this method of manufacturing, however, is the fact that neither at its inception nor in its present form does it take due cognizance of the human factor.

This analysis does not mean that the entire method should be abandoned. There are several things that can be done to improve the internal workings of the operation and, at the same time, meet productivity goals. Adoption of these corrective measures is not likely to increase production, but at least they will stop the skid that seems to be beginning.

The primary corrective action needed is to restore a strong sense of job satisfaction in the workers. However, this cannot be done merely by making changes in wage rates, working conditions, work rules, company policies, or administrative practices. It is true that these factors may be a major cause of DISsatisfaction (the Herzberg theory of motivation), but improvements in them will not make the workers like their tasks. If a task is boring, monotonous, and unsatisfying before any of these things are improved, it is no less boring after they are changed.

Real job satisfaction, according to Robert N. Ford of A.T. & T., must come principally from the task itself. To insure this, the task must have designed into it true work motivation factors. These are: (1) A chance for achievement as measured in the worker's terms, rather than just in management's terms. (2) A chance for recognition associated with this

WRITING FOR THE "REAL" WORLD   139

achievement. (3) A chance for increased responsibility as a result of his performance. (4) An opportunity to grow in knowledge and competence at the task. (5) A chance to advance to a higher rated or more important task.

These are the things that the unhappy production worker wants. The lack of these things is what underlies the unrest that is prevalent throughout industry today. The worker's basic subsistence needs for food, shelter, security, and the like (see Maslow's hierarchy of needs), are being adequately met by the comparatively high wage rates that are almost universally in effect. But money, etc., is not enough to satisfy the worker's human needs. These can be satisfied only if he has the opportunity to achieve and grow psychologically—that is, to move toward self-fulfillment. If he cannot do so in the job he now holds, he will go elsewhere if possible. If he feels that he cannot leave, he is likely to persist in his present rebellious pattern, antagonistic to the objectives of his employer. Such a situation is really an armed truce in which periodic walkouts may be expected, together with poor quality of goods produced. The growth of this sort of thing is all too evident in the contemporary industrial scene.

Up to this point in the development of industrial production, managements have vigorously exploited the services of engineering, cost-accounting, and marketing, but only relatively recently have they begun to look upon the behavioral sciences as a source of help. In the meantime a giant, complex productive system has developed and its growth has been based on inadequate precepts. Those precepts have largely grown out of economic and physical sciences. It is understandable that the behavioral sciences were relatively ignored up until recently because their development has followed that of the other sciences. Their relevance is now becoming clear. Thus, management will have to begin to redesign the productive system on the basis of more comprehensive precepts. The new design must embrace the now rich contribution that may be drawn from the behavioral sciences along with that of older sciences.

It is our belief that the past trend in industry toward greater and greater work simplification and mechanization affects most workers to a considerable extent—that is, their productivity is much reduced. Of course, it affects some more than others. Perhaps as many as 30 per cent may be relatively unaffected, because of a great need for the money or because they have formed an attitude of restricted needs, bordering on an orientation of resignation. On the other hand, there seems to be 30 to 40 per cent who are restless and who have high need levels and high expectation levels. It is these workers who will react openly and sometimes vigorously to kinds of work that is to them meaningless. The remaining

30 or 40 per cent will probably not remain neutral, because they will respond to the complaining of the restless group, even though they are not of themselves particularly discontented.

Management must be concerned with the under motivation of at least 60 to 70 per cent of their employees. Even the 30 per cent who "accept" the present type of work are also less productive than they would be if they had more meaningful work, as can be brought about through job enlargement or job enrichment. It is false logic to argue that because an attitude survey shows a small percentage of complaint, those who do not complain are productive, or even like the nature of the work they are doing.

Is the Problem Widespread?
A. A. Imberman

The most popular song on the reformers' hit parade today is called the Blue Collar Blues. A new Federal report, *Work in America*, provides the music. This report is the product of a Special Task Force appointed by the U.S. Department of Health, Education and Welfare.

What are the Blue Collar Blues?

They are a disease that is said to kill all workers subject to division of labor, job simplification, and repetitive operations. Obviously, it will kill assembly workers first, affecting the numberless industries that use some form of assembly fabrication. Secondarily, the Blues will kill process company employees—including workers in chemical plants, refineries, papermaking, glass, rubber, utilities of all sorts, distilling, and so on. Third, it kills white collar employees in banks, insurance companies, and other service establishments.

How does the division of labor and job simplification injure workers?

By turning them into "inhuman" robots. Their tasks are narrow and repetitive; they have no control over their work speed, because it is controlled by a moving line or other work flow procedures. Such employees have no chance to think ("to realize their potential"). They are subject to someone else's whims and desires. As a result, they turn bitter because their lives are "empty of significance." The same dread symptoms are to be found among process plant workers who must watch dials and monitor automatic processes, and among typists in an insurance company pool or mail room clerks in a bank who have the same forms to fill out or the same routines to follow every day.

What is the cure for this alarming disease?

By giving every employee "autonomy" over his job, letting him determine how it ought to be done, at what speeds, and giving him responsibility for the quality of his output. In most instances, the job ought to be expanded. Instead of an employee soldering the same two wires over and over again, or inserting the same automotive part, or sewing the same sleeve, or machining the same piece, or making the same casting, or watching the same gages, or filling out the same form letters—the employee will be permitted to take on two or three related functions so that his job is expanded and "enriched." He can then proceed at his own pace. In order to accomplish all this, all jobs in plants and offices will have to be "restructured" and "redesigned" so that the employee has more freedom to express himself at his work ("The redesign of jobs is the keystone . . .").

In redesigning jobs, emphasis must be on workers deciding on: ". . . their own production methods . . . the internal distribution of tasks . . . kinds of recruitment . . . kinds of supervision . . . what additional tasks to take on . . . [and] when they will work." All this would permit the worker "to achieve and maintain a sense of personal worth and importance, to grow, to motivate himself, and to receive recognition and approval for what he does."

How is that to be accomplished?

Every factory job, every process plant assignment and every white collar task will be scrutinized for its repetitive (i.e., "inhuman") aspects, redesigned, and enriched. The Federal Government will spearhead the movement by virtually outlawing such repetitive jobs and then subsidizing the transition. This "job enrichment" will also require a similar redesign of our school and college curricula, particularly their vocational and career aspects, and a redesign of our business training.

Won't this change in production methods increase costs?

Obviously. But that is where Federal subsidies come in. The Federal Government would have to finance the interim costs ("All of these training and research efforts could be funded under existing authority lodged in the Departments of Labor, Commerce, and Health, Education and Welfare"). Those costs would be in the billions. In addition—if the same products or services are to be produced under the proposed methods with every employee performing the job as he thinks best, at his own pace, and to his own quality requirements—the production costs would be several times present costs. That too, would have to be met by Federal subsidies.

Is all this proposed seriously?

Yes indeed. One indication that the proponents mean business is that one major Federal agency, the Department of Health, Education and Welfare, appointed a "Special Task Force" on the subject. The resultant report, *Work in America,* issued in December 1972, made all these recommendations and more—and was reported in every newspaper in the land. All quotations above are from this HEW report. Unions are beginning to take up the cry of "humanizing the job" and will undoubtedly ask for something at the bargaining table, if they can figure out what "humanization" to ask for. Here are some straws in the wind:

The reasoning of the [UAW] union leadership on the [Blue Collar Blues] work issue is that since it is not feasible to do much on the assembly line to improve jobs without making American cars unable to compete with imports, they should try to get the next best thing: more time off. [Agis Salpukas, *The New York Times,* Feb. 18, 1973.]

More time off . . . is the only way that the monotony and strain of these assembly jobs can be eased: longer vacations, more paid holidays, and the shorter work week with no reduction in pay . . . [United Electrical Workers Union, *UE News,* Nov. 13, 1972.]

My own researches on this subject of the Blue Collar Blues were completed a few months ago. Our study covered 3,800 hourly factory workers, by far the largest sample ever used in any study on this subject. In summary, our finding on the subject of Blue Collar Blues was that most employees (about 80 per cent) are *not* dissatisfied or unhappy with assembly work, while about 20 percent are.

This result on the very limited extent of Blue Collar Blues was far from novel. It jibed with the earlier reported findings of Elmo Roper, Ray Wild, George Strauss, Eliezer Rosenstein, Mitchell Fein, Harold A. Wolff, Milton R. Blood, Charles L. Hulin, and many other well-known researchers. The only significantly different element about my study was the larger number of employees covered, and the geographical and industrial diversification. Nobody else had covered as many as 3,800 assembly workers; nobody else had taken the study to five different industries in five different states. My point in mentioning the research literature is to provide background for my own conclusions on this subject.

More specifically, I have now tested the Blue Collar Blues theory in interviews with 3,800 hourly employees in five different factories in Ohio, Illinois, Massachusetts, South Carolina, and Missouri. My finding is that there is very little evidence for the theory that factory workers are alienated by their repetitive assembly jobs and desire "richer," more varied, and more responsible tasks.

From 79 to 88% Were Satisfied

I found that at most only 21 per cent of the hourly workers would like broader jobs; in some plants the percentage was as little as 12 per cent. On the other hand, the vast bulk of the hourly workers (ranging from 79 to 88 per cent) were satisfied with their assembly jobs. They expressed *other* dissatisfactions, but these had little to do with narrow versus broader jobs.

The data arose out of our normal program of interviews in five client plants that used some variety of assembly fabrication. In those five plants the jobs were (more or less) narrow and repetitive; both men (60 per cent) and women (40 per cent) were involved; black (31 per cent over all) and white. All 3,800 were hourly workers. The plants respectively manufactured nonelectrical machinery, electronic equipment, furniture, radio and TV components, and automotive parts.

In all cases, the employees interviewed were asked what suggestions they might have to make their job situations happier, more productive, and more satisfying. In analyzing the thousands of interview responses, most employees were found to prefer jobs with *less* demand for high-quality, with *less* direct responsibility, with *less* troublesome variety, but with *more* money.

In a Massachusetts nonelectrical machinery plant, while the theory told us that blue collar workers should respond favorably (high satisfaction and low absenteeism) to jobs that are more complex and have more responsibility and variety, we found that only 12 per cent preferred broader jobs. Most of the employees preferred the same jobs that they held, but with even less responsibility; about one-third of the employees were indifferent.

In a South Carolina furniture plant we found that the employee attitude toward the job enrichment theme was strikingly similar with only one difference. Most of these employees had rural backgrounds and hence valued independence on the job more than urban workers. As a result they tended to complain about "close" supervision, about being nursed, supervised, and policed. But they had no more preference for "enriched" jobs than did the employees elsewhere.

In an Illinois radio and TV component plant with urban workers, we found that there was a high preference (82 per cent) for repetitiveness and working on a small part of a product. In addition, another value of the assembly-line task was described at some length. The employees here valued "social intercourse" on the job. While they worked repetitively on a small operation, they tended to work in groups where conversation helped enliven the day. "Visiting" on the job was pleasant to them, and so long as they turned out the required quota, their foreman (or fore-lady) had no objection. These employees also felt that enlarging their jobs would require more attention and rob them of their opportunities for "social intercourse." This had been mentioned in other assembly situations, but not in all.

In a Missouri automotive parts plant, and also in an Ohio electronic equipment plant—both with highly automated assembly lines—the employees hit a new note. A high percentage (48 per cent) of these employees were black. Most of these employees evinced not only a liking for assembly line operations, but made reference to a rationale not en-countered before. Among the disadvantaged—white and black—who came from poor or limited backgrounds in cities, and a good number of rural and small town workers, our study found that they regarded assembly-line work as a step upward. It enabled them to acquire a limited skill quickly, to become what they regarded as semi-skilled workers—a step up from janitors, laborers, porters, and others who presumably have no skills. Without the narrowness of the assembly line operations, these workers would be reduced to unskilled laboring or janitorial jobs. With assembly fabrication, they could achieve a measure of skill in a short time that differentiated them from the lowly, "muscle-men" (as one de-scribed it), and gave them some claim to status among their peers in their communities.

A review of notes from interviews in dozens of plants previously covered by myself and staff members indicated that our findings in the five plants were nothing new. The same story, once you started digging for it, was revealed in many other plants.

How does all this jibe with the HEW report, *Work in America*? The report was a comprehensive, cut-and-paste compendium of past academic studies—but *only of those studies that purport to find a great groundswell for job enrichment*. No others are cited. Moreover, if you tunnel under the great moraines and stalagmites of words in that report, you will find that virtually all the companies cited are smaller companies, with so-called job enrichment in limited areas of production. No mass production is involved in any example.

In my speeches around the country before employer groups, I find that many employers shrug off the movement for job enrichment and the re-structuring of American industry as silly utopianism. They may be making a grievous error. There is enough worker dissatisfaction in factories, proc-ess plants, and white collar establishments—witness the parade of union-ization in nonunion plants, and the strikes in union plants—that could generate quite a movement for redesign of all jobs. It may bring chaos into American industry under the spur of misguided concern of the reformers.

What these reformers mistake for a job enrichment mandate is really worker frustration with some of the management oversights about working conditions and environment. Judging from my long consulting experience in industry, I find that the sharpest complaints that the worker has about his job are: (1) Supervisors who don't know how to supervise, are abusive, unfeeling, dictatorial, and unhelpful. (2) Poor plant or office management that is responsible for the inept scheduling of materials, poorly maintained machinery, unhappy working conditions (lights, heat, drinking water, dirty toilets), unbalanced inventories (the line shut down and the workers sent home because the parts manager wanted to maintain a small inventory), wrong sizes of parts, poorly machined parts that don't fit, ignored safety regulations, arbitrary management policies, and so on. (3) Nobody asks the employees' opinions about anything.

There are tested remedies for all these dissatisfactions. How these worker complaints in union plants cause wildcats and strikes—and their remedy—is discussed in a short study entitled, "You Too Can Enjoy a Strike." How these worker complaints in nonunion plants lead to votes for unionization—and how to remedy that—is discussed in another short report entitled, "Is Your Company Vulnerable to Unionization?". Either report is available free on request to the author at 209 S. LaSalle St., Chicago, Ill. 60604.

Management Must Show Concern

The typical factory employee would like to do a day's work for a day's pay, if management would just show more concern for him. This attitude has nothing to do with money. But when it comes to job enrichment, this is not part of the desires of most (about 80 per cent) of the hourly assembly workers.

As for the other 20 per cent—the ambitious, mobile employees—they *do* have legitimate complaints, and it is mainly these people that the critics of assembly work are talking about. The complaints of most of these employees would vanish if their managements listened to their employee sentiments; paid attention to better selection and better orientation; and provided some reasonable job posting and job promotion ladders combined with an honest in-house training program.

EXERCISES

VOCABULARY

autonomy	staccato	wellspring
feasible	cacophony	emanate
diversify	inexorable	agenda
evince	evaluate	concerted
compendium	concept	irrespective
moraine	segment	curtail
stalagmites	commensurate	milieu
utopia	feedback	manipulate
arbitrary	engender	regimented
subconscious	authoritarian	momentum
manifest	allocate	ethic
epitomization	revert	motivation
inevitable	compliance	inception
utilize	prerogative	cognizance
concomitant	integrate	precepts

QUESTIONS (JACKSON)

1. Substitute more commonly known synonyms for the "big" words in this essay. Do these substitutions change the essay in any way?

2. This essay begins with a description of an assembly line. What is the controlling idea in the paragraph? Is this a good way to begin this essay?

3. Read through the Jackson essay once; then try to state in a sentence of your own the author's main point.

4. Is this essay mainly an attempt to describe factory conditions or to give us information about what is going on in factories, or is the author trying to persuade us to accept an opinion or idea?

5. What kind of audience was this essay written for?

6. This essay has seven sections. Copy down the sentence that signals the beginning of each section, and summarize briefly in your own words what the writer says in that section.

7. Find examples of description and cause-and-effect organization in the essay.

8. Does the author give us specific examples of "work dissatisfaction"? What other examples does he supply?

9. List the various kinds of evidence the author uses to support his ideas.

1. Would Imberman agree with Jackson's points about worker dissatisfaction? Explain.

2. This essay breaks into three main sections. Describe the content of each section.

3. What sentence gives us Imberman's main topic? Why doesn't he say this earlier in the essay? Does he agree with the federal report (*Work in America*)?

4. What kind of evidence does Imberman use to support his point?

5. Identify paragraphs in which Imberman provides specific examples.

6. Which essay do you consider more convincing? Why?

7. Which essay did you find easier to read? Explain what characteristics made that essay easier to read.

8. Find statements in the Jackson essay and the Imberman essay that seem to contradict each other. Which one does the most effective job of developing and supporting his ideas?

THE SPECTER OF FULL EMPLOYMENT
Robert Lekachman

As we embark on Year One of the Carter Era, it is perhaps permissible to wistfully recall that its chronological predecessor was the 200th anniversary of the Declaration of Independence, Adam Smith's *Wealth of Nations*, and Edward Gibbon's *Decline and Fall of the Roman Empire*. To postpone anticlimax no further, 1976 was also the thirtieth birthday of the Employment Act of 1946.

Antiquarians can testify that the new statute was the emasculated survivor of the Full Employment Bill of 1945, which threatened concrete action against unemployment. All that the Employment Act specifically did was create the Council of Economic Advisers and the Joint Economic Committee of Congress, two of Washington's more talkative and less influential groups. The act's wordy preamble did, it is true, promise something called "maximum employment," but it never paused to explain what that might be and how it was to be attained.

Since 1946 we have staggered through a couple of recessions courtesy of Harry Truman, three sponsored by Dwight Eisenhower, and two conferred upon their country persons by Richard Nixon and Gerald Ford. During the 1950s, which those of hazy recollection now glorify as a veritable Golden Age, unemployment averaged around 5 per cent and general economic growth lagged enough to provide a winning issue for John Kennedy in 1960. A combination of Kennedy-Johnson tax cuts, subsidies to the Pentagon, the war on poverty, and, not least, the Vietnam public works program, turned the 1960s into a better than average decade for jobs. In the 1970s things are back to normal or worse.

This abbreviated business history does call attention to a puzzle, at least for the naïve. For thirty years it has been declared national policy to run the economy rapidly enough to give every American willing and able to work a job roughly commensurate with his or her skills if not expectations. All political candidates extol the work ethic and dutifully recall hard boyhoods spent jerking sodas, shining shoes, delivering newspapers, or digging up peanuts. In the course of the late, unlamented Presidential campaign, Carter was no less eager than Ford to get people off welfare rolls onto payrolls, to recall the felicitous language of the departed Nixon. Certainly no shortage looms of things to be done and goods and services to be supplied. A community whose median income hovers around $14,000 and in which average families are noticeably worse off than they were two or three years ago, has not lost interest in getting more income to buy cars, houses, and vacations in the sunny South or the snowy North.

The Uses of Unemployment

Men and women want to work. Work, private and public, is there to be done. How come, a wandering rationalist might ask, the work and the workers are not happily married? Well, as the radicals of my youth were wont to intone, it is no accident that we tolerate as a nation years of 7, 8, even 9 per cent general unemployment and horrifying rates of teen-age joblessness which among urban blacks exceed, by some estimates, 50 per cent.

The brutal fact is that unemployment at "moderate" rates confers a good many benefits upon the prosperous and the truly affluent. If everyone could be employed, extraordinarily high wages would have to be paid to toilers in restaurant kitchens, laundries, filling stations, and other humble positions. Whenever decent jobs at living wages are plentiful, it is exceedingly difficult to coax young men and women into our volunteer army. Without a volunteer army, how can the children of the middle and upper classes be spared the rigors of the draft?

Unemployment calms the unions and moderates their wage demands. Business periodicals have been noting with unconcealed gratification that last year's contract settlements between major unions and large corporations were considerably less expensive for employers than those of 1975, even though union members were steadily losing ground to inflation. When people are scared about losing their jobs, they work harder and gripe less. In more dignified language, absenteeism declines and productivity ascends.

Better still, factory and office workers, alert to potential layoffs and plant shutdowns, are unlikely to nag unions and employers to make work more interesting, and less menacing to health and personal safety. It cannot be mere coincidence that in Sweden, where job enrichment and plant democracy have had their greatest success, unemployment is practically zero and astute management of their economy protected Swedes even from the worldwide economic crisis of 1973–75. The new government, elected on the fortuitous issue of nuclear safety, has promised to extend even further the social benefits for which Sweden has become celebrated. American employers preserve themselves from Swedish experiments in good part by keeping the industrial reserve army plentifully manned.

Nor is this quite the end of the tale. The hunger of communities and regions for jobs and tax revenues has allowed large corporations to extort an endless assortment of valuable concessions from local and state governments, either as blackmail to keep existing installations or bribes to lure new ones. Few major corporations pay their fair share of property taxes. Propaganda by oil, steel, chemical, and paper industries has noticeably slowed the pace of regulation to protect the environment. Leonard Woodcock, who knows better, has allied himself with the major auto companies in seeking to postpone the application of the next wave of auto standards, entirely out of concern for the jobs of his UAW constituents.

By contrast, full employment on a sustained and assured basis (the system can stand a spell of full employment so long as all parties understand that it is temporary) presents an embarrassment to the movers and shapers of American plutocracy. To begin with, full employment is the most efficient agent of equitable income redistribution which is at all politically feasible in the United States. Full employment sucks into the labor force men and women who now struggle on welfare, food stamps, Social Security, and unemployment compensation. It pushes up the wages of low-paid people whose position is scarcely less precarious than that of the unemployed. It is an especial boon to blacks, Hispanics, teenagers, and women—last hired and first fired in expansion and recession alike. A long spell of full employment would substantially narrow existing wide differentials between the earnings of these groups and those of white males. In a time of layoff and business contraction, affirmative action is a mockery, but when there is full employment the cry for justice is heard more sympathetically by members of a majority whose own security is not threatened.

These repercussions are severe enough to alarm gentlemen in their clubs and boardrooms. The threat, I suspect, is still more grave. For men of property the charm of the 1970s lies in the way economic adversity has cooled the campuses and shoved American politics, already the most conservative in the developed world, still further right; one only has to look at Gerald Ford of all people after Watergate and the Nixon pardon, and in the middle of a messed-up economy, very nearly winning the Presidential election. This could not have happened without general apprehension and dampened expectations of the efficacy of action by any national administration. As one comedian commented upon the stockmarket decline which preceded the election, investors were selling out of deadly fear that one of the candidates would win. Lift the burdens of apprehension and apathy from the psyches of ordinary folk and—Who knows?—they might entertain radical thoughts of inviting the rich to share rather more of their capital gains and inheritances.

It goes without saying that it is scarcely respectable for the rich and their mercenaries, lawyers, economists, politicians, public-relations types, and so on, to openly proclaim their affection for unemployment, although among friends they tend to be more candid. One requires a respectable rationale, a convenient theory that combines apparent concern about the sufferings of the unemployed with actual capacity to avoid any action realistically calculated to alter their status.

My colleagues (I am an economist, but I am confessing, not boasting) have risen to the challenge. As their apologetic runs, we can't proceed sensibly toward universal job guarantees, even in the cautious, timid shape of the Humphrey-Hawkins Full Employment Bill, a revival of the 1945 original effort to write a serious job guarantee into law, because of the horrifying menace of more inflation. That menace is among economists embodied in a marvelous construction interred in the textbooks under the rubric of the Phillips curve.

The provenance of this notion that democratic societies must choose between inflation and unemployment deserves a paragraph. The late A. W. Phillips, a British economist who taught for much of his career in Australia, published in 1958 an article catchily entitled "The Relationship Between Unemployment and the Rate of Change in Money Wage Rates in the United Kingdom, 1862–1957." Phillips's data appeared to demonstrate that, as unemployment rose, wages increased less and less rapidly. The man said nothing at all about prices, price inflation, or the manner in which rising wages might or might not be translated into commensurate increases in the cost of living. Nevertheless, his findings were rapidly extended in statements like this typical textbook pronouncement: "Low rates of unemployment tend to be associated with high rates of inflation and, conversely, price stability or low rates of inflation tend to be associated with high rates of unemployment." Triumphant conclusion: "There seems to be a trade-off between employment and the price level."

Economists shifted from Phillips's cautious conclusions about unemployment and wage rates to the words just cited very simply. After all, wages and salaries, including those of executives and other overpriced folk, amount to about 70 per cent of business costs. Wherever competition reigns, employers have no choice except to pass along plumper labor costs to their customers in the shape of higher prices. The line of causation is direct: low unemployment stimulates wage demands, higher wages enlarge business costs, and these in turn lead to higher prices. It's an indisputable pity, but if we are to restrain demand inflation, we simply must operate the economy at what an MIT economist, Robert Hall, has recently labeled the "natural" rate of unemployment. A bit hard on those selected to serve their country by losing their jobs, but their patriotic sacrifice is nothing less than a valuable public service.

Let us absolve A. W. Phillips of blame for the intellectual sins committed in his name and look calmly, on its merits, at the Phillips curve in its modern guise. It is to start with an embarrassingly inaccurate explanation of recent stagflation—the malignant combination of persistent inflation and high unemployment. To those untutored in economics, the causes of a good part of current inflation have nothing at all to do with the Phillips curve. Out there in a world mostly beyond American control, OPEC has been busy quintupling petroleum prices, the Russians have been bidding up the cost of food in American supermarkets by vast grain purchases, and the world market for American farm products, temporary fluctuations aside, has been exerting steady upward pressure upon domestic food supplies.

These external shocks initiated an inflationary surge in 1973 and 1974. In spite of the sharpest recession (1974–75) since the 1930s, that inflation continued, somewhat abated in 1976, and gave ominous signs of spurting once more by the end of that year. Here is the real embarrassment for Phillips curve groupies. Their mechanism has simply failed to work. Unemployment has escalated and stuck at the highest recorded levels since the Great Depression. Wages have risen more slowly than the cost of living. Productivity is improving. Nevertheless, prices continue to rise. It has proved perfectly possible to suffer simultaneously from severe inflation and still more severe unemployment and factory underutilization.

As it happens, there is a reasonable explanation at hand for events so baffling to partisans of inflation-unemployment trade-offs. Clearly, inflation is not a simple matter of translation of higher wages into higher prices. Rather, it is an aspect of the distribution and concentration of market power among suppliers and sellers, abroad and here at home, who are in a position, within generous limits, to set their own prices for the goods and services that they sell. In both recession and expansion, sellers with market power have chosen to charge more, even if, as a result, they sell less. Businessmen and respectable mainstream economists who judge full employment to be inflationary are utterly correct. It is only their reasons that are wrong.

Prices rise during both phases of the business cycle because in recession businessmen who enjoy monopoly or quasimonopoly power over their markets push prices upward in order to maintain their profit margins. When better times come, businessmen seize the opportunity to improve their profit margins. As a fair example, recall that during 1974 and 1975, two of the auto industry's worst years since the 1950s, General Motors and its amiable rivals marked up auto sticker charges an average of $1,000 per car, even though the customers were reluctant to buy. The rarer the customers, the larger the profit that needed to be attached to the selling price of each unit. Now that sales are behaving more wholesomely, prices continue to rise. Why not get more when the customers are willing to pay more? As in autos, so in steel, aluminum, and a long list of other industries in which one, two, three, or four dominant corporations set prices and conduct orderly markets unblemished by unseemly price rivalry. The manufacturers have company. In the delivery of health services, a pleasant cartel of health insurers, hospitals, medical societies, and complaisant federal authorities has propelled medical costs higher at twice the pace of general inflation. The television monopolies have raised the charges for network time, and the university professors who lecture and consult have done rather better than the inflation rate. Lawyers have long judged advertising and price competition two serious breaches of legal ethics. Food prices rise partly because of the widening profit margins of food processors.

Worse Than the Disease

The diagnosis dictates the choice of remedies. One is as old as the 1890 Sherman Antitrust Act: break up the monopolies and end price-fixing in restraint of trade. The remaining true believers in antitrust would cheerfully fragment the large corporations, which, either by themselves or in combination with one or two peers, dominate many markets. Alas, the nonprogress of former Sen. Philip Hart's oil divestiture bill in the last Congress and its dim prospects in the new one are the latest evidence of the political futility of this tactic. Although no technical reasons justify the size of Exxon or General Motors, the public is yet to be persuaded that small is beautiful.

The only feasible alternative is control of key prices and profit margins in the very large proportion of the economy where old-fashioned competition is celebrated only by banquet speeches. Such controls were imposed during World War II and the Korean War. It is a historical curiosity that John Kenneth Galbraith, who was a price administrator, and Richard Nixon, who briefly served as a compliance attorney, drew diametrically opposite conclusions from their respective experience. Galbraith continues to believe that price control is both necessary and feasible. Nixon preached the wickedness of interference with private markets, but nevertheless suddenly froze prices August 15, 1971, and followed the ninety-day freeze with a year or so of more flexible but astonishingly successful wage- and price-hike limitations. As the Nixon experience suggests, wage controls generally accompany price controls. There recently has been the rub. The wage controls in 1972 and 1973 were considerably more effective than the price controls, for two excellent reasons. The Nixon controllers, probusiness to a man, were far more eager to check union demands than to interfere with business earnings, and employers gladly cooperated with Washington to police the wage-rise limits. Seldom did patriotism pay better.

The fact is that in the United States (England is, of course, quite a different matter) mandatory price controls over concentrated industries and the health sector, together with voluntary wage guidelines, would probably work very well for a time. American unions are, after all, both weak and conservative. The path to full employment without inflation is impassable without a firm incomes policy and the statutory authorization of price controls administered by individuals who believe in what they are doing.

Does the political will to shape a national full employment policy exist? It is difficult to answer yes to that question. Last year full employment struck a Democratic Congress as sufficiently radical to bury Humphrey-Hawkins. For, as has been noted, full employment means diminishing long-standing inequalities of income, wealth, and power; inviting the black, brown, young, and female to the American celebration; and controlling the rapacity of doctors, lawyers, giant corporations, and other reputable extortionists. After full employment who will iron Russell Long's shirts, clean up after the Lutèce diners, and do the world's dirty work? Settle the job issue once and for all, and even American unions will begin to entertain dangerous thoughts about job redesign, codetermination, and similarly radical Swedish and German nonsense.

The fine Christian (and occasionally Jewish) men whom the good Lord has placed in the seats of authority and the halls of the mighty know that there are far worse phenomena than unemployment. One of them is full employment.

Jobs were the most frequently reiterated of Carter's campaign themes and the President's squeak to victory required essential aid from blacks, Chicanos in Texas, the AFL-CIO, and aggrieved New Yorkers persuaded that Ford, not the *Daily News* headline writer (a great man), had actually told their city to drop dead. The ingratitude of Presidents is as notorious as that of princes, so there is no certainty that the new Chief Executive will automatically move toward genuine full employment, as distinguished from the moderate stimulation of a quick tax cut. Carter cautiously, reluctantly, and belatedly endorsed Humphrey-Hawkins, in the wake of his ethnic-purity blunder. He repeatedly emphasized his preference for job creation in the private sector and his desire to avoid expanding the weight of federal activity. At that famous luncheon at 21 for Henry Ford II and other corporate heavyweights, Carter promised that he would study the tax code a year or so before making recommendations for revision to Congress—the same tax code that he had described before less affluent audiences as a disgrace to civilization.

Nevertheless, there is some reason to believe that Carter will pursue more expansionary tax and spending policies than did his predecessor. Even businessmen who mostly voted for Ford are concerned about the continued sluggishness of the economy. When retail sales falter, profits are threatened and the long-awaited boom in investment never occurs.

It appears that the "pause," "lull," or just plain old recession has gone further and lasted longer than is needed to serve the laudable purposes which unemployment serves.

A genuine commitment to sustained full employment demands a good deal more than a temporary tax cut or a brief loosening of the federal purse strings. The United States will move toward a coherent high-employment economy at the same time as it becomes politically feasible to diminish the power of great wealth and reduce inequalities of income and wealth.

The fate of George McGovern in 1972 and Fred Harris in 1976, two brave souls who rose to the perils of open discussion of such political dynamite, makes it depressingly plain that Americans continue to admire the people and institutions that make life harder for them than it need be. As Prof. Walter Burnham of MIT pointed out last year, the missing 45 per cent of the American electorate who don't turn up on Election Day in Europe vote Labor, Socialist, or Communist.

All my life my country has suffered from the absence of a significant political Left. As I trudge through middle age toward the golden years of senior citizenship, I glimpse even less hope of the emergence of a democratic socialist party than I did during the late 1930s and early 1940s when, at least in Manhattan, revolution was in the air.

Until a credible left rises in the United States, unemployment will be a little higher when the Republicans are in the White House, a little lower when the Democrats take their turn. Genuine full employment, decent jobs at decent wages for every man, woman, and youth interested in working, has been a myth, is a myth, and will stay a myth so long as every four years voters choose between one party minimally to the right of dead center and a second minimally to the left.

EXERCISES

VOCABULARY

specter	affluent	plutocracy
radical	rigors	equitable
intone	astute	precarious
wont	fortuitous	repercussions
confer	extort	efficacy
apathy	psyche	candid
mercenary	rubric	provenance
malignant	abate	ominous
partisan	cartel	fragment
rapacity	reputable	reiterate
laudable	credible	guise
myth		

QUESTIONS

1. What are the benefits of moderate unemployment as explained by Lekachman?

2. Do you think the first six paragraphs contain adequate evidence to support the author's position? What types of evidence does he use?

3. Identify instances of paragraph development by detail, by reason, and by example.

4. Is this essay intended to describe, to explain, or to persuade?

5. After explaining the problem, the author proposes a solution. What is the solution? What evidence does he offer that it will work?

6. Does the author see any hope for the future? What in his opinion is required to resolve the situation explained in the essay?

THE DYNAMICS OF POWER:
RECENT TRENDS IN MECHANIZATION
ON THE AMERICAN FARM

Sam B. Hilliard

IF ANY characteristic of American agriculture can be singled out as being especially representative of its dynamic nature, it is mechanization. The American farmer has distinguished himself consistently from other farmers throughout the world by his willingness to experiment with his tools and buy new ones. During the last two-thirds of the 19th century he showed an unrestrained eagerness toward virtually any innovation that crossed his path.[1] The 20th century has seen a continuation—even intensification—of this zeal, with the result that American agriculture now is the most mechanized and has the highest productivity of any in the world.

To the student of American agriculture or history, the story of mechanization is a familiar one, and innovations such as the steel plow, the reaper, hybrid corn, and the cotton harvester have become part of the accepted lore. However, the extremely rapid, almost explosive, increase in the rate of technological developments in the field during the past two decades has led to an equally rapid change in the number, size, and types of machinery that populate the agricultural landscape. This "revolution" is well known to farmers and other persons within the complex system of farm-related business (often referred to as agri-business); but the rapid transfer of population out of the agricultural realm and the concurrent rise in other, more spectacular, aspects of our national life, such as space exploration and computer technology, have led to a neglect of the dynamics of farm technology. This is not to say that the history of agricultural technology has been neglected. One has only to peruse the pages of *Agricultural History* or *Technology and Culture* to see a blossoming of attention. However, the greatest interest seems to be focused toward early developments, leaving a gap in our knowledge of the immediate past. Far too many people regard "farm mechanization" as the culmination of a series of technological achievements, not as a continuous process in which we are still engaged. Consequently, many fail to appreciate the drastic changes that have occurred during the last two decades.

This paper attempts a brief analysis of some of the most recent de-

FROM *Technology and Culture*, Vol. 13, No. 1 (Jan. 1972), pp. 1–14.

[1] For an account of how easily the farmer accepted innovations, or was duped into them, see E. W. Hayter, *The Troubled Farmer, 1850–1900: Rural Adjustments to Industrialism* (DeKalb, Ill., 1968), pp. 145–208.

velopments in agricultural machine technology. It does not delve into the
field of "specialized" machinery such as vegetable and fruit harvesters and
nonrolling machinery.[2] Rather, it concentrates on the power revolution
with its thrust toward larger tractors and the increased use of self-propelled
machinery. Seemingly, the two are different, but they represent two facets
of the power revolution, since they both add to the farm operator's arsenal
of power. It also looks at the dynamics of farm technology as it responds
to the power revolution.

The roots of the power revolution go back to the steam era, when man
first began to use inanimate power for traction work. The steam engine
saw farm service in the United States early in the 19th century, but its
use was confined primarily to stationary or portable applications involving
belt-transmitted power, such as powering threshers, sawmills, and grist
mills. During the latter half of the century, a gear or chain drive was added
to the basic portable engine and the vehicle became self-propelled, though
for years the engine continued to require a team of horses or mules to
steer it safely. Further refinements were added, and, as farming moved
westward where large-scale operations were more practical, the engines
became larger. During the 1880s most traction engines were in the 8–20
hp range, but by the 1920s engines of 30–40 hp were common, and some
were much more powerful. Although the horsepower claims of most engines were modest, they were "monsters" in size and extremely slow and
awkward. For example, in the early 1900s, J. I. Case of Racine, Wisconsin,
marketed an engine that measured some 16 ft long, 8 ft wide, and weighed
8 tons. Despite the impressive size, it was rated at a meager 20 hp and
crept along at about 2½ miles per hour.[3] Because it needed no boiler, the
development of the internal-combustion engine permitted a substantial
reduction in tractor size. The decrease in size, however, was not immediate since the first petroleum-powered tractors were patterned closely after
their steam predecessors and were similar in both outward appearance and
size.[4] In time, the elimination of the bulky steam boiler proved to be revo-

---

[2] See, for example, Wayne D. Rasmussen, "Advances in American Agriculture: The
Mechanical Tomato Harvester as a Case Study," *Technology and Culture* 9 (1968):
531–43.
[3] R. M. Wik, *Steam Power on the American Farm* (Philadelphia, 1953). The "steam
buff" is referred to F. Clymer, *Album of Historical Steam Traction Engines* (New
York, 1949), an excellent source for photographs of old engines, both European and
American.
[4] For an excellent pictorial account of the early gasoline tractor, see R. B. Gray and
E. M. Dieffenbach, "Fifty Years of Tractor Development in the U.S.A.," *Agricultural
Engineering* 38 (1957): 388–97. See also R. B. Gray, "Development of the Agricultural Tractor in the United States," U.S.D.A. Agricultural Research Service, Information Series no. 107 (Washington, D.C., 1954). Part 2 of this work is published
by the American Society of Agricultural Engineers, Saint Joseph, Michigan.

lutionary, and engineers began designing tractors that reflected the size and weight advantage of the smaller power unit.

In the years following World War I, tractor size decreased markedly, and many manufacturers entered the highly competitive field. By the late 1930s the "small" farm tractor had become widespread. The best known of the machines developed for the small to medium farm was the Fordson, designed by Ford Motor Company to be the "tin lizzy" of the farmstead.[5] Ford had its competition, though, and the 1920s and 1930s saw an increase in the number and type of small tractors marketed. This was the period during which experimentation was rampant, and virtually every conceivable style was marketed: special plowing machines, cultivating machines, front-wheel-drive tractors, tricycle wheel arrangements—these and a host of other weird vehicles appeared on the scene. However, most were short-lived, and by the late 1930s only three basic types remained popular: the tricycle, the standard four-wheel tractor, both being driven through the rear wheels and steered by the front wheels, and the crawler (track-laying tractor).[6] However, the crawler was limited primarily to giant operations or cases where slope and soil conditions required extra stability or traction. In most areas it has never made up a large segment of the machines used on farms.

The shift from the huge "monsters" of the early 1900s to the smaller units of the 1930s and the 1940s reflected several changes in technology and farm operation. The elimination of the steam boiler allowed great reduction in size; thus a small, light, highly maneuverable machine became technically feasible. The development of rubber tires permitted greater versatility, speed, and comfort. With such characteristics it was adaptable to many more farm tasks, such as, planting, cultivating, mowing, and raking. Therefore, it became a much more suitable replacement for the horse and mule than was any of its predecessors. Furthermore, its small size, near-universal utility, and relatively low cost made it economically feasible for a much larger group of farmers than its huge steam or gas predecessor. In fact, the huge potential market among small- to medium-scale farm operations probably was the most important stimulus to the emergence of the small tractor.

During the early 1940s, war activities impeded further development, but the postwar period saw a continuation of the previous trend. It is worth noting that the *smallest* farm tractors ever developed were offered in the few years following World War II. The Farmall "Cub" (Fig. 1),

[5] R. M. Wik, "Henry Ford's Tractor and American Agriculture," *Agricultural History* 38 (April 1964): 79–86.
[6] Actually, most tricycle tractors have four wheels, but the two front wheels are spaced quite close together, giving the machine a tricycle appearance (Figs. 4 and 12).

FIGURE 1. *The Farmall "Cub" cultivating a single row in a slightly gullied and very weedy cotton "patch." It is the only surviving member of the post-World War II minitractors. Note that the engine and power train are offset to the left to give the operator an unobstructed view of his work. Its puny 10 horses severely limited its heavy work, but its small size and open design allowed the operator to "manicure" the row being worked. (Courtesy of International Harvester, Chicago, Illinois.)*

the Allis Chalmers "G" (a rear-engine machine), and the Massey-Harris "Pony" (all around 10 or 12 drawbar hp) marked the extreme in the minitractor movement (except, of course, for the garden and estate models which are so popular among suburbanites today) and were designed to mechanize even the smallest of farm operations.

This trend toward small machines was a logical one. Given the agricultural conditions of the 1940s with the large number of small farms, many of which were unmechanized, and the relative success enjoyed by the "small" machines of the 1930s, one could only have concluded that previous trends would continue and that the market for small tractors

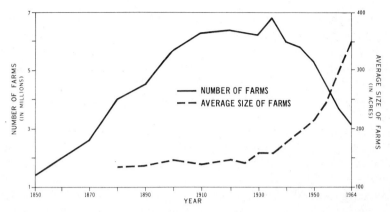

FIGURE 2. *Number and size of farms in the United States, 1850–1964. Source: U.S. Census and Census of Agriculture. (Chart drawn by Cartographic Laboratory of Southern Illinois University.)*

would increase. As late as 1957 the large number of small farms still looked attractive to some as a potential market.[7] But even as Gunlogson wrote, it was obvious that the former trend would not continue. In fact, the reverse became true; the demand was for larger machines, and the market for small tractors declined drastically. A number of factors were involved in this reversal, but the most important was the decline in numbers of small farms. This trend started during the late 1930s, but its effects were most notable after World War II. The zenith in farm numbers was reached before 1940, and the precipitous decline in numbers did not occur until the late 1940s, corresponding closely with the increase in farm size and the thrust toward higher-powered tractors (Fig. 2). Millions of small farms still existed throughout the 1940s; for example, approximately 54 per cent of all farms in 1949 reported less than 50 acres of cropland harvested.[8]

The rapidly changing conditions during the early 1950s spelled the doom of the small tractor market. Post-World War II farm commodity prices showed little improvement over those prevalent during the war itself, and farmers saw a slow but steady inflationary trend in which the cost of fertilizers, machinery, and other goods rose. Concurrently, there was a decline in farm labor and a corresponding rise in farm wages, a fact

---

[7] G. B. Gunlogson, "Needed: A Substitute for a Team of Mules," *Agricultural Engineering* 38 (1957): 162–63.
[8] U.S. Census of Agriculture for 1950, General Report, vol. 2.

that added to farm costs and stimulated mechanization. Caught in this cost-price squeeze, the farmer reacted in a number of ways. Older farmers simply quit, either by turning over their operations to sons or by renting or selling to those who remained. However, many of the younger farmers were not inclined to sit on the small "family farm" as it had existed in prewar days, but made optimistic efforts toward increasing their incomes. Some increased the productivity of existing holdings by going into truck cropping, poultry, or other high-value specialities, but this proved to be only a temporary expedient as those fields soon felt the same cost-price pinch and were forced either into larger, more efficient operations or bankruptcy.[9]

As a result of all these factors the number of large farms increased markedly while the number of small farms declined. During the period 1940–64, the average size of all farms jumped from about 175 acres to almost 350 (see Fig. 2). The increased scale of farming resulted in a sharp increase in the power necessary to operate each farm unit. This demand for more work could have been accomplished simply by adding more units (tractors, combines), but additional units meant more labor, and labor was leaving the rural areas at a phenomenal rate. The answer was obvious. Large-scale operations meant larger machines—perhaps not physically larger but machines whose output per man-hour input was higher. The results of this demand have forced change of an unprecedented magnitude and transformed the American farm into a new entity. In order to demonstrate this, let us look at the machinery that was available to the farmer in the immediate postwar years and compare it with that of today. For the sake of convenience, the years 1949 and 1969 are chosen as examples.[10]

The experimentation of the 1920s and 1930s resulted in a consensus as to the tractor types best suited to farm conditions of that time. Of course there were variations between regions and among farm sizes, but the two basic wheel types mentioned above were almost universal (the crawler was used to some extent, especially on large operations in the West). Sizes ranged from the 10-hp Farmall "Cub" (Fig. 1) to the Massey-Harris "55" (Fig. 11), which developed over 60 hp. Most manufacturers offered four or more basic sizes, and in some cases, but not all, each size was offered with optional wheel arrangements and accessories (Fig. 3). Except for the huge (over 45 hp) machines, one could purchase a given size in either a "standard" four-wheel model or a high-clearance, "row-crop" model de-

---

[9] This point is argued very well in E. C. Higbee, *Farm and Farmers in an Urban Age* (New York, 1963).
[10] The basic data source is the *Red Tractor Book 34th ed., 1949–50* and *53rd Annual Farm and Industrial Equipment Red Book* (Kansas City, Mo., 1949).

TRACTOR MODELS
BY HORSEPOWER

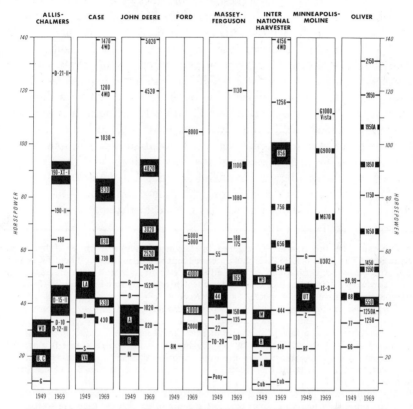

FIGURE 3. *Tractor models offered in 1949 and 1969 by major American manufacturers. Models are indicated by lines or dark shaded areas in columns under each manufacturer's heading with separate columns for 1949 and 1969. Dark shaded areas indicate range of power covered by more than one engine or transmission option. Specific models are indicated by letter or numbers (Allis-Chalmers "WD"; Oliver "77"; and John Deere "4020"; or Case "930"). Sources: Red Tractor Book 34th ed., 1949–50 and 53rd Annual Farm and Industrial Equipment Red Book (Kansas City, Mo., 1949). (Chart drawn by Cartographic Laboratory of Southern Illinois University.)*

pending on the intended use.[11] Ferguson and Ford were the only exceptions, with each offering one (almost identical) tractor.[12]

The chart of Figure 3 lists the model offerings of the major American manufacturing firms for both 1949 and 1969. The models are arranged by "belt" and "PTO" horsepower.[13] Looking at the tractors manufactured in 1949, we find a substantial variety available to the farmer, but some limitations should be noted. There were no tractors offered in "row-crop" style above 45 hp; most were in the 20–35-hp range. Furthermore, there were a number of very popular models in the under-25-hp range with many adapted to "one-row" operation (see Fig. 1).[14] Rated according to "plow size," most models could handle from one to three 14-inch plows, with a few capable of four- to five-plow service. As mentioned earlier, most of the four- to five-plow tractors were not row-crop methods, and their use was limited to plowing, discing, or pulling combines. Unquestionably, most 1949 farm tractors were designed for small to medium farms. This was the largest market, and the manufacturers catered to that demand.

---

[11] For example, the model "Z" offered by Minneapolis-Moline in 1949 had four variations. The ZTS was a "standard," wide-front-wheel machine. The ZTE was a wide-front-wheel machine but with an adjustable front axle and high clearance for row-crop work. The ZTU had a tricycle wheel arrangement while the ZTN was a tricycle with only one front wheel (a true tricycle).

[12] These two tractors grew out of the revolutionary Fort-Ferguson machine developed in the late thirties. It featured an integral, hydraulically operated implement lift which was attached to the implement by three arms. This "3-point hitch" in time has come to be adopted by all the major manufacturers and is now the basis for "interchangeability" among implements and tractors manufactured by different firms. The 3-point hitch can be seen on the Ford in Fig. 5 and the International in Fig. 7.

[13] The terms need clarification. The University of Nebraska has been conducting tests for some fifty years on farm tractors. Among other things, they are testing for horsepower, which is an index of tractors' ability to do work. Belt horsepower is one measure of output using the conventional flat belt and was the method used in evaluating the 1949 models, but at the present time tests are by PTO (power take-off) horsepower. There has been a drastic decline in the use of tractors for "belt work" (sawmills, hammer mills, wood saws, threshers) and a corresponding increase in the use of the PTO, hence the abandonment of the belt test. Both are quite comparable, but neither should be confused with "drawbar horsepower," which is a measure of the tractor's "pulling power" and usually is somewhat lower than the belt or PTO rating. (In 1949, the drawbar figure varied among models from 71 to 93 per cent of belt horsepower.) Drawbar horsepower is quite different from other measures such as "manufacturers estimates" (usually a carefully tuned laboratory model stripped of all accessories). Many gasoline engines also are rated in "Brake Horsepower" (BHP), which is the effort expended in braking an engine turning at specified revolutions per minute. Steamers usually were rated according to a theoretical formula based on steam pressure, speed, and piston bore and stroke.

[14] A tractor designed for one-row cultivation must have a four-wheel arrangement allowing it to straddle the row being cultivated (Fig. 1). Two-row operation requires either a tricycle arrangement (Fig. 4) or adjustable wide front wheels (Fig. 5). Four-row cultivation poses no additional problem to wheel arrangement, since both outside rows are outside both the front and rear wheels.

Due to the lack of data, the regional variation in tractor size and type cannot be demonstrated in detail, but some rough generalizations can be made. The 20–35 hp models were common in the Midwest, and most were row-crop machines, either tricycle or high-clearance, wide-front-wheel models. The latter gave better stability, but the tricycle was a favorite since it permitted easy upfront mounting of a cultivator or corn picker (Fig. 4). The larger machines found a market on the plains, especially on wheat farms, where large acreages demanded more power without the necessity of row-crop adaptation. Too, where large, pull-type combines were employed in the grain harvest, the extra power was necessary. Other applications for the heavy, industrial-type tractor were the large-scale operations in the Far West where high power was needed and in the plantation

FIGURE 4. A Farmall "Super C" with front-mounted cultivators handling two corn rows. The tricycle wheel arrangement permits easy mounting of cultivators and eliminates the need for adjusting front wheels to fit row widths. Despite the upfront mounting, the cultivator has rear shovels to plow out the wheel tracks. (Courtesy of International Harvester, Chicago, Illinois.)

South where tractors often were used only in plowing and seedbed preparations. Since a substantial proportion of the southern cotton crop was
cultivated by mule power, there was less need for row-crop models.

The thrust toward mechanization in the South took a somewhat different, though no less revolutionary, tack than the rest of the nation, and it
deserves special comment.[15] Prior to World War II the region lagged far
behind other areas in number of farm tractors. Many of the machines that
did exist were used for belt work on sawmills and threshers or as traction
machines for heavy plowing. Planting and cultivating were still the domain
of the cropper and his mule. After the war two events served to shake the
Southerner out of his century-long lethargy toward mechanization. One
was the increasing scarcity and cost of farm labor, and the other was the
development of a workable cotton harvester. Both stimulated a shift from
mule to inanimate power of unprecedented rapidity. This shift occurred
in the immediate postwar years, and differed markedly depending on location within the South, size of holding, and crop emphasis. In the plantation areas, where sharecropping was well entrenched before the war, the
shift was to machines designed to handle the huge acreages created by the
neoplantation movement.[16] In many cases, though, the shift from sharecropping to the neoplantation system occurred prior to the initial mechanization; thus, there were no small tractors to replace. The shift was made
directly from mule power to large tractors with no intermediate stage.

The eastern portion of the South, especially the hill country, was an
area of small- to medium-size farms, often owner operated. Many farmers
grew neither cotton nor corn in large quantities, and the demand was for
a highly maneuverable one- to three-plow tractor capable of adapting to a
variety of chores and conditions. The one-row models were quite popular,
but the machine that proved itself most adaptable was the Ford. With
wide (but adjustable) front wheels and a low center of gravity, it was well
suited to hill farms, yet could be adapted to row cultivation (Fig. 5).[17]

Since 1949, economically viable farming units have increased steadily in
size—and so has the size of tractors. Farm tractors sold in 1949 averaged

---

[15] H. R. Tolley and L. M. Church, "Tractors on Southern Farms," U.S.D.A. Farmers'
Bulletin no. 1278 (Washington, D.C., 1936).

[16] M. C. Prunty, Jr., "The Renaissance of the Southern Plantation," *Geographical
Review* 45 (October 1955): 459–91.

[17] The model listed on the chart is the "gray" Ford-Ferguson. However, a split between Ford and Ferguson led to their marketing different but competitive models;
both were similar to the prewar Ford-Ferguson. Ford's machine, the famous "red-
bellied Ford," became a familiar part of the rural landscape in the East and Hill
South, and it established the company as a major competitor in the implement field
(Fig. 5). Ferguson developed his own line but later merged with Massey-Harris (a
Canadian firm) to become Massey-Ferguson.

FIGURE 5. A Ford handling two bottoms in Texas soil. The plow is attached to the tractor by three arms which can be raised or lowered hydraulically. It features a four-wheel stance and an unusually low profile. Compare it to the tricycle in Fig. 4. (Courtesy of Ford Tractor Operations, Birmingham, Mich.)

some 29 hp, but by 1968 this average had increased to over 70 hp. Arranged in three size groups, tractor production for fifteen years is shown in Figure 6. In 1953, some 62 per cent of all wheel tractors were in the under-35-hp class, but by 1967 this figure had declined to a mere 7 per cent. Concurrently, the percentages for tractors rated 50 hp and over were 23 in 1953 and 67 in 1967. More detailed data show that the largest-selling group in 1968 was the 90–100-hp range. Moreover, this trend toward higher horsepower is almost sure to continue in the future, as the greatest percentage gain in 1968 was in the over-100-hp group.[18]

In Figure 3, showing the major American-made tractors by manufacturer model and rated horsepower, note the differences between the machines marketed in 1949 and 1969. Three are especially outstanding. (1) The great range of models developed by each manufacturer. All pro-

[18] In addition to the remarkable increase in power, there has been a concurrent shift away from gasoline and distillate fuel toward diesel power. Diesel engines were installed in only 6 per cent of the wheel-tractor units in 1953, but by 1967 this had increased to 61 per cent. In the 80-hp-and-over size, diesels accounted for 90 per cent of all units shipped (U.S. Census of Manufacturing, Current Industrial Reports, calculated in Implement and Tractor, December 21, 1968, pp. 25 and 42).

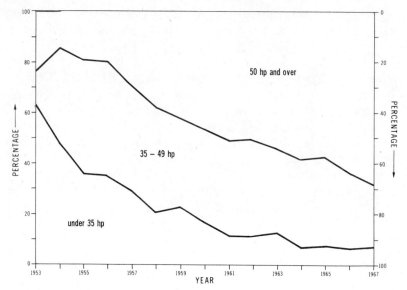

FIGURE 6. *Production of wheel tractors by horsepower class. Note the increase in the percentage of machines over 50 hp and the corresponding decrease in the under-35-hp class. (Drawn by Cartographic Laboratory of Southern Illinois University.)*

duced more models in 1969 than in 1949: some offered twice as many. Ford showed the greatest increase. Manufacturing only one tractor in 1949, by 1969 its line had grown to six. (2) The drastic increase in power. Of the 1949 farm tractors, only one boasted of over 60 hp, but in 1969 a total of forty-two (⅔ of all models) were in that range. (3) There were many fewer small models offered. In 1949 many of the row-crop models were in the under-30-hp range, but in 1969 only three were left in that category.[19] Of the minitractors that blossomed in the late forties, only the "Cub" remains. One-row cultivating tractors are all but extinct except in specialty operations. In fact, the two-row holds its own only where small fields or highly contoured hillsides limit machine size. In the Midwest and plantation South, hedgerows and fences have been rearranged to create fields large enough to accommodate multirow equipment. Of course, in the West and Southwest large fields were common from the onset of settlement. In all these areas the trend is toward larger machines. Six-

---

[19] These figures exclude a host of imports that have hit the market recently, most of which fall into the 20–70 hp range. One could argue that the imports fill the gap left by American manufacturers as they abandoned the small tractor field, and there is merit in such a contention. But since the imported machines are relative newcomers it is too early to be sure.

and eight-row planting and cultivating units are commonplace, a number of twelve-row units are in operation (Fig. 7), and a sixteen-row unit is currently being marketed.

Even before this proliferation of planter and cultivator sizes, the imaginative operator never felt constrained by the manufacturers' offerings. Long before the eight- and twelve-row implements were sold, many farmers were multiple hitching to increase their planting and cultivating capacity. Part of the trend toward more rows is due to the increasing prevalence of narrow-row planting, especially in corn growing. In the last decade, 3–4-ft corn rows have given way to narrower ones; 30–40 inches is considered standard, but during 1967 and 1968 many were going to 26- or even 20-inch rows. A machine planting twelve 20-inch rows covers the same width as one handling eight 30-inch rows.

The power revolution was a response to several stimuli (larger farms, costly labor), but the power itself has encouraged changes in farm tactics and operations. In addition to providing the ability to pull more plows or plant more rows, increased tractor power has spawned a host of develop-

FIGURE 7. A twelve-row rig cultivating knee-high corn. Being too wide to transport as shown, for road travel it is pulled sideways, using the two wheels shown on top. Note the tractor's dual wheels which are spaced so as to straddle a corn row. (Courtesy of International Harvester, Chicago, Ill.)

FIGURE 8. *A John Deere "5020" using a tandem hitch. With around 130 hp, it handles a disc harrow and a six-row planter with ease. Note that each planter has hoppers for fertilizer, seed, insecticide, and herbicide. (Courtesy of Deere and Co, Moline, Ill.)*

ments designed to increase efficiency. Multiple hitching now allows several operations simultaneously. In a single trip across the field one can apply liquid fertilizer via tractor-mounted saddle tanks and pull a traditional bottom plow followed by a tandem-hitched harrow for discing. In other applications, chisel plowing, discing, and planting are done in a single operation. Moreover, the planting process itself involves several operations with seed, fertilizer, insecticide, and herbicide being applied simultaneously (Fig. 8). Related to this multifunction operation is the attempt toward minimum tillage. There is an increasing feeling among agricultural scientists that soil compaction is undesirable, and that excessive trips across a field should be avoided. Thus, multihitching not only saves time and fuel, it lessens soil compaction.[20]

High power also has encouraged another kind of innovation not related to plowing and cultivating. In forage harvesting, the wide availability of

[20] It should be noted, however, that packing the soil is not always considered an evil. Some years ago, "wheel-track planting" was in vogue as it placed seeds in a medium that encouraged sprouting, but with multirow operations this dubious advantage is eliminated.

large tractors has encouraged field chopping. Whereas ensilage formerly was hauled in to be chopped and blown into the silo, the practice now is to cut and chop in the field, blow it into a forage wagon, and then haul it in where it is power-unloaded into feed bunkers or a silo. Most of the recent developments in chopping and related machines were made possible by large tractors capable of powering heavy choppers *and* simultaneously pulling a huge wagon (Fig. 9). The same trend also struck the corn-harvesting system when field shelling became feasible, but the tack has been somewhat different. Instead of relying on powerful tractors with shelling attachments, the job has been taken over by the self-propelled combine equipped with a corn header.

Finally, there is one other feature the higher-power tractor has brought to the farm scene—speed. If one is performing an agricultural operation, there are two basic means of increasing output (other than decreasing the losses associated with wheel slippage, turning, and other inefficiencies): increasing the width of ground covered each trip and decreasing the time taken to perform each trip. Thus an operation taking a width of 60 inches

FIGURE 9. A *Massey-Ferguson 1130 (90 + hp) pulling a Gehl chopper and wagon. The chopper's size is deceptive, since it requires tremendous power to operate. The chopper is equipped with a pickup head for handling windrowed forage and a fan to blow the chopped forage into the covered wagon. (Courtesy of Gehl Brothers, West Bend, Wisc.)*

traveling at 2.5 mph could be doubled two ways, either by increasing the swath to 120 inches *or* moving at 5 mph. Obviously, it also could be accomplished by any combination of the two. Therefore, high-powered tractors have increased the range of speeds at which one can operate and stimulated the development of implements to withstand such speeds.[21]

The demand for higher power also has created its own problems, one of which is traction. As power increased, the necessary traction was maintained by raising tractor weights and increasing tire size. There is no limit to tire size on non-row crop machines, but where cultivating is done it is a different matter. Tractors in the 70–90-hp range commonly wear 16–18-inch rear tires (width), but with the trend toward narrower rows extremely wide tires are not feasible. Even with 16-inch tires, cultivating 26-inch corn rows is difficult, and 20-inch rows are impossible (this would leave only 2 inches on each side of the rear tire). Most manufacturers minimize the problem by installing narrower tires initially, but add another set to make duals for heavy work (see Fig. 8). A recent innovation is to space the dual rear tires so as to straddle a row. This permits the duals to be left on the machine for row-crop cultivation (see Fig. 7). Even with this aid, many engineers see 140–180 hp as a practical limit for the traditional tractor style and are experimenting with four-wheel drive machines. Several are currently being marketed, but most are not aimed at the row-crop tractor buyer (Fig. 10). However, the technology of agriculture is so dynamic that the problem of tire width versus row width may not be with us forever. Narrow rows and the widespread use of herbicides have been so successful in controlling grasses and weeds that the cultivating process itself may be eliminated. Within the next decade we may see both soybeans and corn planted with a grain drill in 6–8 inch rows like wheat, with no cultivation at all. In some areas this is being approached through the recent system of "minimum tillage."

As the traction wheels have changed, the choice of front-end design has moved away from the tricycle toward the wide-front-style, especially among the higher-horsepower sizes. A spokesman for International Harvester estimates that 80–90 per cent of the machines in the over-70-hp class have wide front wheels today as compared with 28–30 per cent in 1949. Below 70 hp, the figure is approximately 70 per cent as compared with 15–18 per cent two decades ago.[22] An official of J. I. Case reports a similar trend. In one tractor size Case shipped 84 per cent with tricycle front wheels in 1949, but in 1968 tricycle shipments totaled only 17 per

---

[21] Several manufacturers have announced models specifically engineered for high-speed operation. They offer a higher power-weight ratio than the traditional models and have matched implements designed to operate at speeds of 5 mph and higher.
[22] Personal correspondence with Mr. W. F. Overman of International Harvester, Chicago, Illinois.

FIGURE 10. An International "4156" four-wheel-drive tractor pulling
nine bottoms in stubble. Note the wide tires, too wide for row-crop
cultivation. The cab is becoming quite common on the larger tractors;
it provides comfort in both winter and summer.

FIGURE 11. A *Massey-Harris model 14 pull-type combine harvesting wheat. The model 14 was available in 12–16-foot cutting widths, and its threshing mechanism was powered by a 48-hp Hercules engine. It is drawn by what appears to be a Massey-Harris "55" tractor. Note the wheel arrangement and front axle of the tractor, decidedly not suited for row-crop cultivation.* (Courtesy of Massey-Ferguson, Des Moines, Iowa.)

cent. Considering all tractor sizes, Case shipped 95 per cent of its 1968 output in wide-front-wheel models.[23]

It is obvious that the power revolution has greatly altered the farm tractor, its appearance, size, and ability to do work. But in some cases the revolution has created multifunction machines which have become units in their own right, and we have the beginnings of the second part of the power revolution, self-propulsion.

While the tractor was undergoing a drastic change in its capabilities, other implements were transformed into completely new units. The most notable of these is the combine. By the late forties the self-propelled combine was an accepted innovation but had by no means displaced the pull-type machine. In 1949 there were thirteen SP models available with from 7- to 16-foot heads (their cutting widths), but many were simply modifications of existing pull-type models. The pull-type model still reigned supreme on the small- to medium-sized operations; for example, fourteen models were offered with cutting heads of 7 feet or less. Large pull-type

---

[23] Personal correspondence with Mr. C. N. Arnold, general sales manager, agricultural equipment, J. I. Case Company, Racine, Wisconsin.

machines still existed, though, as ten models with heads of 12 feet or larger were manufactured. In fact, the largest combines offered (20 feet) were pull-type rather than self-propelled (Fig. 11).

The relative merits of the two machines are not immediately apparent, since so much depends upon their application. In general, the SP offers these advantages: (1) It is self-contained and therefore much more maneuverable than the cumbersome pull-type machine. (2) Being self-powered, no tractor is needed to tow it. This cuts down on manpower needs and releases the tractor for other work, a factor more important on general farms than on wheat farms where little other work is carried out at harvest time. (3) For custom threshermen, the single unit offers greater mobility in that it can be truck-transported quite easily. (4) With interchangeable heads it can be adapted to multicrop harvesting more easily than the pull-type.

Despite some attractive advantages of the SP, the pull-type has managed to hold its own on many operations because its cost is far less than that of a comparable SP, usually less than half. This makes it available to many small operators who harvest small acreages and cannot justify the expense of an SP (Fig. 12). It also has been tenacious in the specialized wheat area, since the demand for tractor time during harvest season is minimal.[24] Despite these special applications, in the decade or so following 1949 the SP came to dominate the market. In 1967 some 42,000 units were sold, of which less than 4 per cent were pull-type units. Furthermore, data on the sale of combines by size have been available since 1964, and they indicate a trend toward larger combines as well. For example, only 10 per cent of the 1964 SP machines had cutting heads of 20 feet or larger, but two years later this figure had increased to about 28 per cent.[25]

The factors behind this overwhelming acceptance of the SP machine are numerous. The inherent advantages of the SP over the pull-type have been discussed earlier, but reasons for the rapid shift are much more complex, and farm organization has undergone profound changes in order to take advantage of the situation. During the past two decades combines have been developed to accommodate a wide variety of grains. Traditionally equipped to cut and thresh the small grains, the newer units handle soybeans, sorghums, sunflowers, and corn—in fact, most seed-yielding plants. Beans can be harvested using the cutting head normally used for small grains, but most combines now can be had with interchangeable corn heads for cutting and shelling corn and a pickup attach-

---

[24] By 1967 the market for pull-type machines had almost vanished, yet the leading states in which such machines were sold were Minnesota and the Dakotas.

[25] Farm and Industrial Equipment Institute, *Reports*, February 8, 1966 and February 16, 1968. Data after 1967 are not comparable to those earlier years as the manufacturers began reporting combines by groups based on price rather than cutting widths.

Figure 12. *An Allis Chalmers "WD" pulling an "All Crop" combine. A small, light draft machine, it became a favorite of the small farmer. Having "grown up" with one, I can attest to its omnivourous nature; it can thresh anything from lespedeza to garter snakes. (Courtesy of Allis-Chalmers, Milwaukee, Wisc.)*

ment for a variety of seed-yielding plants. Thus, a single machine now can be used to harvest three or more crops with only minor changes.

The technological and economic adjustments to this breakthrough have been profound. Perhaps the most obvious effect was the increased market for SP machines with a concurrent decline in pull-type combines. With a multipurpose machine available, the medium-sized farm operation could justify its cost. This was especially true in the South and Midwest as soybean acreage increased.

A second result was the decline of the corn picker. Sales have been declining since the early 1950s, and there is evidence that the picker will go the way of the steam tractor. Estimates for Illinois indicate that the corn acreage harvested by corn pickers was surpassed by combine-harvested corn in the mid-sixties.[26] Field shelling was seen as a distinct ad-

[26] *Implement and Tractor,* January 7, 1969, p. 30.

FIGURE 13. *The versatility of the SP is due in part to its interchange-able attachments. Only minutes are needed to change from grain cutting head (center) to eight-row corn head (left) or pickup at-tachment (right). (Courtesy of Massey-Ferguson, Des Moines, Iowa.)*

vantage, and other machines were built to perform the job (shelling attach-ments and picker-shellers), but the great advantage of having a multipur-pose SP probably will complete the rout of the picker.[27]

Field shelling also stimulated the development of a new group of products catering to handling shelled corn as opposed to ear corn. Grain wagons (power or gravity unloaded) or grain-tight truck boxes move the grain from the field; auger elevators (as opposed to chain-type) move the grain into metal bins (the replacement for the wooden or wire crib); and due to the higher moisture content of field shelled grain, the grain dryer has emerged. Figure 14 indicates the relation between the multipurpose

[27] There may be some exceptions, such as the growers of hybrid seed corn who want their corn harvested in the ear. Just how long this constraint will last is open to question.

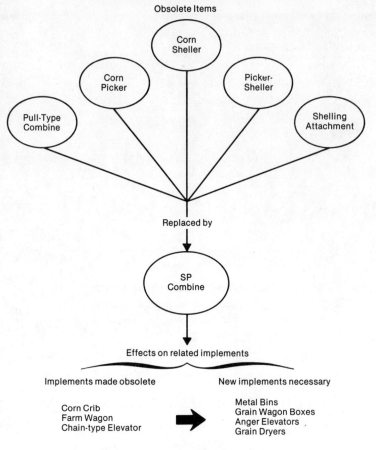

FIGURE 14. *Impact of SP combine.*

SP combine and implements it stimulated as well as those it is making obsolete.[28]

The self-propulsion revolution has not been limited to the combine. Forage harvesters, corn picker-shellers, mowers (now the windrower or swather), hay balers, hay wagons, cotton pickers, and a number of other specialty items are now marketed in SP models.[29] The one most successful

---

[28] I wish to acknowledge my debt to Messrs. Mark Zimmerman and Geo. H. Seferovich of *Implement and Tractor* for their stimulating ideas. Figs. 3 and 14 are based in part on work they have done.

[29] The cotton picker (not the stripper) is one machine that did not go through the "pull-type" stage. It evolved full-blown into an SP machine. It did, however, go through one stage in which one-row pickers were marketed to fit existing tractors. But the installation is so complex and time consuming (it involves turning the

FIGURE 15. *The windrower or swather which cuts, conditions, and windrows forage or small grains in one operation. It has gained wide acceptance in the Dairy Region. (Courtesy of Owatonna Manufacturing Company, Owatonna, Minn.)*

(judging from the manufacturers who jumped into the market) is the windrower (Fig. 15). It takes the place of the mower, side delivery rake, and (usually) the hay conditioner, and has gained wide acceptance in the dairy and other haying states. Its companion is the SP forage harvester. One trip over the field with a windrower followed by a chopper with a pickup head and the forage harvesting is done.

Other machines have been developed to mechanize the forage harvest. A SP baler is being marketed currently, as well as a SP bale loader that picks up and stacks bales onto a wagon. The bale thrower (tosses the bales from the baler into a towed wagon) had been marketed for several years. However, the future of the haying-implement market depends so much upon the direction cattle and hog feeding goes. Field chopping for forage and mechanized feeders may spell the doom for baled hay, but there is always the possibility that field "cubing" machines may make forage chopping obsolete.

---

tractor around, mounting endless paraphenalia on it, and operating it backward), that it is rapidly giving way to the SP models.

If we look back on the developments over the past two decades and try to extract the key trends, two are especially notable: the revolutionary surge in power and the trend toward self-propelled (specialty) machines. In fact, a closer look reveals that the trend toward self-propulsion is simply another facet of the thrust toward power, since the SP machine simply adds to the farmer's power arsenal. The well-equipped farm operator of today appears to be more convinced than anyone that the key to his farming future lies in his ability to multiply his own effort. Consequently, his machinery investments reflect this commitment. With his tractor (or tractors) tripled in power; his combine, swather, and forage harvester or baler self-propelled; and his materials handling equipment motorized, the American farmer now commands more sheer power than any other farm operator has ever done at any time. If his past record is any indication, this is only the beginning.

EXERCISES

VOCABULARY

mechanization	concurrent	hybrid
innovation	arsenal	precipitous
zeal	inanimate	consensus
peruse	facet	inherent
expedient	zenith	meager
transform	intermediate	

QUESTIONS

1. Identify the sentence in the first three paragraphs that states most clearly what this essay is going to talk about.

2. Paragraphs four through eight share a common pattern of development. What is it? Summarize in your own words the main idea these paragraphs are intended to explain.

3. Find examples of the following strategies: description, cause and effect, comparison, and classification.

4. This essay is divided into two main sections. What is the subject in each? Identify the transition paragraph leading from the first section to the second.

5. In the section of this essay on self-propelled machinery two techniques of organization are dominant. What are they? Find examples.

6. Select a suitable paragraph and list the words and phrases used to make smooth transitions within that paragraph.

SWIFT JUSTICE ON THE JOB
Ben Fischer

GRIEVANCE arbitration is virtually a unique American labor-management institution. It is a private judicial system created by unions and companies, embodied in collective bargaining agreements and free of government controls or interference (except as all private actions are subject to law suits based on fraud and similar criteria).

Some form of dispute settlement is inherent in any contractual agreement. Generally, in the United States and throughout the world, allegations of contractual violation are matters for courts or other government created tribunals.

Our own labor-management arbitration arrangement is very special because it is private, not inspired by government and not subject to significant outside interference.

If the arbitration process is not doing its job for the parties, it is to these private parties—labor and management—that one must look to assess the blame. Efforts by arbitrators to fix up the process are doomed and of questionable propriety except as they are asked to consult with the parties for advice based on their specialized experience. Efforts of university-based research or government agencies designed to change arbitration are useful only as they may furnish ideas or information to labor and management. But there's no escape—it is unions and management who must monitor the arbitration institution, nurture it, adjust it, adapt it to the varied needs of varied parties.

When referring to unions and management in this regard, it is important to indicate where the decision-making should rest. The advocates who personally try cases are not the ideal decision-makers. They are too close to the trees to see the forest. They often have a self-serving axe to grind; too often they tend to evaluate the status of arbitration arrangements in terms of who wins and who loses. This tendency can overlook the broader impact of the quality, integrity and long-range effects of arbitration performance.

For instance, a union may win cases where back pay is forthcoming and lose cases where fundamental contract rights are at issue. This winning of back pay may look good in the union paper or in the report to the union meeting; but taking the two as a whole, with the loss of the fundamental contract rights, the best interests of the employees have not been served.

FROM *Viewpoint*, Vol. 4, No. 3 (1974). Reprinted by permission.

Policy-Makers Should Have Chief Role

Thus, it is appropriate that arbitration be shaped by the union and company policy-makers, usually by those who play the decisive role in the collective bargaining process itself and in the overall implementation of contracts. They are more likely to see the problems from the inside looking out, instead of from the outside hardly aware of what are truly the stakes.

This emphasis on control of arbitration reflects a belief that no single system is right; each relationship needs its own system depending on a wide range of variables: In fact, the need in a particular relationship can change due to a change in circumstances such as personalities, collective bargaining atmosphere, grievance procedure and other factors.

Most of the general efforts to "fix up" arbitration have been ineffective. General programs to streamline arbitration have met little success and unimpressive results. General efforts to train new arbitrators by universities or appointive agencies have had little demonstrable effect toward improving the process. In any event, the recent attempts to generally improve the arbitration process have been very limited and have made hardly a dent on the onrushing problems. (It should be noted that there are a number of specific, tailored programs which have been useful in their individual situations.)

What are the problems most commonly surfacing? We will try to list a few we have experienced or observed during a full generation of arbitration experience:

1. The mode of arbitration tends to be fixed without regard to the specific cases and the needs of the parties. Thus, procedures and personnel appropriate for handling major disputes over contract interpretation are also used for day-to-day shop problems. A case of minor discipline over a routine infraction can absorb experts and involve time and expense all out of proportion to the problem at hand. Each party may hire counsel or assign highly trained professionals to appear before a prestigious arbitrator. The costs are great. The time lapse is out of line with reason. The actual proceeding takes on forms which leave the grievant and his supervisor cold because they become minor actors in a matter which really should involve them and not some institutional clash or joust between professional advocates.

Even the decision reflects the distortion of the procedure. It is common for a routine case to be decided by a lengthy award, sketching background, practice, evidence, precedents, and what not. What the grievant wants is a decision addressed to him and to his foreman, not to the history books or the commercial arbitration services.

This developing picture results in widespread disenchantment, not only among union members but also in management circles. The complex and time-consuming route required to get a decision in a simple case is not defensible. It serves only those who are cynical about the financial benefits they personally derive from these complexities or those who doubt the value of arbitration as a proper judicial system. There are indications that some employers who wanted overly expensive, prohibitive, frustrating arbitration as a means of discouraging employee challenges of management decisions are having a change of heart. Employers are increasingly recognizing the constructive contribution that is made by a procedure which fully permits fair and expeditious resolution of disputes.

Frustration Can Flare

2. This observation leads to another consideration. A grievance and arbitration procedure which results in frustration and a feeling of employee helplessness does not aid management. Insofar as the welfare of the business is concerned, a poor procedure is costly in the long run. Not only does it tend to interfere with work performance, it also complicates good-faith collective bargaining.

Many strikes and bargaining failures can be traced to a general state of employee dissatisfaction rather than objection to specific terms of a proposed new agreement. It is at bargaining time that accumulated employee frustrations and anger can result in an employee's desire to punish the employer. Contract rejections, strikes and whatever weapon may be at hand are easily resorted to under such circumstances.

3. Insofar as any union and company (or industry) is seeking stability in bargaining relations, the prestige of arbitration among the employees and with management is often decisive. Surely, if an effort to resolve differences over contract terms by arbitration is under consideration it is important to have the participants not generally angry over the institution of arbitration. Dissatisfaction with grievance arbitration makes resort to arbitration of contract terms more difficult.

But even if contract terms arbitration is not desired, grievance arbitration plays another important role in arriving at collective bargaining agreement terms. Many bargaining issues do not lend themselves easily or readily to solution by precise contract language especially in multi-plant or multi-company bargaining. The only "out" available to the parties may be, and often is, some general language which creates a framework or guidelines for resolving specific incidences that occur during the term of the agreement. Such general language may be acceptable if the parties feel that disputes over specifics will be subject to resolution by a fair and competent arbitrator. If no such faith exists, the achievement of a solution is made much more difficult.

A common example is discipline. Many contracts require discipline to be "fair" or for "just cause" or "proper cause." Such broad criteria leave wide latitude for an arbitrator. The alternative is to write rules which are detailed, complex and usually rigid. This alternative overlooks employee equity in specific cases and may well confine management to do no more than the rule proscribes and also no less because its own deviation from the rule may be construed as its abandonment.

Dependability Is a "Must"

The history of bargaining and arbitration is replete with the impact of arbitration's reputation on the ability of bargainers to come to terms. If arbitration of grievances cas be relied on as dependable, the negotiators have an easier time in arriving at acceptable accommodations, perhaps settling on broad guidelines instead of reaching impasse in the process of spelling out precise clauses or rules which cannot practically be spelled out without creating serious inequities.

Our conclusion then is that grievance arbitration needs more concerted and systematic attention by labor and management leadership.

The experience of the Steelworkers may be of some value to those who seek ways to improve arbitration performance. In 1971, the basic steel negotiators agreed to an experimental Expedited Arbitration system. It resulted in 14 area panels of relatively young, inexperienced but qualified men and women serving as arbitrators in every steel and iron ore center.

There are more than 200 panel members, assigned in rotation by an administrative officer in each area. Most of the panel members are relatively young, mostly lawyers or law professors. Representatives of both management and labor recruited the panel members with cooperation from law school deans. The arbitrators are available on virtually an instant basis. Hearings are informal. Decisions are brief and made within several days of the hearing. There are no briefs or transcripts.

The representatives who present the cases are plant-level company and union officials. The decisions do not set precedents. The cases are relatively non-technical, involve non-complex issues such as discipline, fact disputes, one or very few employees.

The steel companies participating in the program all have permanent arbitrators who continue to handle cases dealing with novel issues, incentives, job classification disputes and complex contract interpretation problems as well as discharges.

The System Works

Two and a half years of experience have demonstrated that the expedited system works well. It has helped alleviate some clogged grievance situations. It has improved the reputation of arbitration at the plants where it has been used most. It has aided the grievance procedure's efficiency in a number of plants by providing a means of prompt resolution of grievance disputes.

The Steelworkers are currently arranging similar programs in the aluminum and can manufacturing industries. These are already underway but months will be required to extend its coverage for these far-flung industries.

Discussions will start soon with at least one major copper company to explore use of Expedited Arbitration.

Significantly, the Industrial Union Department of the AFL-CIO is engaged in efforts to develop a similar Expedited Arbitration system in Columbus, Ohio. This pilot program is intended to be multi-union, multi-company, multi-industry. If it succeeds, it could pave the way for blanketing the country so as to make expedited arbitration available for virtually all unions and companies desirous of using this method.

If these programs—steel, IUD and others—succeed, there will be a new look in grievance arbitration. It will have a number of consequences including:

1. Ready access to inexpensive, informal, expeditious arbitration of routine grievances which the parties themselves cannot resolve.
2. A better total labor-management atmosphere which could have important by-products—better morale, improved productivity and more constructive collective bargaining.
3. Involvement in the labor management scenes of hundreds if not thousands of new faces as arbitrators.
4. Possible recruitment of very able, talented new personnel as arbitrators because they will not have to run the traditional gauntlet—to become an experienced arbitrator you must first be acceptable and to be acceptable you must first become experienced, an improbable if not impossible dilemma.

With the tremendous growth of demands for arbitration, a new kind of recruitment is essential. Not only do more private parties desire arbitration and not only is the incidence of resort to grievance and arbitration procedures growing but unionization of public employees has precipitously engendered tremendous new demands for arbitrators, fact-finders and mediators.

If our nation is to have a viable system of collective bargaining, we cannot afford to neglect the challenge—labor and management must provide the solutions to getting enough arbitrators and proper use of arbitrators in a manner best able to serve their mutual and respective interests.

EXERCISES

judicial	joust	replete
criteria	cynical	impasse
propriety	latitude	transcript
monitor	equity	gauntlet
viable		

1. What is the author's purpose in this essay?

2. Identify places where the author uses examples. Do these examples help clarify his point?

3. What technique of organization is used to discuss the problems currently part of the arbitration procedure?

4. After he discusses the problems, does Fischer propose a solution? What is it?

5. In which paragraph does Fischer relate the Steelworkers' system of arbitration back to the problems he discussed earlier?

6. Find an example of cause-effect thinking and writing.

THE NEW MILITANCY:
A CRY FOR MORE

O NE of the minor economic miracles in the past couple of years has been the quietly cooperative spirit of U.S. labor. As living costs sailed skyward and corporate profits rose sharply, most of the nation's biggest and toughest unions accepted relatively moderate contracts that added little to the rapid pace of inflation. But that remarkable show of patience has now ended. The American workers' mood has turned increasingly bitter lately, and wage demands have climbed steadily higher.

Last week, in the middle of the most important contract talks of the year, the 120,000-member United Mine Workers went out on strike and quickly won one of the fattest settlements in labor history, a 50% raise in wages and benefits over three years. In the light of labor's understandable frustration with both inflation and recession, the increase could well set a new high goal for other unions to shoot for, with grave consequences for the economy and the nation. Last year most unions were accepting wage-and-benefit increases of little more than 6% in the first year of contracts. During the first six months of 1974, the average settlement climbed to between 8% and 9%, and by September to 11%. The miners' success in achieving 14% to 15% for the first year could easily presage even higher inflationary demands and more disruptive strikes by other unions.

The mine settlement is certain to lift the price of coal—as well as steel, electricity and myriad consumer products—adding further to oppressive living costs, which are now rising at an annual rate of close to 12%. The pact must still be ratified by the entire membership, a new union procedure that will take between eight and ten days and guarantees that the strike will paralyze the mines for at least three weeks. U.M.W. President Arnold Miller has repeatedly stated that his men will not return to the pits before the voting is completed.

Despite the stupendous size of the package, there was little jubilation among the miners in the humpbacked hills and crooked hollows of Appalachia, where most of the nation's coal is dug. Many of the men reckoned that they deserved still more. By last week's end, the union's Bargaining Council, made up of key officers, had not yet approved the contract and ran into surprisingly long arguments over its fine points. Meanwhile, the outcome of the membership-wide vote was uncertain.

The U.M.W.'s policy of allowing every member to cast a secret ballot

---

F R O M *Time*, November 25, 1974. Reprinted by permission from *Time*, The Weekly Newsmagazine; Copyright, Time Inc.

on industry-wide contracts at last brings the miners into the mainstream of progressive unionism. Until now, the final decision on major mine contracts was made at the top. Under the plan, the first vote is cast by the Bargaining Council. The schedule then calls for the agreement to be explained to 800 delegates from the local unions at a meeting in Pittsburgh late this week. The delegates will then take the 58-page agreement back to their local headquarters, where it will be explained in great detail to members before they vote. The union hopes to distribute a copy of the contract to each miner for study, and Miller has insisted that the agreement be written in plain language.

The settlement will cost the companies an estimated $1.25 billion. Only about a third of the package will be in pay increases, which will go up 9% in the first year and 3% in each of the next two years. That will jack up the top pay scale for miners from $50 a day to almost $58 over the life of the contract.

The U.M.W. also won its first cost of living escalator, which workers in steel, auto and other industries have had for years. The formula will increase base pay by 1¢ an hour for every .4 rise in the consumer price index, up to a maximum 20¢ a year. That could add almost $24 a week to wages over the next three years.

The biggest gains for miners were in benefits, which had been extraordinarily skimpy. The agreement calls for a dramatic $900 million increase in royalties paid by companies to support the union's health and retirement plans; the payments will jump from the present 80¢ per ton of coal dug to $1.55 by 1977. The money will increase pensioners' payments from $150 to as much as $375 a month and greatly expand health and hospital care for disabled miners, widows and children.

Other benefit enrichments include company-paid disability insurance of $100 a week for up to one year, five days of paid sick leave, v. none now, three more paid holidays in addition to the present nine and a new $75-a-year allowance for work clothes. The U.M.W. also scored well on improving safety measures. Every miner will get the right to leave any area that he considers unsafe, and the companies agreed to bear the cost of four comprehensive mine inspections each year by the union's Miner Safety Committee.

The big settlement comes at a time when the Ford Administration is struggling with raging inflation, rising unemployment and a steadily declining economy. Even a three-week strike will hurt. Coal-hauling railroads —including the Penn Central, Norfolk & Western and Chesapeake & Ohio—have laid off more than 2,500 workers. Thousands more have been let go by U.S. Steel and Republic Steel, which need coal to produce. Most electric utilities, which burn about two-thirds of the nation's coal, have adequate stockpiles for a relatively short strike. But the Government-owned Tennessee Valley Authority was so low on coal that it asked the communities it serves in seven states to cut their street lighting in half for the duration of the strike. In all, a three-week coal stoppage would cause a loss of more than $5 billion in the sagging gross national product.

The nation's real output of goods and services has declined for the past nine months; the drop is expected to continue at least until mid-1975, thus marking one of the longest slides since the Great Depression. Last week, with the election over, the White House ended its verbal contortions and permitted Presidential Press Secretary Ron Nessen to concede what most non-Government experts already knew: the U.S. is now in a recession. Alan Greenspan, chairman of the President's Council of Economic Advisers, added that the economy had stood up fairly well until late September, but "some time in the past four to six weeks there has been a marked weakening." The economy is likely to get worse in the next few months.

A most ominous factor is labor's new and growing restiveness. Until recently, labor militancy had been muted in large part because more and more workers were covered by cost of living escalators. In the past year alone the percentage of union members covered by such clauses jumped from 40% to just over 50%, bringing the total to more than 10 million people. Many workers lulled themselves into believing that these escalators would keep their wages in line with prices—but they did not. The average U.S. worker's buying power in September was down 5.2% from a year ago and down 7.4% from 1972.

Then the growing specter of recession cast a lengthening shadow over the economy, layoffs spread, and by the end of September, 5.5 million people were out of jobs. The unemployment rate is now 6% and is expected to scoot up to 7% or more by mid-1975. Though the ax is falling in many industries, no group has been harder hit than the auto workers. A combination of consumer uncertainty, high gasoline prices and substantial increases in 1975 model prices sent car sales skidding to an annual rate of 6.2 million in October; at that pace, auto sales for the year would be the lowest since 1961.

As a result, the 1.4 million-member United Auto Workers union reports that as many as 150,000 of its members are out of work. The number may soon swell to 230,000 because Chrysler Corp. is expected to take the unprecedented step of closing down virtually all of its U.S. assembly plants for five weeks beginning Dec. 2. Says U.A.W. Vice President Irving Bluestone: "The auto industry is not in a recession—it's in a depression." In Bluestone's arguable view, auto demand would quicken somewhat if General Motors, Ford and Chrysler lowered their prices and the oil companies reduced the cost of gasoline by taking lower profits. Reflecting labor's new anger, Bluestone, a militant unionist, adds: "If the oil firms continue to gouge the public, then we'll call for regulation of the industry or, if need be, its nationalization."

Fortunately for the nation, the bargaining calendar for the next year is relatively light, and none of the big pacesetters like steel and autos are up for contract talks. Yet there are a number of important, potentially explosive negotiations in the wings. Bargaining will begin next week for the railroad workers' contract, which expires at the end of December. "We gotta get more money, no question about it," says Al Chesser, president of the United Transportation Union, one of the railroad brotherhoods.

The rail workers are aiming for a three-year 45% to 50% increase in wages alone. At present they earn an average of about $45 a day. The railroad workers are also worried about job losses. Like other craft unions, the rail unions have historically responded to this threat by jiggering contract work rules that limit the amount of labor one man can perform and thus spread more work around. That featherbedding, of course, guts productivity and lifts inflation even higher.

The construction workers will be coming to the bargaining table early next spring, and they will press for skyscraping settlements. Other union members with contracts expiring next year—airline mechanics, insurance workers, oil and refinery employees and the 600,000 postal workers—will be out not only to catch up with prices but to get ahead of them, thus further fanning inflation.

Robert Nathan, a member of *Time's* Board of Economists and a leading labor specialist, is frightened by the intensity of the anger that he finds among union people. "There is talk of violence and rioting in the street," says Nathan. He believes that inflationary pressures will become so great that unions that have already signed settlements without an escalator clause will be back to reopen their contracts in order to get one. "If I were an employer," says Nathan, "I would be receptive to such demands." The alternative, in his view, is worker slowdowns and sputtering productivity.

Beyond the bargaining table, labor is using its clout more and more on the political front. Its aim: to push through the new Congress, which takes office in January, a long list of legislative proposals. Many of the newly elected legislators had the solid support of top labor chieftains—and their $3 million campaign kitty. Now AFL-CIO President George Meany has passed the word that these Congressmen are honor bound to reciprocate or face labor's wrath in the next election.

High on labor's list of priorities is the national health security bill sponsored by Senator Edward Kennedy of Massachusetts. The most expansive of several plans before the Congress, the Kennedy bill would establish a federally funded hospitalization and medical plan for all U.S.

citizens. In addition, the union leaders want: (1) curtailment of imports of clothing, electrical goods and other foreign items that compete with U.S. products; (2) tax reform aimed at the rich and the big corporations; (3) expansion of Government financial aid to the mortgage market; and (4) the repeal of state right-to-work laws, which weaken labor's authority by permitting nonunion help to work in unionized shops.

Labor has enough influence in the new Congress to get much of what it wants, but it still could be stymied by President Ford's veto power. Thus Meany and his lieutenants are gearing up a major drive to put a more amenable man in the White House in 1976. Says Meany: "We just can't wait for the economic theories of [Federal Reserve Board Chairman] Arthur Burns or these other people to bring us out of this thing. The unemployment picture is getting worse and worse. It adds up to a national disaster."

If workers in many industries are angry, none have more justification than the men who mine America's coal. For decades, the miners' bargaining strength had been reduced by the nation's increasing reliance on oil and natural gas, which now supply almost 80% of U.S. energy needs. As coal demand diminished, company profits shrank, and miners' wages and benefits lagged behind those in other industries. But coal's prospects have changed dramatically in the past year in the face of quadrupled petroleum prices. Last fall's Arab oil embargo raised supply worries everywhere and prompted a rapid switch to coal.

Today coal is king, and orders are running far ahead of the companies' ability to fill them. Voracious demand has enabled mine operators repeatedly to renegotiate prices upward. Contract coal now sells for an average of $15 per ton, almost double what it was a year ago. Noncontract coal (spot purchases) has leaped by as much as 1,000%, to as high as $120 per ton. The rise in company profits is colossal. For example, in the third quarter, Consolidation Coal (owned by Continental Oil) earned $15.9 million, up from $200,000 in the same quarter last year, and Island Creek, the third biggest company (owned by Occidental Petroleum) went from a loss last year to a profit of $35.2 million. The oil industry has a big stake in coal; petroleum companies now control 70% of the nation's reserves, which total 1.3 trillion tons. Indeed, the U.S. has about half of the world's known deposits and is often called "the Saudi Arabia of coal."

The mine operators contend that after years of slumping sales, they are entitled to the higher prices that the surging demand for coal has brought. This year coal companies' return on investment will average about 23%, v. an average of 12% for the rest of industry. Last year, however, the return in coal was only 9%, and the year before 7%. Coalmen assert that the cost of the new labor contract also justifies increased prices. Most important, company officials note, they will need massive amounts of capital to meet the Government's goal of almost doubling production in the next ten years.

Though the miners insist that the companies can well afford to grant them their rich package without an inflationary boost in coal prices, they doubt that that will happen. Says Lou Antal, president of U.M.W. District 5 in Pittsburgh: "Every time in the past when they've given us two bucks, they raised the price of coal by three."

Much more than prices and wages was at stake in last week's confrontation. The union had its future, possibly even its very existence, on the line (the Steelworkers union has long been ready to swallow up the miners). Two years ago, the miners ended a half-century of bullying and often exploitative union rule when they elected a reform slate of former miners, headed by Miller. Since then, the new leaders have entirely rewritten the union's old, restrictive constitution and have given back to the locals the right to elect their own officials instead of having them rammed down from the top. Yet democracy is a fragile bloom in the coal fields, and Miller needed a resounding negotiating victory to strengthen his still tenuous grip on the presidency as well as prove that miners can govern their own affairs. "We have to show that we're not just a bunch of dumb asses," he says.

Such talk would probably have brought a haughty sneer from John L. Lewis, the union's legendary leader from 1920 to 1960, whose autocratic legacy still burdens the U.M.W. In his early days, however, Lewis was a mighty force for progress. Only a decade or so before he took over the union, much of the nation's coal was dug by youngsters, some barely into their teens, who labored in appallingly dirty, unsafe conditions for only a pittance. Lewis was the Paul Bunyan of unionism, standing up to companies, courts and even Presidents with fiery bombast. When Franklin Roosevelt threatened to bring out the U.S. Army to break a U.M.W. strike in 1943, Lewis replied with classic defiance: "They can't dig coal with bayonets."

In the '30s, Lewis made the U.M.W. the battering ram of organized labor, the strongest union in the nation. But he ran the organization like a feudal fief, stripping the membership of all elective power, making all decisions himself and swatting down any opposition. He bought a bank for his union, loaned money to troubled coal companies, and acted as the final arbiter for the entire industry, labor and management alike.

W.A. ("Tony") Boyle, a Montana local chief who came to the Washington headquarters in 1948, succeeded to the presidency in 1963. He tightened the dictatorship. But the union became a shambles, membership fell off, and corruption and terror tactics grew. Boyle and his cronies milked the union's pension and health funds for their own purposes. Bob

Wingrove of Moundsville, W.Va., a Boyle opponent, recalls: "I was threatened many times. They used to call up my wife and ask, 'Are your kids in school? Are you sure?' Then when I'd come home, my wife would be crazy with worry. I had my phone taken out. I carried a gun."

Finally, Boyle's leadership was seriously challenged in a 1969 election by Joseph ("Jock") Yablonski, a member of the U.M.W. executive board. Yablonski lost the election, but for daring to defy the leadership's code of blind loyalty, he, his wife and daughter were brutally gunned to death in their beds on New Year's morning 1970—on the orders, it later came out, of Tony Boyle, who was eventually convicted of murder and is now in prison. The murders sent shock waves of indignation across the coal fields. Shortly afterward, Miller, who had risen to prominence in West Virginia as president of the insurgent Black Lung Association, was chosen at a meeting of anti-Boyle factions to succeed Yablonski and lead the reform movement.

In the Government-ordered and monitored election of 1972, Miller's campaign took on the air of a crusade, attracting the support of widely diverse groups, including poverty-fighting VISTA volunteers. He beat Boyle by 70,000 votes to 56,000—the first time in recent labor history that any upstart from the rank and file had ousted the president of any major U.S. union.

To the miners of Appalachia, Miller has become a symbol of new possibilities in their lives. Like Miller, they are mainly of Anglo-Saxon stock. On the whole, they are proud, patriotic, sometimes violent and yet often deeply religious. For them, the mines are generally an alternative to grinding rural poverty. Those who do not flee to the city love the raw, knobby hill country and the sense of freedom from urban constrictions and pressures.

The miners today lead far better lives than their fathers did, both in and out of the pits. Gone is the image of the fatalistic miner mournfully characterized two decades ago in Tennessee Ernie Ford's rendition of *Sixteen Tons:*

> *You load sixteen tons,*
> *What do you get?*
> *Another day older and deeper in debt.*
> *Saint Peter, don't you call me 'cause*
> *   I can't go—*
> *I owe my soul to the company store—*

Still, among major industries, mining is the most dangerous work in the U.S., running far ahead of construction, which is the second most hazardous. So far this year 122 miners have been killed on the job and thousands more injured. Part of the problem, Miller asserts, is that the federal mine-safety inspectors have not been strict enough with the companies.

Many miners lose an eye, and many more lose fingers; the Mining Enforcement and Safety Administration estimates that three out of every five miners who have been in the pits for 20 years or more have lost a finger in a conveyor belt or some other machinery. In addition, 215,000 miners are disabled by black-lung disease, caused by breathing coal dust. Says Miller: "A miner who gets black lung gives up ten or 15 years of his life. And it's a helluva way to go. It took my stepfather five years to die of it, and in all that time he couldn't breathe when he lay down in a bed. The only rest he got was sitting in a reclining chair."

The dangers that miners face routinely each day would be considered harrowing by most American workers. At the Shoemaker Mine near Benwood, W.Va., for example, a miner's day begins at the bathhouse, a big stark room with showers. Miners' work pants, boots, jackets and gloves are in buckets hung from the high ceiling on ropes that look like stalactites. After changing, the men hang their numbered brass tags on a board at the mine entrance; a tag that is still there after the shift ends alerts the rest of the crew that a miner is missing.

Next the miners descend in an elevator to the mine, far below the surface. There they file into a tiny rail car for the ride to the mine face, the wall of solid coal at the end of the tunnel where the coal is actually extracted. During the four-mile journey, the beams from the lamps on the miners' hats bore through the darkness, picking up eerie, abandoned passageways, diggings of another day. The foreman carries a small naphtha lamp; if the lamp's flame flares up, it indicates the presence of flammable methane gas and the threat of fire; if it goes out, it means that the oxygen has been depleted to dangerous levels. Each man has clipped to his belt a small canister with an hour's supply of oxygen.

As the men near the mine face, visibility diminishes, and the air thickens with black dust. The miners begin to clear their throats and spit. The area around the mine face looks like a small construction site, with piles of boards, bolts, rails, ties and electrical power equipment. The wires on this equipment are regularly checked lest a miner be electrocuted. Facing the wall of coal is a continuous coal mining machine called "the beast." The machine's whirling blades chew into the seam with a roaring noise like an avalanche, spewing chunks of coal back into waiting coal cars, which are equipped with robot-like "gathering arms" that channel the flow. The load is then trundled back along the tracks and automatically unloaded onto a conveyor-belt system that lifts the coal to the surface.

When the machine has dug ahead 4 ft. or so, it pulls back. Then two members of the crew bolt boards in place on the mine roof to support it; drilling holes for the bolts is one of the most dangerous jobs in mining because the unsupported roof can easily give way. When the supports are up, the mining machine goes back to work, and the process is repeated over and over until the shift ends. For all the hazards, miners insist that there is a great deal of satisfaction in coal mining. Says Miller, a third-generation miner: "There are always going to be dangers. After a couple of years, you learn to accept the realities of mining."

Veteran miners know how much those realities have improved. For example, Raymond Echard, 58, has spent four decades in West Virginia mines. When he started out at age 13, he loaded coal for 17¢ per ton— earning about $4.40 a day. Companies then forced miners to buy their own picks, shovels and other equipment and did not even provide fans to blow away the coal dust. Echard lost a thumb coupling coal cars and injured his back three times. Yet he encouraged his grandson to get into the mines. "I told him it was a good job," says Echard. "Coal's the thing of the future."

Off the job in their small communities, miners generally do not live as well as auto workers or steelworkers, but they have begun to enjoy more of the amenities of middle class life. Bob Wingrove, 49, a miner for 27 years and the popular president of the U.M.W. local at the Ireland mine near Moundsville, speeds to work in a sports car, returns each evening to his modest frame house, which he is renovating. On days off, he drives to Pittsburgh, 90 minutes away on Interstate 79, for concerts or sporting events.

Neither Wingrove nor his brother "Peach," 36, was dissuaded from mining because of their father's death in a mine fire in 1966. Although Peach was disabled for a year after a roof fall, he still works the mines, and today he lives fairly well. To supplement his income of about $12,000 last year and to help save for retirement, his wife works in an enamelware plant. Last summer the couple and their three teen-age daughters vacationed in their travel trailer for two weeks at South Carolina beaches. "Mining's getting better," says Peach. "I know I'm not going to be a millionaire. But as long as things go the way they are, I'm not complaining."

Many young men choose to follow their fathers and brothers into the mines. Pat Callebs, superintendent of the giant Shoemaker Mine, has hired miners with college degrees. "I asked one of the college men if he'd like to train for a management job," says Callebs. "He told me, 'Nope. I like what I'm doing just fine.'" Callebs tries to hire sons, brothers or cousins of miners; they know what they are getting into and usually stick with the job.

Dick Parsons, 20, has been in the pits for two years, earning $47.25 a day as a roof bolter at Ireland. He is a member of what older miners call the industry's "Pepsi generation"—young, eager, willing to work topsy-turvy schedules to build seniority that will put them in line for permanent day-shift jobs. Two weeks ago, he slept days and worked nights. Three weeks ago, he worked days. A month ago, he worked the 4 P.M. to midnight shift. On summer weekends, he and his wife Martha go camping in the Appalachians. His two older brothers are also miners. Parsons' goals are set. "I'd just like to live a nice peaceful life and raise a nice small family," he says.

Yet many miners and their families still live in skittery, weather-bleached houses in scores of coal-camp villages that are little more than rural slums. Life is worst for retirees on minuscule pensions; they spend their last years living from hand to mouth. "You know, $150 a month barely pays your heat and utility bills," argues Miner Jim ("Catfish") Barlow, 27, of Moundsville. Adds co-worker Rod Lash, 24: "The old guys got stuck. They didn't get what was coming to them. But it doesn't make sense for us to take that too."

The union's fat new settlement should go far in righting many of the inequities that miners have long been forced to live with. Whether it goes far enough to satisfy the rank and file is still uncertain. Like the rest of organized labor, they are fed up with waiting to catch up with inflation. Miller believes that labor's problems go well beyond issues of wages and to the very heart of the union movement. In his view, labor leaders and their membership have grown too complacent, too willing to accept the status quo. "We are all guilty," says Miller, "because we sat back and waited for someone to do something."

The gathering threat of a wage explosion is already raising fresh cries in Congress and elsewhere for a return to some form of wage-price controls. Even Meany has said that he is willing to accept controls, provided that they keep as tight a lid on prices as on wages. On this and other issues, big labor, bolstered by its new political muscle, is now moving into open conflict with President Ford and his top economic aides, who vigorously oppose any further Government intervention and most of the other measures that the union chiefs want. The stage is set for what could well be two years of turbulent confrontation between labor and the Ford Administration over how to meet workers' rising demands for a better shake in a troubled economy.

EXERCISES

VOCABULARY

presage	comprehensive	bombast
disrupt	duration	insurgent

myriad	contortion	stalactites
stupendous	concede	amenities
progressive	ominous	inequity
militancy	restive	arbiter
mute	reciprocate	harrowing
virtual	amenable	deplete
embargo	voracious	dissuade
tenuous	autocratic	turbulent

QUESTIONS

1. What details and examples does the author give us to support the statement "The American workers' mood has turned increasingly bitter lately, . . ."?

2. Is this essay totally objective? Do the writer's attitudes and opinions show through at any point? Find examples.

3. Why does this essay focus on the mine workers' problems more than on the problems of some other profession?

4. This essay uses narrative development effectively. Find two examples of narration. What are these narratives intended to demonstrate?

5. Read the section on persuasion in this text. Find examples of different types of evidence in this essay. What type seems to be most effective?

6. Pick out the key sentences in the essay that signal the introduction of a new topic. Describe the transitional devices the writer uses to move smoothly from one topic to the next.

7. Make a list of the various cause-and-effect relationships discussed in this essay.

SCIENCE, TECHNOLOGY, AND DEVELOPMENT:
A NEW WORLD OUTLOOK

Glenn T. Seaborg

THERE is a singular significance to this inter-American meeting in the interest of advancing science. This hemisphere was long known as the New World. It was considered the new frontier where freedom—physical, spiritual, and mental—would follow new opportunities to be envisioned, grasped, and developed. Many of those opportunities were realized. Many are in the process of being fulfilled. And hopefully this conference will contribute to that fulfillment.

But much as we believed—and still believe—in the opportunities that exist in this hemisphere, I think we must redefine our concept of the New World. Today we must think of the New World in terms of the entire world, as a community of mankind whose future lies in pursuing the belief that knowledge—universally obtained, widely shared, and wisely applied—is the key to the viability of the human race and the earth that supports it.

We at this conference are advocates of that belief. We are interested in the advancement of science because we know that it will result in the advancement of man. What I want to discuss now are some of our reasons for this belief and a rationale for putting science and technology to work more constructively and humanely on an international scale. This has become truly the main scale on which we can now measure the success of science. Nations may advance their national scientific progress. Temporary power and prestige may flow from such progress. But we now see the world evolving into an ecologic, economic, and ethical whole. Science and technology have created the conditions leading to this viewpoint, and they have created the instruments to observe it; and if they have fostered many of the problems related to it, they are also capable of giving us the knowledge and tools to solve these problems. My convictions about such an international humane role for science have been reinforced by my visits to more than 60 countries during my tenure as chairman of the U.S. Atomic Energy Commission.

This conference on Science and Man in the Americas is built around ten central themes, and of these perhaps the most basic is "science, development, and human values," for this deals most broadly with the human condition.

FROM *Science*, Vol. 181, No. 4094 (July 6, 1973), pp. 13–19. Copyright 1973 by the American Association for the Advancement of Science. Reprinted by permission.

Call to Action

There has been a commendable move by scientists and engineers in the last few years toward a greater concern about the social impact of their work, accompanied by a redirection of their efforts into areas more directly applicable to practical contemporary problems and the promotion of human welfare. But this effort has been largely confined to the domestic scene. That there has as yet been no concurrent widespread activity on such problems on an international scale is somewhat surprising in view of our traditional interest in this arena. The theme of this talk is a call to my colleagues in science and engineering to expand their action to the international scene. If we want to see our children live in a world of peace based on the fulfillment of human needs and the recognition of human dignity, we must over the coming years make every effort to narrow the gap between the developing and the developed countries through the achievement of a worldwide unified economy. This goal should be among our highest priorities. I shall conclude my remarks with a few suggestions of how we scientists and engineers might improve our means for helping to achieve this goal.

Unifying Force

Why are science and technology the leading forces in an evolutionary unification of man? One reason is simply the universality of a scientific truth once it has been accepted as such by the science community. We may compete as well as cooperate in search of a scientific discovery; but once that discovery has been made, revealed, and confirmed it belongs to all mankind.

The sharing of such knowledge today is an enormous international enterprise. Each year now there are held more than 100 major international scientific congresses, and several hundred smaller ones. Some 60 intergovernmental organizations and more than 250 international non-government organizations deal with science and coordinate global scientific activities. The world shares its scientific and technical information in some 100,000 journals printed each year in about 60 languages, and the number of such publications continues to grow. Even more important is the increase in the numbers of those educated and trained to use them and to apply the knowledge they bring. Together with our colleagues in the arts and humanities, we in the scientific and engineering communities are in the forefront of forging a global civilization.

A second unifying element of science and technology lies in the demands of the earth itself and in our need to work together to understand it and its life-giving resources more fully. This is one of the central themes at this meeting. We now recognize that the earth—its oceans, its atmosphere, its polar lands—forms a most magnificent laboratory in which we must work together to understand the complex dynamic system of forces that create our weather, supply our food and water, and provide us with resources to improve our lives. These forces recognize no political boundaries, and we must explore them together and share our knowledge of them. We have been doing this in a number of ways, through many international organizations and programs. They are too numerous to even list, but perhaps a few examples are in order.

At this moment scientists from several nations are aboard the deep-sea drilling ship *Glomar Challenger* taking cores of the earth's crust from beneath the ocean floor, examining them for clues to the earth's climate, life, and movement of past ages. More than 50 scientists from 17 countries have participated in this work. More than 6,000 samples of deep-sea sediment cores have been taken in 25 voyages. Already this research and evidence from other international geophysical programs has radically revised our theories about the surface of the earth and the formation of the continents.

Under the title of the Global Atmospheric Research Program a vast armada of ships and aircraft of nine nations will take to the tropical zone of the Atlantic Ocean next year in the first of a series of research projects to gain vital information on the conditions that generate the weather over much of our inhabited land areas. This first experiment will employ 25 research ships, 12 instrumented aircraft, 9 geostationary and polar-orbiting satellites, special balloon and buoy systems, and the World Weather Watch network of land stations in some 30 countries. It will be one of the largest international research experiments ever conducted, with its huge amount of data to be managed and collected by a global telecommunications system.

Another example of international cooperation in science takes place on the frozen waste of Antarctica where there have been developed over the years more than 60 research stations to gather data on fields ranging from astrophysics to glaciology to marine biology.

International Cooperation in Science and Technology

I could go on to give numerous other examples of international scientific programs in which scientists from many nations are working together —sharing resources, facilities, and information—to enlarge our understanding of the planet and its resources. But I want to turn to the kind of international cooperation in science and technology that I believe may be most significant in the years ahead, namely, the work that will determine the course of national development.

Science and technology, wisely directed and strongly supported, must assume a more central role in the development of individual nations and in advancing our international systems of exchanging resources, products, and services. It becomes more obvious every day that from an environmental, economic, and ethical viewpoint we cannot afford merely to drift into future development, nor can we let the state of the economy and "the invisible hand" of the international market alone determine the fate of man and the earth. Science and technology can reveal a more rational course for planning our future and give us the means to provide for all men without plundering the planet. It should be possible for the developing nations, without significantly restricting their aspirations, to avoid the environmental blunders that are now plaguing the developed countries and to bypass some of the economic and social problems that have accompanied the development process in the past.

Much of that course has been, or is being, charted by scientific organizations that are already well established or are in the process of being formed. Foremost among these, of course, are the organizations of the United Nations—UNESCO, the Food and Agriculture Organization (FAO), the World Health Organization (WHO), the World Meteorological Organization (WMO), the U.N. Industrial Development Organization, the International Atomic Energy Agency, the International Labor Organization (ILO), the new U.N. Environmental Program to be headquartered in Nairobi, and several other U.N. groups. It is to be hoped that the governments of an even wider range of countries will bring their scientists into these activities. Of great importance, also, is the support being given to the planning and implementation of technological development by the Organization for Economic Cooperation and Development (OECD) and by the international monetary organizations—the International Bank for Reconstruction and Development (the World Bank), the Inter-American Development Bank, and the newer Asian Bank.

The newest addition to the bodies of experts that are concerned with worldwide development, and one which should someday make a major contribution to the course of development, as I am advocating it here today, is the International Institute for Applied Systems Analysis, which will be located in Vienna. This institute, a nongovernmental organization founded by the scientific academies of 12 nations, will support about 100 research scientists who will come to grips with the major interrelated problems of our times. They will investigate urbanization, transportation, communications, energy sources, environmental problems, allocation of natural resources, and several other problems, using the methodologies of systems analysis and operations research, advanced management techniques, and computer technology. They will work not only toward a solution of the problems gripping the developed nations, but in anticipation of those that could befall the developing countries. Hopefully their analyses, models, and warnings will be effectively brought to the attention of the world's political leaders and their significance will be understood, heeded, and acted upon.

The conference here in Mexico, though it purports to deal with the problems of this hemisphere, nevertheless encompasses the subjects with which all the international organizations I have mentioned must become involved. It is to the credit of those in the Consejo Nacional de Ciencia y Tecnologia (CONACYT) and the American Association for the Advancement of Science (AAAS), who jointly planned this conference, that these subjects have been so well covered. Special recognition should go to President Echeverría, the Mexican host government, and the Mexican science community, all of whom are making, through the vehicle of CONACYT, a notable effort to link local science to local development.

Population and Food Supply

Let me turn to some brief discussions of these critical subjects and their relation to each other, as well as to the role of science in development. Of first priority are the problems of population and food supply and those of health and medical services. In the limited time at my disposal I have chosen to focus on the former, which should not be taken as any indication that I regard the latter as less important. A number of the technical symposiums at this conference are devoted to a discussion of health, illness, and disease.

Central to any discussion of development is always the dual matter of population and food supply, and these are considered in two of the central themes of this conference. In some respects it can be pointed out that almost all other human and environmental problems spring from this crucial relationship. The problems of urbanization and the urban-rural balance, together with their effects on labor and employment, hinge on this. The problems of land use, land distribution, and the development of arid lands and tropical forests are related to the same matter. And the problems of the depletion of resources and the deterioration of the environment can be shown to be strongly tied to the issue of population and food supply.

Fortunately, in recent years, great strides have been made throughout the world in recognizing and acting upon the problems of population. We now have a far better grasp of the demographic, social, and economic aspects of population growth as well as better physiological means to deal with that growth. In many areas·of the world there are indications that populations are being stabilized and that with a well-organized and sustained program of family planning the birth rate of a country can be regulated according to its best interests.

But neither these hopeful signs, related to some successful population programs, nor the reduced concern over food supply due to the success of higher yield corps should make us overconfident that we are solving the population or hunger problem. Much more needs to be done to turn some hopeful signs and some temporary victories into a more sustained success —one based upon recognition that we are dealing with a series of dynamic processes and relationships and not a group of simple problems that can be solved for now and all times.

If we turn to the matter of food supply, with all of its ramifications, we can readily see why this is true. The first aspect to consider is the viability of the high-yield crops produced by the "Green Revolution." We recognize now that such plants, though they are currently a great boon to mankind, are, like all plant strains, subject to new diseases and pests that are continually evolving. We must therefore be constantly vigilant and active in developing and banking new genetic strains that have the desired characteristics, yields, and food qualities and could be resistant to new strains of diseases and pests that might evolve to destroy them. The Food and Agriculture Organization is, of course, aware of this and is encouraging the establishment of national and regional "gene banks" to maintain seed and plant collections so that the characteristics of the various strains can be preserved.

The "Green Revolution" must become, in a sense, the "Green Evolution," with new research and development always under way. In addition, we must conduct an international effort to spread to many more areas of the earth the benefits of this type of agricultural research and development. Much more research will be required to breed strains that will thrive in a variety of conditions, particularly the cereal grasses which, directly and indirectly, supply three-fourths of all of man's food. The FAO estimates that, with continual introduction of locally adapted new varieties, the high-yield technology so successful today can be applied to one-third of the cereal acreage of the developing countries by 1985. However, to achieve this goal will require great commitment on the part of governments, scientists, and farmers throughout the world. Much credit is due, and continued support should be given, to the FAO for its work under the International Plant Protection Convention in setting up a network of regional plant protection organizations to strengthen cooperation in controlling destructive pests and disease. They are also developing a computerized data system to match fertilizer and herbicide application to soil properties, for rational use and the prevention of pollution.

It is an appalling fact that, at this time of increasing food production, as much as a quarter of the world's food never reaches the consumer because it is destroyed in storage, in transit, or in the market by insect pests, rodents, bacteria, and mold. In some areas the loss runs as high as 80 per cent of the supply produced. We must develop and promote ways to avoid these tragic losses. We must create and apply technologies, particularly in the developing nations, to preserve and store grains and other produce efficiently and economically for longer periods of time, so that in bountiful times surpluses can be saved for periods of poorer yield due to unforeseen circumstances. Development of methods for the preservation of food, together with the provision of means for transportation and distribution will help correct its maldistribution—a plethora of one kind of food at one spot with a dearth in another place not too far away.

Nutrition is another aspect of the food problem that demands more attention. It is estimated that today there are more than 300 million children who, for lack of sufficient protein, suffer retarded physical development and who may well, also, be impaired in mental and behavioral development. The health and productivity of a large segment of the world's adult population may be similarly afflicted.

The result is affecting present and future generations. It is trapping them in a form of self-perpetuating poverty. The nutritional well-being of its people is essential to a nation's economic development, not to mention its social and human development. In the years ahead the world's scientific community must intensify its efforts to improve nutrition and public understanding of what is now known. Indications that this can be done are encouraging. Several nations and international organizations have placed nutrition on their development agenda. Three countries in particular—Columbia, India, and Tunisia—are to be commended for their pioneering efforts to establish a national nutrition program. Their work should be studied and, wherever applicable, their methods emulated.

With greater confidence that total food demands can be met through the Green Revolution, more attention should be turned to the breeding of more high-protein crops, to the production of meat, dairy products, and fish. Two agricultural research centers in Latin America that are making major contributions in developing better sources of protein are the International Maize and Wheat Improvement Center (CIMMYT) here in Mexico, and the International Center for Tropical Agriculture (CIAT) in Columbia. The important work of the Institute of Nutrition of Central America and Panama (INCAP) and its collaboration with U.S. universities and private food industries should not be overlooked. INCAP research emphasizes the interrelationship between malnutrition and childhood disease. It is an outstanding regional program.

Food technology research is making significant strides in the enrichment of foods and in the creation of new foods and food supplements, but the problems of transferring their success to the poor, rural areas of the world remain.

One source of protein that should be given more attention is inland fish farming. There are indications that this may be the most efficient way to produce the highest yield of protein per pound of feed. Some research projects in fish culture are reporting remarkable results with protein yields far greater than poultry farming. This is particularly significant at a time when there has been a decrease in fish catches at sea in certain parts of the world. We now recognize that we have a greater international responsibility to protect the world's oceans from pollution and to use their resources far more wisely. It is encouraging that a U.N. Conference on the Law of the Sea is being held this year in Santiago, here in the Western Hemisphere.

Numerous new ways of approaching the food situation could be considered more seriously in the coming years. For example, the history of agriculture indicates that of the approximately 350,000 plant species described by botanists only some 3,000 have been tried as a source of food. Today only a dozen or so of these provide, directly or indirectly, 90 per cent of the world's food supply. We need to know much more about the potential for developing other varieties of foods and for producing more food in both arid and tropical lands. Most of the accumulated knowledge in agriculture has been gained in temperate zone countries and is not applicable to other lands. We particularly need to support more research in tropical agriculture, in areas and under conditions where, ironically, man has great difficulty producing food while nature sustains life so abundantly. Have we been taking the wrong approach in the tropics? I was intrigued a few years ago to hear a Latin American scientist suggest this when he stated (1):

> We must study wildlife in our Amazon Basin, where trees play a principal role. . . . We must compare tree-eating animals with those that eat grasses. It is fascinating to speculate on what will be found out about the giant leguminous trees so abundant in our jungles, for these are capable of association with a multitude of terrestrial and air-borne organisms for the better utilization of nutrients from the soil and air. They also utilize multiple layers of the soil, and create microclimates more tolerable to animals. Above all, they are extremely efficient in photosynthesis. Perhaps we should try to perfect what nature is already doing so successfully instead of trying to make her do things for which she is not prepared. Perhaps we should develop a technique for efficient animal nourishment from trees. Also promising are the possibilities of our use of the tremendous quantity of solar energy available in the tropics.

In repeating this statement I am not recommending that we abandon research on the more conventional approach to tropical agriculture (and neither was the scientist who made the statement). But perhaps we can pursue more than one approach in developing tropical agriculture in some areas of the world.

The same holds true in our development of the arid and semiarid lands, another central theme of this meeting; such lands represent almost a third of all the world's habitable land. At present arid lands support about 150 million people. Much more could be done to develop these areas and make them more productive and capable of sustaining a larger proportion of the world's people under better living conditions. A principal problem is, of course, insufficient fresh water. Some 60 developing nations must look forward to increasing difficulty in meeting water needs. Many of these countries border on the world's oceans and could benefit by the development of an economic desalting technology. It is unfortunate that much more support is not being given to this promising technology.

For a number of years I, and many of my colleagues in the nuclear energy field, believed that abundant, economical energy through nuclear power might hold the key to the development of some arid seacoast regions. We envisioned the use of that energy to desalt seawater and to provide power for a highly scientific agriculture and specific industries as a basic means of developing and supporting those regions where certain conditions—such as acceptable soil and temperatures—prevailed. Unfortunately, the economics of nuclear power has not yet reached the point where that concept can be pursued vigorously. We still hope to see the time when the idea of the Nuplex (the nuclear agro-industrial complex) will be successfully developed. In the meantime, other fields of research and development related to arid lands are being explored. Some of these regions lie over large supplies of underground water that could be tapped if energy and the right technologies were made available. Many also receive a small amount of rainfall that could be used more scientifically to better agricultural advantage. Israel has provided the world with an outstanding example of how this can be done. Some of her techniques of irrigation are even being adopted in my own country in order to use water more efficiently and effectively.

Now why have I devoted so many of my remarks to this point on matters of food and agriculture? There are two major reasons. The first is that the physical health of a nation's people is basic to its development—to its economic growth, its social advancement, and even its political stability. Aside from the purely humanitarian aspects of eliminating hunger, a people who are sufficiently fed and properly nourished can better ward off debilitating disease, can be more productive, and will be more likely to make a contribution not only to their own country but to the peace and progress of the world. A second reason has to do with the way in which nations develop and the important matter of how patterns of development will affect the future—particularly the matter of rural-urban balance.

This in turn will affect important, related matters such as employment, education, and almost all the economic and environmental aspects of growth. Let me spend a few minutes in trying to relate these various factors.

Problems of Urbanization and Industrialization

It has been estimated that more than two-thirds of the people of the developing nations depend directly on agriculture for employment. Though many of these countries seek to emulate the ways of industrial nations, they are basically agrarian economies. In the past the pattern of progress has usually been associated with a parallel shift of population from rural to urban areas. One of the major questions to be faced in the remainder of this century is whether this pattern will—or can—continue. Certainly it cannot continue in the way it has. In many of the advanced nations the urban implosion has created serious problems—social, economic, and environmental. Rural areas have decayed and urban areas have undergone cancerous growth with sprawling suburbs surrounding deteriorating inner cities.

But such problems in the advanced nations pale before those that could take place in the developing nations, should their rural-urban shift continue at its present rate. With urban populations in these countries now totaling about 600 million, it is said that they could increase to 3 billion by the end of the century. Such a 400 per cent increase within one generation would be disastrous. Consideration of this leads all who think seriously about the future, not just of the developing nations but of the whole world, to wonder whether one of the central questions the scientific and technological community faces in the years ahead is creating ways—perhaps an entire system of development—through which the less developed world can rapidly advance without attempting to repeat the process and pattern of industrialization and urbanization that the developed nations followed. Developing nations must not strive to be carbon copies of developed nations. And to the extent that they seek to industrialize, they should not follow—and do not have to follow—the same route to industrialization.

This is an extremely sensitive and difficult matter. It is sensitive because some developing countries view even its consideration by others as an attempt on the part of the industrial countries to control their status, to restrain them from seeking an advanced and competitive position. It is difficult because, even with their consent and fullest cooperation, to prevent the developing countries from experiencing the urban implosion with all its subsequent explosive problems would require an enormous international effort in rural development, in education, in the creation of new kinds of light industry, and in researching and developing a whole range of technological and social innovations about which we have only begun to think. Should we attempt all this, it would also require a vast change in our global economic and political arrangements, based on a degree of cooperation, integration, and planning that can, at best, be achieved only over a long period.

In the absence of any grand master plan to accomplish this in the near future, it is at least encouraging that some international steps are being taken to prevent many of the harmful conditions associated with industrialization. For example, the U.N. Advisory Committee on the Application of Science and Technology to Development has prepared a report designed to provide developing countries with guidelines for the rational utilization of their resources. The U.N. Industrial Development Organization is providing technical assistance in the analysis of environmental aspects of industrialization. The new Environmental Program of the U.N., organized as a result of the Stockholm Conference, will also be focusing heavily on these problems. And the new International Institute for Applied Systems Analysis, which I mentioned earlier, will no doubt contribute some serious thinking and helpful ideas on these matters.

But what things can be done to alleviate the human problem associated with the massive migration from rural to urban areas to prevent—as Barbara Ward puts it—the cities from "silting up with workless multitudes"?

It has been estimated that during this decade the developing nations will face the incredible task of creating productive jobs for more than 300,000 people each week. Whether this can be accomplished remains highly questionable. According to World Bank economists, it would take twice the growth rate of the 1960's—9 to 11 per cent annually—to be able to employ in the developing countries those seeking work outside of agriculture. It would also require that agriculture retain about one-third of its own labor force increases.

Energy Supply

This means, in the years ahead, we must see two related massive efforts take place to solve the employment problem per se and to solve it significantly outside of major urban areas. One effort should be in agricultural developments based on methods, technologies, and land use that are perhaps less capital-intensive and more labor-intensive than those in many developed nations, but nonetheless just as highly productive. The other should be an important move toward rural industrialization—small and light industry that will provide high employment and low environmental impact. Much of this industry might be closely related to agricultural and other natural products. These would not be energy-intensive industries; but, nevertheless, power and rural electrification would play a major role in their success, as well as in determining the standard of living of the communities that provide their manpower. It is therefore essential—and urgent—that we move ahead with our energy technologies, nuclear (including fusion) and nonnuclear, to provide sufficient economic power wherever it is needed.

We should make every effort to find ways to use solar and geothermal energy and to search for cleaner and more efficient applications of fossil fuels. Aside from its longer range possibilities of generating economic electricity, solar energy might be used sooner in a variety of ways to meet other energy needs—for heating, cooling, and local industrial and agricultural processing. Nonnuclear energy for development is one of the central themes for this conference.

One of the most difficult things we will have to do, and do soon, is to seek ways to ensure that all the peoples of the world share more equitably the vast human benefits that energy can bring. It is estimated now that less than 50 per cent of the world's population uses close to 90 per cent of its commercial energy. This fact alone is a major reason for the great chasm between the advanced and the less developed nations of the world. It is no mere coincidence that there is a relationship, when comparing these groups of nations, between the electric power consumed per year per capita and such items as life expectancy and literacy, not to mention the gross national product.

New Frontiers in Human Relationships

We must be just as creative and innovative in our social, political, and economic thinking as we are in our planning and use of science and technology. Furthermore, we cannot deal with human and technological matters in any but the most integrative, interactive way. We may therefore find that in the years ahead we may not be able to make the maximum use of our science and technology in the cause of man unless man, in his various nations and societies, is willing to change many of his tradition-bound ways, free himself of many prejudices and outmoded ideas, and explore new frontiers in human relationships as well as take bold steps forward in his exploration and application of science and technology.

This is not meant to be a rejection of the past—of all tradition, of national heritages and cultures—but an affirmation for the future, a future in which the best of all traditions and cultural achievements can be carried forward to be enjoyed and treasured and shared by coming generations. A healthy mankind does not have to be a homogenized mankind. A global civilization can contain much diversity and decentralization and still function effectively as a system. In fact such diversity will provide the system with the vigor and strength that is typical of a species that is infused with genetic variety.

Environment and Natural Forces

The kind of human development that I have been discussing can, of course, take place only if man wisely uses science and technology to understand and learn to live with the natural forces of this planet—another central theme of this meeting. The environmental movement we are experiencing signals our recognition of this, and I believe we are responding to the warnings that have been issued on environmental matters. Great challenges have been thrown to the world's scientific and engineering communities. There is the challenge of more fully understanding the effects of man's impact on the biosphere. There is the challenge of developing materials and products that minimize that impact. There is the challenge of creating a civilization bent upon recycling, which will maximize the use of all resources rather than deplete and degrade finite supplies. It is up to the world's scientists and engineers to exercise great leadership, not only in focusing the attention of their communities and countries on these problems but in developing practical solutions that can be rapidly put into effect by industrial and political leaders. The problem of the industrialization of the developing countries in a humane and sensible way provides a great challenge to the world community of scientists and engineers.

Living with the forces of the planet means also fostering a better understanding of the destructive capacity of the earth—its ground movement and weather—and designing human habitats to minimize the loss of life and property during nature's rampages. This can be done. For example, earthquake engineering (another central theme here) is becoming successful in designing buildings to withstand sizable tremors. It is important to note that two large buildings that survived the recent Managua earthquake with only interior damage had been designed by experts trained in earthquake engineering. Other buildings surrounding them were reduced to rubble.

We are also making progress in understanding our global weather so that we can make longer range forecasts and give more advanced warnings of storms. More accurate forecasts and longer range forecasts can save millions of dollars annually in property damage and crop losses as well as reduce the loss of life and human misery caused by severe weather. Of greater importance, such forecasts—for example, of the behavior of the monsoon in South Asia—could help farmers plant their crops at the right time to take advantage of the steady rainfall. Without such forecasts, they are liable to plant their seeds at the first rain and then lose them if the monsoon rains stop for several weeks, as they often do. Study and limited experimentation are taking place in weather modification (one particularly successful experiment has helped in preventing local hailstorms), but extensive weather modification involves so many complexities that it is probably many years away.

Education and Research

In conclusion, let me focus briefly on the human force that will be necessary to carry out much, if not all, of the change demanded to create a livable future. That force is organized knowledge; and it is transmitted by education. It is education, perhaps more than any single factor, that will determine how we survive—the way in which developing nations develop, the quality of life in all nations, and the extent that human freedom and dignity flourish in a complex and highly organized world. Our global civilization will be shaped more by the activity and content of its classrooms, books, and television screens than by its forges and factories. One of the central themes at this meeting—opportunities in education —is devoted to this key subject.

While the growth and direction of higher education remains an important matter, it is far overshadowed by the need to combat the illiteracy and ignorance of a large portion of humanity. Are we winning this struggle? We are making progress but the outcome is still in doubt. In the 1960's educational growth rose steeply in the developing countries. It is encouraging that much of this growth took place in Latin America where more than 250,000 primary school classrooms were built and more than 1.3 million teachers were added to the primary and secondary schools. During my own tour of Latin America 6 years ago I witnessed much that attested to the quality and effort of education there.

Throughout the developing world the number of students enrolled in formal schooling rose 6 to 7 per cent annually during the previous decade. Yet, by the end of that period, nearly 300 million children between the ages of 5 and 14 were not enrolled in school. Aside from other factors, the cost of education is a major deterrent to its necessary growth in developing nations. It has been estimated that, relative to their incomes, it costs most low-income countries five to ten times as much to provide primary schooling for a given proportion of their population as it costs the high-income nations. This is also true proportionately at secondary and higher levels. Reasons for this include the rate of population growth that has raised the fraction of school-age population, the relatively higher teachers' salaries, and the higher costs of school buildings.

But much can be done by educational research and technology to improve this situation. Attempts are being made to use satellite and television technology to bring basic education to remote and rural areas. These should be supported, and efforts should be made to improve teaching systems and materials and to produce and distribute equipment as economically as possible. Traditional education will have to change and give way to new ideas in order to meet the new needs emerging today. One of these needs is to relate schooling to rural development, to produce local populations and leaders educated to improve conditions in their regions and yet who are willing to work cooperatively and productively with the central government.

At the higher levels of education, much work is being done in the developing nations to focus on the development of scientific capabilities to serve their own unique needs. During my 1970 trip to six African countries I was impressed by the quality of this work in which small but dedicated cadres of men and women in each country were engaged, and I urged, in an article in *Science* (2), that more support and cooperation be given by other nations to their efforts in education and research. Education to spread developmental knowledge—whether in the form of basic literacy, instruction in sound hygiene and health practices, or the application of new agricultural techniques—has only begun and yet must be advanced rapidly. This represents a major challenge in the years ahead. And efforts to meet it should be strongly supported by the scientific community who, perhaps more clearly than any other group, can see the consequences of failure.

Some of this support will come from a number of recently planned international organizations. In my article in *Science* I urged the creation of an International Science Foundation; this had also been suggested by Roger Revelle and by Robert Marshak and Maurice Levy and, as a result of their efforts and those of others, such an institution (the International Foundation for Science, IFS) for the support of research in developing countries is in the process of being created. The newly formed International Federation of Institutes for Advanced Study (IFIAS) also represents a positive move in this direction and the various moves toward the concept of the World University or various forms of the International University could help fill this need. And the older International Council of Scientific Unions, together with the individual International Scientific Unions, has certainly played an important role for many years in fostering scientific education and research on an international scale.

Despite the progress of these various efforts, science is pursued today primarily in countries that together constitute only a quarter or less of the world's population. Besides the loss of the vast human resources that remain untapped in scientific research, the benefits of research are largely confined to those countries that pursue science. There is thus created great disparities in the human condition and hence a contribution to worldwide political instability. I believe this is an arena which the international scientific community should enter in a more effective and meaningful manner.

Plan for Action

The main requirement is a widespread rededication to this goal of international science by scientists and engineers on a worldwide basis. One method of implementing such an effort is through the many Associations for the Advancement of Science in the countries throughout the world. These are in general noncommercial, nonpolitical associations of scientists and engineers and of other people interested in science and engineering. They are nationwide and include all of the natural and social sciences within their domain. Their membership is in general open to all without restriction as to scientific qualifications and, typically, there are organized affiliations with many other associations and societies. Thus these Associations are, in varying degrees, representative of organized science in the countries in which they operate and can act with the great authority inherent in their membership. There are at present some 40 associations of this type with a wide variation in their names.

My greatest familiarity and influence, and point of contact from this point of view, is with the American Association for the Advancement of Science in the United States, a cosponsor of this meeting in Mexico City. One of my first acts when I was elected to a position of leadership in this organization was to move toward the creation of an Office of International Activities. One of my specific motivations was the large response to my call for increased cooperation between U.S. and African scientists in my article in *Science*. I felt that this favorable reaction indicated a large potential interest. In attempting to respond to these offers to help in the development of African science and these requests for information, I felt a strong need for a nongovernmental international center, in addition to the Foreign Secretary's Office of the National Academy of Sciences, which did its best to try to help. Additional recent steps toward increased international involvement of the AAAS have taken the form of agreements, either in effect or under negotiation, for cooperation with individual associations of other countries.

I believe that the time has come for the American Association for the Advancement of Science to move further into the international field. Perhaps the next step might be to join with our sister national associations of science in Latin America and Canada to create a true American Association for the Advancement of Science—an association in which the term *American* would represent its broader and true meaning. This might be followed in due course by a joining together of the national associations of science in an International Association for the Advancement of Science (or perhaps an International Association for the Advancement of Science and Technology). There are, of course, many degrees of affiliation that can serve as a start and which can develop into closer and closer affiliation with the passage of time.

This is my farewell address, which is given, in the tradition of a long line of predecessors, as past president and present chairman of AAAS. It is difficult, and perhaps not even desirable, for presidents to make any lasting impressions on AAAS. My immediate predecessors have launched the Association in important and exciting new directions—toward broader membership and increased emphasis on the use of science and technology in the promotion of human welfare. Let me dare to hope that I can help us to move more quickly toward broader international involvement. Should this be the case I feel confident that the demonstrated international interests of my successors, Leonard Rieser and Roger Revelle, will ensure the maintenance of any momentum in this new direction.

I have tried to review what I believe are among the most important issues we in the world of science must face if we are to make science work more fully in the best interest of humanity. The task ahead for science and technology is not made easier by the doubts that many have over the aims and accomplishments of these two forces. There are too many who view the objectivism, determinism, and rationalism of science as threats to humanity and who see in technology only a behemoth out of control and destined to destroy its creators. We in science must prove these ideas false, not merely to justify the existence of intelligent human life, but in order to fully enroll science and technology in the effort to preserve and improve all life on earth. Nothing less is at stake in the struggle to make science and technology successful in the cause of mankind. To this end, I hope, and I believe, we are entering the world's greatest era of international science cooperation. Let it be an era of increasing goodwill among all nations and one that will bring peace and contentment to men, women, and children throughout the world.

References

1. A. Bacigalupo, Puerto Rico Nuclear Center Tenth Anniversary Symposium, 30 to 31 October 1967.
2. G. T. Seaborg, *Science* 169, 154 (1970).

EXERCISES

VOCABULARY

universal	priority	terrestrial
viable	evolution	stability
advocate	dynamic	implosion
rationale	telecommunications	equitable
prestige	plunder	deterrent
aspiration	developing nations	disparity
urbanization	systems analysis	inherent

purport	arid	debilitate
depletion	demography	agrarian
ramification	plethora	alleviate
dearth	emulate	habitat
collaborate	ironical	cadre
implement	behemoth	

QUESTIONS

1. Is the main purpose of Seaborg's address to persuade, to explain, or to describe?

2. Find the sentence that most directly states the unifying theme of the address.

3. In the section on paragraphs, we describe three basic ways of developing a paragraph: detail, reason, and example. Find examples of each in this article.

4. Seaborg devotes much of his address to speculating about the future. In our section on cause and effect, we discussed speculation. Find some examples in the essay of speculative thinking and writing.

5. Reread the section devoted to the world's food supply. How does Seaborg organize his discussion of this complex subject? How does he relate this discussion to the central theme he is developing?

6. It is even more difficult for an audience listening to a speech to make the connections between ideas than it is when reading an essay. Find instances where Seaborg helps his audience see the connections among his ideas and where he makes clear transitions to his next point.

THE SEARCH FOR TOMORROW'S POWER
Kenneth F. Weaver

Nuclear Power Brings New Problems

The most immediate solution [to our energy problems], of course, is the nuclear reactor, which taps the mighty energy released when uranium atoms fission, or split. Twenty-eight commercial nuclear power plants are already operating in the United States, including the pioneering plant at Shippingport, Pennsylvania, that went on line 15 years ago. Forty-nine additional plants are under construction, and another 67 are on order. When all the new ones are completed, they will add more than 30 per cent to the Nation's 370-million-kilowatt total capacity.

Nuclear power plants bring their own problems. Even more than conventional generating plants fired by fossil fuels, they produce large amounts of waste heat. Safeguards must be provided against leakage of radiation from the reactor itself, and also from the radioactive wastes that the process produces.

Finally, there is a scarcity of inexpensive uranium. According to the Atomic Energy Commission, relatively low-cost nuclear fuel will probably be exhausted by the end of the century if we continue to build only the types of nuclear power plants operating today.

Fortunately there is a major development in nuclear reactors that may meet some of these problems. It is the liquid-metal fast-breeder reactor. To understand how it works, you need to know something about the conventional water-cooled reactor now in use.

Fast Breeder Makes Its Own Fuel

If you could examine the core of a conventional reactor, you would find it made up of thousands of zirconium-alloy tubes, called pins. About twice the thickness of a lead pencil and usually 12 feet long, they are inserted into the reactor in bundles. Constantly bathed with water, these pins hold a mixture of ordinary uranium 238, which does not fission, and a small amount of the scarcer uranium 235, which is the actual fuel. Heat given off when uranium atoms split is carried away by the circulating water and used to produce steam for a turbine generator, just as in a coal- or oil-fired plant.

One pound of uranium, about the size of a golf ball, stores as much energy as 15 carloads of coal. But in the water-cooled reactor barely one per cent of that energy can be tapped.

F R O M *National Geographic* (November 1972). Excerpted by permission.

That's where the breeder reactor comes in. The alchemist of old, who sought to turn base metals into gold, would have been entranced by the breeder, for it transmutes elements, producing more fuel than it consumes.

Pins holding uranium 238 are placed around the core. As atoms split in the core, they give off heavy nuclear particles called neutrons, which bombard the uranium in the core and in the blanket. Some of these atoms absorb neutrons and are converted to plutonium 239, which will fission.

The mixture of uranium and plutonium can be used as a nuclear fuel. After its energy is depleted, it can be reprocessed and returned to the breeder, and still more fissionable fuel will be produced. This process can be repeated until up to 40 times as much energy has been extracted from the raw material as can be produced in a conventional reactor. Thus with the breeder there is no longer a shortage of nuclear fuel.

The breeder offers other advantages. It is more efficient than the conventional reactor; it converts more of the nuclear heat to electricity. Thus it produces less heat loss and less radioactive waste, which is difficult and dangerous to dispose of. Also, the breeder operates at much lower pressure, so there is less chance of leakage of radioactive gases.

For these reasons, the Atomic Energy Commission and the power industry are moving rapidly to develop the breeder for commercial use. President Nixon, in his energy message last year, called the breeder "our best hope today for meeting the Nation's growing demand for economical clean energy." He called for a commitment to complete a successful demonstration breeder by 1980.

EXERCISES

VOCABULARY

fossil	entrance	radiation
deplete	turbine	conventional
transmute	uranium	convert
alchemist		

QUESTIONS

1. Examine the first four paragraphs. Where do we find out what the main topic of the essay will be?

2. What is the controlling idea in the first paragraph? What method of paragraph development is used in this paragraph?

3. What is the controlling idea in the second paragraph? What method of development is used here?

4. The word *finally* is a transition word. What information goes before this final point? Why is the fact of "scarcity" discussed last?

5. What is the key difference between the two types of reactors?

6. What strategy of organization is used in telling us about the two kinds of reactors?

7. The paragraph beginning, "The breeder offers other advantages" relates to an earlier paragraph. Which one?

8. The author gives us a great deal of information in relatively few words. Do you think the essay is unified (sticks to the point)? If not, where does the essay break down? If so, how does the writer manage to gain unity?

SOME DOWN-TO-EARTH MEDICINE WE'VE LEARNED FROM OUR FLIGHTS INTO SPACE

Lawrence K. Altman

OVER the last 12 years 35 Americans have been hurled into space from Cape Kennedy launch pads. Each of the men in the Mercury, Gemini, and Apollo programs was backed up by the most elaborate and sophisticated machinery ever devised and built. As you might expect, the same thoroughness that designed the hardware to put an American on the moon by the end of the Sixties also governed the selection of the healthiest, most stable, and fearless band of astronauts the country could produce. Most of them were ex-test pilots, who sought out and were accustomed to danger and risk.

Although the primary purpose of the space program was to put a man on the moon, not to carry out medical or psychological experiments, scientists two years ago made an important and still mysterious discovery about potassium losses in astronauts during space flight that has already helped develop lifesaving techniques used in post-operative care, and for treatment of heart disease, diabetes, and serious traumatic injuries.

In the psychological realm, at least three of the astronauts came back from the moon to find their sense of themselves drastically changed. One found it difficult to accomplish even the most ordinary daily acts like choosing what to wear. Two others found new meaning in religious and spiritual concerns.

One of the most important medical discoveries coming out of the moon program was the fact of significant potassium loss during space flight. Potassium, a naturally occurring and vital body chemical, plays a key role in speeding nerve impulses through the body. Among other functions, it helps muscles contract and is required to make the heart beat in a forceful, rhythmic cadence.

Potassium deficiency, on the other hand, can produce a variety of subtle symptoms: tingling sensations in the skin, muscle weakness, and apathy. If the patient suffers small losses of potassium over a long period of time, his kidneys, heart, and bowel can be permanently damaged. If the loss is severe at any one time, paralysis and death can result.

Potassium losses—which doctors often call K losses, after the chemical symbol for potassium—during Apollo flights were not discovered until after the Apollo 15 astronauts splashed down in the Pacific in August of 1971. During the flight two of the astronauts—David R. Scott and

FROM *Today's Health* (April 1973).

James B. Irwin—had several abnormal heartbeats while working on the moon and afterwards on the return flight to earth. The astronauts themselves were unaware of the momentary irregularities, called atrial bigeminy, but they were picked up in Houston on electrocardiograms relayed by telemetry.

After-splashdown tests on Scott and Irwin showed that they had lost large amounts of potassium—at least 15 per cent of the K normally present in their bodies. Only then could space agency physicians link the K losses with the irregular heartbeats.

No one yet knows precisely why space flight causes this potassium loss. Charles A. Berry, M.D., director for life sciences at NASA's Manned Spacecraft Center near Houston, and his colleagues, have put forward a complicated theory that involves the increase in blood flow caused by conditions of weightlessness, and the effect of that increased flow on a series of hormonal reactions ending in a loss of body electrolytes, including potassium and sodium. (Electrolytes, in biochemistry, is the name given to substances that separate into ions when in solution, thus making them electrically conducting. This process of separation, which occurs in the bloodstream with necessary electrolytes such as potassium, sodium, and magnesium, plays an important part in body functioning. Thus, any impairment of electrolyte balance, which is maintained by the kidneys, can be damaging to health in a wide variety of ways.)

Since the end of World War II, so much complex knowledge has been gained about electrolyte balance that many medical centers and hospitals now have doctors who specialize in maintaining electrolyte balance.

This knowledge has helped doctors add decades of useful life to many kinds of patients, including those suffering from such complications as congestive heart failure resulting from arteriosclerosis; diabetics recovering from a condition known as acidosis, which results from a severe loss of insulin; those undergoing bowel surgery for cancer or nonmalignant diseases like ulcerative colitis and regional enteritis, which are chronic diseases of unknown cause that inflame the intestines and produce diarrhea; and victims of automobile accidents and other serious injuries.

The impact has perhaps been greatest in the medical and surgical care of the very young and very old—because pediatric and geriatric patients are especially sensitive to small changes in electrolytes like potassium. Electrolyte balance is especially important in the drug therapy of older Americans. For those who take digitalis, for example, losses of potassium can interact with the drug to bring on digitalis toxicity, which can be instantly fatal.

The new knowledge about chemical balances in fluids of the body is just as important in post-operative care. It is not just the techniques of the surgeon that has made modern surgery so successful. Perhaps even more important to recent surgical advances has been the post-operative fluid and electrolyte care that is essential to the recovery of patients from operations that seriously disturb the body's physiology. Often the success of the surgery depends largely on the doctor's ability to apply the results of automated electrolyte tests and to juggle the potassium levels so that the body's biochemistry is kept in its delicate state of balance.

Such surgical patients have benefited greatly from bedside application of basic metabolic research findings made from test tube and animal experiments, and NASA's Dr. Berry contends they could benefit further from space medicine research.

The Apollo flights also provided new evidence that the human body is one of the most adaptable of all organisms. Twenty-seven American spacecraft have blazed off the Cape Kennedy pads, launching men for more than 3,521 hours of space flight. These 27 manned flights have carried 35 astronauts, some of whom have flown two or more times. Of the 59 American and Russian astronauts who have spent a total of more than a year and a half in space, none has suffered medical difficulties serious enough to prevent him from functioning.

Fifteen years ago, when man knew little about physiology in space, some scientists were predicting an almost endless list of medical catastrophes that might beset astronauts. Perhaps, it was speculated, their hearts would beat so fast on liftoff that the rapid rhythm would prove fatal. Or serious anemia would result from loss of too many red blood cells. Or weightlessness would cause kidney stones to form as calcium was leached from the bones, turning the skeleton to jelly. Or muscles might atrophy, or wither away.

None of these dire consequences resulted. Astronauts' hearts responded to the physiologic demands—the heartbeat of astronauts ranging from a high of 180 during liftoff to a remarkable low of only 28 beats a minute while they slept in space, compared to a "normal" heartbeat on earth in the 60s or 70s.

Cardiologists were also surprised to learn that astronauts' hearts shrank in space. The doctors still do not know if the smaller size results from loss of muscle fibers and cells, or loss of body fluids, chiefly water and potassium, which seems to be an inevitable consequence of space flight.

Needless to say, their bones did not break. Though they lost some calcium from their bones, kidney stones did not form. Some astronauts did suffer brief episodes of nausea and vomiting. Others had head colds, which are worse in space than on earth because in zero gravity mucus cannot drain, and an astronaut can damage his ears by blowing his nose too hard.

Just as the problem of potassium loss did not become apparent until after splashdown, so too the psychological problems faced by a few of the astronauts did not show up until after their missions were completed.

Remarkably, there seem to have been no psychological problems at all during the missions themselves. "We've been fortunate," Dr. Berry says, "because we have seen no serious psychological problems in anybody as a result of our actual flight experience—even including long periods of time when an astronaut was alone in the command module and spent a fair amount of time behind the moon, totally out of contact with anybody."

He attributes this result to the fact that "we started with a select group of people who had gone through all the stresses and strains of having been selected as a test pilot and who thereafter had been exposed to a lot of life-threatening situations as test pilots."

"Astronauts are human beings," Dr. Berry says. "Everyone tends to think of them as supermen and they are not. They're just plain old common human beings subject to the same foibles the rest of us are."

Most astronauts appear to have adjusted to the sudden renown, the plaudits, the demands for public appearances that followed their flights.

But for some of them, none of the moon flight training prepared them for the post-splashdown psychological effects of becoming America's newest heroes. The most important of these seems to be a space-age version of the famous malaise that came over Alexander the Great, who, at the height of his conquests at age 29, complained—inaccurately, as it turned out—that he "had no more worlds to conquer."

Coming back from the moon precipitated such a downward psychological spiral for (then) Colonel Edwin E. (Buzz) Aldrin, Jr., who, with Neil Armstrong, was one of the first two human beings to set foot on another world. (Astronaut Aldrin is now Dr. Aldrin, having recently earned a Sc.D. degree in astronautics from the Massachusetts Institute of Technology.) As recently as three years after his epic flight on Apollo II, in fact, Aldrin actually feared for his sanity.

In his Apollo days, Aldrin saw himself as others generally saw him: as a supremely self-confident superachiever, an intense, disciplined harddriver who had almost never failed at anything important he tried to do.

By Aldrin's own account, that self-confidence evaporated in the postflight letdown that is said to have afflicted several American astronauts. It is a phenomenon that some of the nation's 22 moon-venturers apparently were not prepared to confront.

Faced for the first time with a loss of purpose in life, plagued by fear of the risks he might face in any new and unaccustomed lifework, and suffering from an unexpected culture shock that made crowds and personal appearances an agony, Aldrin himself admits that he virtually ceased to function at times. He couldn't get organized and had to let others almost lead him through day-to-day tasks.

"It got to a point where deciding what suit to wear became an overwhelming decision," Aldrin, now a 42-year-old retired Air Force colonel who wears a lush, graying beard that fringes his rugged face like that of a 19th-century New England sea captain, said in a recent interview.

As he spoke, he sipped sangria at lunch in an intimate cafe on the outskirts of Los Angeles not far from Hidden Hills in the San Fernando Valley, where he now lives with his wife, three teenaged children and a menagerie of dogs, cats, chickens, a goat, and an Appaloosa mare. At Hidden Hills, Aldrin is attempting to put together a new life—and a new personality.

He has had to do it with the help of two periods of intensive psychotherapy, including a month in a military hospital, and he still sees a psychiatrist every two or three weeks or so.

A more relaxed Buzz Aldrin now says he is "back on the track, but still not with great confidence."

Aldrin describes his post-flight experiences as "an unanticipated, abrupt change in life style." Before Apollo II, his days had been governed by concise, precise, concrete objectives and his personal life was still under his own control. After Apollo II, there was no objective ahead, and Mr. Aldrin began to lose his grip on both his professional and personal life.

For a year or two, in between the personal appearances he found so burdensome, he looked around "for some little job in NASA I'd be happy with." But mostly, he sat in his office in Houston, answering mail, occasionally attending meetings, and wondering, in his words, "Gee, what'll I do today?"

"You get so dissatisfied that you get in your car and drive down to Galveston and walk on the beach," he said, "but that doesn't help."

Eventually Aldrin was made commandant of the Air Force Test Pilot School at Edwards Air Force Base, California. There his downward spiral into anxious depression accelerated.

"I had been away from the Air Force for 10 years," he said, "and every job has its element of risk. Plus, I was extremely self-critical." This combination of insecurity and self-demand for perfection "started bringing on the problem that eventually put me in the hospital," Aldrin explained.

The problem was diagnosed as "moderate depression" by doctors at Wilford Hall, an Air Force hospital in San Antonio, where Aldrin, beginning in October 1971, underwent a one-month course of drug-aided psychotherapy. But he believes that the very act of seeking help on his own "went a long way" toward helping solve his emotional difficulties.

As part of his treatment, Mr. Aldrin had to examine his life as never before and ask of his Air Force career, "Is this what I want to do?" His answer was no. So he decided to retire from the Air Force, seek a life of less pressure, and explain his story so other Americans might benefit and learn from his experience.

But facing civilian life last July for the first time in 23 years brought on yet another, even more frightening, seige of depression. This time Mr. Aldrin feared that he might be in such a state for the rest of his life. But after two or three visits to a psychiatrist at the UCLA Neuropsychiatric Clinic, the depression lifted again.

Now, Mr. Aldrin believes, he has come through the worst and will be the better for it. He is his own boss. He can control the nature and level of his activities, can dabble in "little projects" here and there. He is gradually relaxing and writing a book *Return to Earth*, which is finished and is scheduled to be published this fall.

However, the nature of an Apollo astronaut's work has given these men a unique view of the world, altering their very consciousness, providing them with perceptions and perspectives that no other American will have —not for many years at the earliest. Dr. Berry comments:

> The total psychological impact of having gone through that ex-perience is great. I don't think you can look at our world in the way that all these crewmen have—and we've been privileged to do that vicariously, too—and not have seen the world in an entirely different context than we do as we sit on earth's surface. That can't help but have some kind of psychological effect.

Two astronauts who reacted to the mystical nature of their flights are Captain Edgar D. Mitchell and Colonel James B. Irwin.

Mitchell said he is trying "to broaden the consciousness of people so that they can see planet earth from the perspective" he had of space. So he has moved toward the exploration. of "inner space" by forming a Houston-based private company to promote scientific investigation of such psychic phenomena as extrasensory perception and mental telepathy.

Mitchell hopes that his enterprise ultimately will help unlock the secrets of "psychic energy" so that humans may communicate with one another in richer, more precise ways.

Irwin's experience was quite different. In his words, he went to the moon a practicing but not especially religious Baptist. The effects of moon flight turned him into an energetic Christian and inspired him to form the High Flight Foundation based in Colorado Springs, Colorado, under whose auspices he travels almost constantly, both in the United States and abroad, carrying two messages—that of science and that of the Gospel.

"I consider that it's God's plan that I had an opportunity to come back and tell people what a beautiful thing we have here on earth; to take care of it; and to try to live in brotherhood, the way Jesus Christ would want us to," Mr. Irwin said.

"Before the flight I was a very quiet, reserved guy." Irwin said. "Now I've changed. You can't shut me up. Now I have something to say."

Irwin believes that he and Mitchell are essentially on the same track. "Ed's going the scientific route," he said, "and when we meet, it'll be interesting." But he added: "I think that Ed's getting in deeper than man was meant to go. He's delving into powers that are really of Satan."

Religious interpretations aside, Colonel Irwin sums up the common experience of several astronauts: "We went to the moon as technicians— nuts and bolts men—and we returned as humanitarians."

After the moon voyagers returned, they were constantly put in the public eye so that their weaknesses, strengths, obsessions and general humanity have emerged as never before. Their differing personalities have grappled in different ways with the transcendent experience of flying to the moon and its earthbound aftermath.

Brigadier General Thomas P. Stafford, who commanded the moon-orbital flight of Apollo 10 in May 1969 and is now deputy director of flight-crew operations at the Manned Spacecraft Center, described to a reporter one of the problems facing the returning astronauts this way:

"You can't let it go to your head. Today's headlines are tomorrow's fish wrappers. Unfortunately, some astronauts have not understood this. Because of one great incident in their lives, they think that anything they say takes on extra meaning."

"There is a tendency to get carried away with yourself," says Colonel David R. Scott, commander of the Apollo 15 lunar-landing missions in July 1971. "You've just got to try to keep your balance."

After their return to earth, Scott and his crewmates (Colonel James Irwin and Major Alfred M. Worden) developed a trick for use when one of the three would "go off on a tangent" while speaking and start talking too long.

"One of us would pass an ashtray or glass of water over in front of the guy," Scott recalled with a chuckle. "That was the signal to shut up."

Perhaps it is this type of common sense that explains why Dr. Berry concludes:

"It's amazing that there haven't been even more psychological effects than have become evident."

But taken on balance, the experience of the space program has been more encouraging than otherwise in what it tells us about the flexibility and resourcefulness of man. That astronauts have been able to adjust so well to the almost completely alien environment of outer space surely ought to give us at least some hope that future explorations of both inner and outer space will give us more reason to rejoice than to despair.

EXERCISES

telemetry	malaise	phenomenon
apathy	plaudits	psychotherapy
cadence	foibles	depression
atrophy	precipitate	perception
obsession	vicarious	perspective
	transcendent	

QUESTIONS

1. The first three paragraphs introduce the subject of this essay. Identify the key sentence that lets us know what the subject of the essay is going to be.

2. The author also tells us in those opening paragraphs how the essay will be constructed around two main topics. What are they? The author summarizes the main information we will get from the essay. Is this an effective way to begin an essay?

3. Why does this essay begin with a description of the physical and psychological qualities of the men chosen to be astronauts?

4. What are the dominant strategies used to present the information in this essay? Pick out some examples.

5. Does Mr. Altman make it clear what the connection is between potassium loss in the astronauts and improved hospital and surgical care?

6. Pick out the sentences that signal changes in topic (transition sentences).

7. What technique does Altman use to change from talking about physiological topics to psychological ones? Find the key sentence and relate it back to a similar sentence earlier in the essay.

8. Does Altman draw conclusions from the glimpses he gives us of psychological problem experienced by the astronauts? If so, what are they?

9. Why did the astronauts (such "stable" individuals) go through such profound psychological changes?

10. Does Altman convince you that the benefits of space flight outweigh the risks and costs involved? What does his last sentence mean?

FROM THE LASER'S EYE:
20 NEW BOONS FOR MANKIND
Forrest Mims

BLIND people may soon be carrying lasers. An engineer in New Mexico has invented a laser travel aid, small enough to fit on eyeglass frames, which projects invisible infrared beams directly in front of the blind user.

If the beams strike a potential obstacle, some of the laser light is reflected back to a sensitive receiver which warns the blind person by triggering a vibrating pin against his finger or sounding a tone in his ear.

This is just one of 20 new highly practical applications of the laser's beam. Until recently lasers were relatively delicate devices designed to work only in laboratories. A few years ago we used to speculate about the future uses of the laser. Today the laser has come of age—we're finally putting it to practical use for the aid of mankind.

Before we get into these applications, however, it's best to first explain how a laser works: Basically, the atoms or molecules of certain gases, crystals, glasses, or liquids are placed between two mirrors and stimulated to higher than normal energy levels. This is done with powerful flash lamps in solid state lasers or with an electrical discharge in most gas lasers.

When some of the excited atoms or molecules begin to drop back to their normal, unexcited state, they give off energy in the form of heat or light. The light energy bounces back and forth between the two mirrors, one of which only partially reflects, and this causes the remainder of the atoms or molecules to return to an unexcited state also and give off more light. In a time period measured in millionths of a second, the light emission becomes strong enough to penetrate the partially reflecting mirror and emerges as a powerful beam of light.

Laser light is usually distinguished by a high degree of *coherence*. That is, it has a narrow wavelength and the waves are in step with each other.

The problem with lasers in the past was that they were too fragile for practical applications because of their glass tubes, carefully positioned mirrors, gas reservoirs and high-voltage power supplies.

But recently, Coherent Radiation demonstrated their new low-cost helium-neon laser by freezing it in a block of solid ice, steaming it with crabs in a kettle of boiling water, resting it under the tire of a 3,000-pound truck, immersing it in a fish-filled aquarium, tying it to a paint shaker and then dropping it with an impact of 200 G's!

The new sturdiness is probably the main reason why scientists have finally been able to put the laser to work. Here's the rundown on the 20 new applications laser scientists have cooked up for us:

1. Lasers are now making work easier for doctors. Surgeons have found that laser photocoagulators are reliable tools for welding back detached retinas, which can cause blindness. The surgeon uses the laser to make a series of tiny welds around the periphery of the separated retinal layer.

2. Lasers also make for bloodless surgery. The great heat from their beams cauterizes exposed blood vessels, thereby making bloodless incisions. Dr. Leon Goldman, a leading laser medical researcher, claims he has even performed bloodless surgery on the human liver, one of the most vascular organs in the body. He and other doctors have also used the laser on patients suffering from brain cancer, stomach ulcers, and cancer of the larynx.

3. In addition to internal surgery, lasers are being used for surface surgery. Skin cancer, skin discolorations and heavily pigmented areas and even embarrassing tatoos can be removed with laser techniques.

In all these cases, the unwanted target area is darker than the surrounding skin and therefore absorbs far more of the laser's radiation. If the skin to be removed is lightly colored, a dark dye is applied to enhance absorption of the laser beam.

4. Dr. Ralph H. Stern of the University of California's School of Dentistry is blasting teeth with ruby and carbon dioxide lasers to prevent tooth decay. Dr. Stern says laser irradiation of the enamel inhibits the demineralization that precedes cavity formation.

5. The military has also fallen in love with the laser. In 1973 military laser orders will approach $120 million, a rise of 14 per cent over 1972 expenditures. Already in use in fighter/bombers are laser-guided "smart bombs."

An operator who sits behind the pilot aims the laser, housed in a pod slung beneath the plane, directly at the target. Keeping the laser on target, the plane orbits the area while a second plane drops a bomb fitted with laser-seeking equipment. The bomb homes in on the spot of bright laser light on the target and makes necessary fin movements to reach the lighted area. The Air Force claims a single laser-guided bomb can do the same job as 100 unguided bombs for a tenth of the cost.

6. Death rays have also been built. These super lasers, financed by the Department of Defense, have already been demonstrated in secret tests and produce enough invisible infrared radiation to burn holes through

tanks and aircraft. (For more on death ray weapons, see August, 1972, *Science Digest*, p. 24.)

7. Solid state ruby and glass lasers are now sturdy enough to be used as altimeters on aircraft and as range-finders on tanks.

8. And lasers are finding their way into space travel. The Apollo command modules used a ruby laser rangefinder to measure the distance from the spacecraft to the lunar surface. The laser shot bursts of brilliant red light at the moon and a sensitive receiver picked up the reflected light. An electronic counter measured the time required for the light to return which was easily converted into distance since the speed of light is accurately known.

9. Another major role for the laser is in communications. The Associated Press is now replacing all of its conventional wirephoto equipment with a laserphoto system designed by Prof. William F. Schreiber of the Massachusetts Institute of Technology. The system records pictures on dry silver photographic paper using laser beams as a light source and needs no chemicals.

10. And you can now talk to someone over a mile away and they'll hear you no matter what the weather conditions. Hughes Aircraft Co. has built a laser walkie-talkie that is used, and looks, just like binoculars.

The laser used in this device is made from tiny semiconductor chips. Lasers made in this way are the sturdiest and most efficient units available. This is because these little lasers convert electrical energy directly into laser light. Most other lasers use at least one intermediate step. For example, the ruby laser must be stimulated by a high-intensity flash lamp, which does not contribute to the laser beam and doesn't even convert all the electrical energy passing through it into light. Semiconductor lasers eliminate this middle man.

Invented in 1962, semiconductor lasers formerly had to be operated with electrical pulses only a few tenths of a microsecond long to prevent overheating. But now a new laser developed by Bell Laboratories can operate continuously from an ordinary flashlight battery.

11. Lasers will also be shooting information into space by 1975. Gilfillan division of ITT is developing a laser that will beam 30 million pieces of information per second to a satellite 22,000 miles out in space.

The Air Force is also developing a special sun-powered laser to provide the long life needed for practical space communications. By means of a series of lenses and mirrors, the device collects and focuses rays from the sun, stimulating material in the laser to produce light beams. These beams are capable of transmitting data, television, voice and other related communications. Also under investigation is the possibility of powering the laser by auxiliary lamps or light-emitting diodes.

12. The world of art is also being affected by the laser. Using holograms, the world's great art treasures can be duplicated for all to see and the holograms can be used as a model to help restore any treasures that get damaged (such as the Pieta which was attacked by a hammer-wielding madman in 1971).

A hologram is a three-dimensional image stored on high-resolution film using a laser light source. When projected into space, a realistic image appears so convincingly that some people believe it's a solid object until they try to touch it.

13. Holography is being used to detect defective automobile tires, to encode and store computer data, and to record multiple displays of print, line drawings and photographs on single pieces of film.

14. On the research side, holography has proved itself in studies of everything from stressed materials to vibrating violins and eardrums. And with the help of ultrasonic waves, holography permits doctors to see inside people and can detect weapons hidden in packages and suitcases.

15. Industrial uses have also been developed for the laser. Modern tunnel digging equipment is now kept aligned by a helium-neon laser mounted at the open end of the proposed tunnel and aimed precisely in the direction the completed tunnel is to follow. Four light-sensitive detectors on the tunnel digger track the laser beam, keeping the digging apparatus on target. As long as the beam continues to illuminate all four cells equally, the machine moves in a straight line. But any change at one or more of the cells means the digger is off track and must correct itself.

16. This same technique was used to guide the dredging barges which excavated the underwater channels for the new Bay Area Rapid Transit System (BART) in San Francisco. A Helium-neon laser gyroscope is also used to monitor the vibration and comfort level of the electronically controlled BART trains.

17. Laser welders can make deeper welds than conventional welders. A deep weld is deeper than it is wide and thereby provides better bonding. Ford has ordered a laser welder that can make three major welds per minute in certain Ford and Mercury underbodies. The laser makes welds ten times as deep as they are wide and can weld 200 to 400 linear inches a minute.

In a related development, General Motors has already installed a 1200-watt carbon dioxide laser for cutting auto parts.

18. Watch makers are using high-power lasers to drill holes in jewel bearings. Some lasers can even penetrate diamond, and Western Electric scientists capitalized on this ability several years ago to drill holes in the diamond dies used to manufacture wire. In a related development, Alcoa

is using a laser system to drill holes in baby bottle nipples. Not only is this process faster, but more sanitary since no residue is left.

19. Finally, carbon dioxide lasers are cutting pants. The English American Tailoring Company uses a half million dollar laser pattern cutter to make custom patterns on an individual basis. The process is computer controlled. And L. Greif & Bros. has a laser cutting system which actually cuts the fabric for men's suits by following directions from a computer. The laser slices the cloth into any specified shape as the fabric unrolls from a bolt at one end of the cutting table.

The twentieth laser development, of course, is the blind travel aid mentioned at the beginning of the article.

What's next in laser technology is anybody's guess. With new applications ranging from detecting and measuring air pollution to remote detonation of explosives without radio signals, lasers may soon find application in almost every area of technology. Consumer uses are in the plans too. Already incredibly beautiful art displays are made with scintillating, bouncing laser beams. Simulated diamond jewelry, a direct result of laser crystal development, is now manufactured by several laser companies. Another company makes coin-operated laser amusement games; still another manufactures laser speed traps for police departments; and laser copying machines are just around the corner.

Several science forecasters have predicted the ultimate: a laser in every living room. With recent developments in laser recording, intrusion alarms, and television displays this prediction is not unreasonable. The 1970's may very well usher in a laser age with implications as far reaching as the effect of nuclear and electronic technology on modern life.

EXERCISES

VOCABULARY

relatively	vascular	technology
speculate	pigment	auxiliary
periphery	inhibit	scintillating
cauterize	infrared	

QUESTIONS

1. This essay begins by talking about blind people. Why does the writer begin the essay in this way?

2. This essay describes how something (a laser) works. Does the writer's description of a process make the laser's operation clear to you?

3. The list of twenty uses for the laser seems random at first, but look more carefully. Into what categories is the list organized? What organizational technique is used here?

4. What kind of audience is this essay intended for? How can you tell?

5. Go over the list of uses for the laser once more. Identify the devices employed to make smooth transitions between the sections.

HOW CABLE TELEVISION MAY CHANGE OUR LIVES

Martin V. Jones

ALTHOUGH there are too many unknowns now to warrant a precise prediction as to the future growth rate of interactive cable TV, the historical statistics covering the growth of conventional television can suggest how fast the interactive TV industry is likely to grow.

Black-and-white television reached its peak growth rate in the 1947–50 period. From 1947 to 1948 the number of sets produced increased by 450%, from 1948 to 1949 by 210%, and from 1949 to 1950 by 148%. In only three years in the 20 subsequent years did the number of monochrome sets produced exceed the 1950 production. The highest number ever produced (1965) was only 12% above the 1950 figure.

Color television has had a somewhat similar pattern. From 1964 to 1965 there was an 80% increase in the number of sets produced and from 1965 to 1966 a 97% increase. The following year the production growth rate tapered to 12% and since then has either declined or grown by only a small per cent.

During the period of most rapid growth (1950–55), the percentages of homes with all types of TV sets increased approximately by an average of ten percentage points per year. Then to get from a market penetration of 65% in 1955 to 90% in 1962 took seven years.

Cable Television has had a somewhat steadier growth. Every year for the last 20 years the number of cable TV subscribers has steadily increased. During the 1952–56 period, the number of subscribers doubled in each of four successive years. Since 1956 the annual percentage growth rate in the number of subscribers has been dependable and substantial, never being as low as 10% or as high as 35%.

The Sloan Commission has pointed out that cable television will reach a market penetration of over 50% by 1980 if it continues to grow in the 1970s at the same rate that it did during the 1960s. Coupling these growth rate figures for cable with those for conventional television, it is reasonable to expect that under favorable conditions interactive TV could achieve a 90% penetration rate in urban areas by 1990.

Many authorities have predicted that the widespread introduction of interactive cable TV into the nation's major population centers will have tremendous social impacts. For instance, Arthur L. Singer, Jr., Vice President of the Sloan Commission on Cable Communications, has

FROM *The Futurist* (October 1973), published by the World Future Society, P.O. Box 30369, Bethesda Branch, Washington, D.C. 20014. Reprinted by permission.

stated that the cable wiring of major cities "will carry with it social, political, and economic implications of unparalleled significance, dwarfing the changes that were brought about by such earlier developments as the development of television itself or by the creation of the present highway network."

No one can speak with any certainty about what the specific impacts will be until it has, at least, been decided as to which potential telecommunications applications will be given priority and under what terms and conditions these services will be offered. However, Paul Baran, in a market study for the Institute of the Future has predicted that by 1989 there will be a $20 billion annual market for two-way home information services. This anticipated market would be spread over 30 highly varied categories, the largest category (video library services) representing about 15% of the total. (See separate article).

Several things about Baran's projections should be noted. First, the magnitude of this potential economic impact can be gauged by the fact that the $20 billion sum approximately equals what consumers currently spend for all electricity and telephone services combined.

As large as this projected sum is, it still omits certain important areas of consumer impact. For instance, Baran did not include any health applications. Although most remote medical-diagnosis applications of interactive TV would not take place in the home, millions of citizens are likely to participate in such applications.

Also, the dollar impact may be a poor indicator of the real social impact in the case of some applications. For instance, although the dollar value of interactive TV services involved in instant citizen voting and referendums may never be large, the political ramifications of such an application could be profound.

Some of the varied short-term and long-term social impacts of interactive TV are shown on the chart on page 238. This exhibit takes some of Baran's projected applications as well as applications suggested by other observers, and speculates about the possible consequences of reaching a 50% market penetration in the nation's 10 largest markets by 1980.

A multi-billion dollar market for interactive TV services will find almost countless applications in the nation's homes, businesses, and government offices. The applications will bring about literally dozens of changes in the public and private lives of the nation.

How Will People Find Time for Interactive Television?

Paul Baran analyzed the applications and impacts of interactive TV from the perspective of a traditional market-research dollar analysis. Another approach would be to examine the question of interactive TV growth possibilities in terms of the citizen's time budget.

The logic for a time-budget analysis is to be found in consumer motivations and life styles. Frequently, consumers, especially those in middle and upper income brackets, will willingly spend more money and at the same time accept a lower quality product in order to save time. One example is the tremendous popularity of TV dinners and other precooked foods.

This characteristic of modern living that people lead brim-filled, busy lives is also evidenced by the fact that they frequently buy more books, newspapers, and reading material than they find time to read. They would like to engage in five or six hobbies or active sports but have time for only two or three. Most parents would like to spend more time with their children than they do. Many people say that they would devote more time to community, church, or professional organizations if there were more hours in the day.

What all this says is this: There are only 24 hours in a day, and for most people these hours are occupied doing something. This means that any new way of spending time, if it is to consume a large block of the citizen's time, must displace something else.

Although citizens do alter their ways of spending time when the logic is sufficiently compelling, these changes in habits are usually small and occur gradually. For instance, consumer time budgets varied rather little percentage-wise between 1900 and 1950.

On occasions new ways of spending time, especially leisure time, do emerge and, in so doing, they command large blocks of the citizens' time. The leading example of this condition during our generation has been television, which now consumes more of the average person's time than any other activity except sleeping and work.

Percent Time Devoted to Major Activities
1900 vs. 1950

Year	1900	1950
Total Time	100%	100%
Sleep	40	39
Work	13	10
School	2	2
Housekeeping	9	5
Child Care	4	4
Personal Care	6	6
Leisure	26	34

(CITED IN: E. B. Sheldon and W. E. Moore, *Indicators of Social Change*, Russell Sage Foundation, N.Y., N.Y., 1968, p. 538.)

These time-budget figures suggest two things. First, it may be in those instances in which interactive TV can save the consumers' time that interactive TV will have its greatest advantage over competitive services and technologies. Second, the present lack of idle time in most people's daily schedules may constitute one of the biggest initial obstacles to people spending a lot of time with interactive TV.

The Analogy Forecasting Method

To estimate the eventual impacts of *widespread* interactive TV on people's time-budgets, we should, ideally, have substantial data from many carefully planned and executed *demonstration* projects. Many such projects are now either in the planning or initial execution stage, but none has progressed far enough to provide enough usable data for a broad analysis of consumer response.

NATIONAL AVERAGE CITIZEN TIME BUDGET
MINUTES PER DAY DEVOTED TO SELECTED ACTIVITIES
1965–1966

Sleep	479
Employment (including commuting)	296
TV	88
Eating	85
Social Activity (visiting, conversation, cultural events, miscellaneous leisure)	73
Home Chores	58
Cooking	55
Personal Care	55
Household Care (including animal care, gardening, etc.)	38
Mass Media (including radio, movies, newspapers, books and magazines, BUT NOT TV)	36
Non-Work Travel	35
Child Care	29
Laundry	28
Study & Participation (study, religion, and organizations)	25
Resting	24
Active Sports and Outdoor'	18
Marketing	18
Total Minutes Per Day	1,440

SOURCE: John P. Robinson, "Television's Impact on Everyday Life: Some Cross-National Evidence" in the Surgeon General's Report, *Television and Social Behavior* (IV), page 419.

Lacking this experimental data base, the next best thing would be to employ what professional forecasters call the analogy method of forecasting, one of the oldest and most widely used of all forecasting techniques. Simply stated, the analogy method uses some similar condition or event on which an information base has been accumulated as a benchmark to project the nature of some future event. There have been many market research applications of this method. For instance, tape recorder manufacturers used statistical data describing the size and composition of the phonograph market as a basis for forecasting the market characteristics of the tape recorder. The manufacturers of hair sprays used the market statistics on other cosmetics as a basis for estimating who would buy hair sprays, and how much. The historical data on vitamin-pill usage has often been used as a benchmark in forecasting likely consumer response to other new food supplements.

The older product or technology whose historical record is used as an estimating base should be as similar as possible to the new product or technology in use characteristics. Second, there should be an ample statistical base covering the older technology.

We have used time budget data reported by John P. Robinson in the U.S. Surgeon General's report *Television and Social Behavior* as a benchmark to estimate how citizens will alter their habits when interactive TV attains widespread usage. Robinson's study furnishes breakdowns of the difference in the time budgets of those who own TV's and those who do not. Using Robinson's data as a base, we have developed an estimate of what the average citizen's time budget would be if interactive TV were applied to the point where it consumes 1½ hours daily of the total time available (See table). This 1½ hours daily is the amount of time that the average citizen now spends with one-way TV.

Finally, we have used the time spent watching one-way TV as a "residual entry." In other words, after making the projected time budget calculations for all non-TV activities, we secured the required balance for obtaining the 90 minutes of daily interactive TV time by reducing the time spent watching one-way TV.

In making these extrapolations, we have assumed that the growth of interactive TV would not reduce the amount of time that the average citizen devotes to any non-TV activity by more than 50%. In many cases, the percentage reductions would be less. To take an example of a maximum 50% reduction, at the present time, on the average, TV owners spend 8.3 minutes daily reading books, whereas non-TV owners spend 14.1 minutes—a difference of 5.8 minutes. In our calculations we have estimated that interactive TV users will decrease their reading time from 8.3 minutes to 4.2 minutes (a 50% reduction) rather than to 2.5 minutes (8.3 − 5.8 = 2.5), a 70% reduction.

A Projected Citizen Average Daily Time Budget Assuming That 90 Minutes Per Day Are Allotted to Interactive TV
(Estimates expressed in minutes per day)

Activities	Present Allotments		Projected Allotments	
	Those Who Do Not Own A TV	Those Who Own TVs	Interactive TV Users	Change
1. Interactive TV	0	0	90.0	+90
2. One-Way TV	11.3	87.6	72.8	−14.8
3. Main Job	253.2	254.2	254.2	0
4. Second Job	4.1	3.7	3.3	−0.4
5. At Work (Other)	10.8	10.6	10.4	−0.2
6. Travel to Work	28.4	28.1	27.8	−0.3
7. Cooking	56.7	55.0	53.3	−1.7
8. Home Chores	58.1	57.9	57.7	−0.2
9. Laundry	32.9	27.9	22.9	−5.0
10. Marketing	18.1	18.1	18.1	0
11. Animals, Garden	17.6	11.5	5.8	−5.7
12. Shopping	6.4	7.7	7.7	0
13. Other Household	20.8	19.1	17.4	−1.7
14. Child Care	16.8	17.9	17.9	0
15. Other Child	10.1	11.5	11.5	0
16. Personal Care	59.5	55.0	50.5	−4.5
17. Eating	84.6	84.7	84.7	0
18. Sleep	491.8	479.3	466.8	−12.5
19. Personal Travel	19.0	18.4	17.8	−0.6
20. Leisure Travel	20.5	16.4	12.3	−4.1
21. Study	18.1	15.7	13.3	−2.4
22. Religion	6.2	3.5	1.8	−1.7
23. Organizations	3.6	5.3	5.3	0
24. Radio	13.2	5.2	2.6	−2.6
25. Read Newspapers	15.3	15.2	15.1	−0.1
26. Read Magazines	5.4	3.9	2.4	−1.5
27. Read Books	14.1	8.3	4.2	−4.1
28. Movies	6.5	3.1	1.6	−1.5
29. Social (Home)	11.7	14.6	14.6	0
30. Social (Away)	33.9	22.4	11.2	−11.2
31. Conversation	19.5	14.5	9.5	−5.0
32. Active Sports	2.6	2.4	2.2	−0.2
33. Outdoors	17.5	15.8	14.1	−1.7
34. Entertainment	3.9	3.9	3.9	0
35. Cultural Events	1.1	1.0	0.9	−0.1
36. Resting	24.8	23.8	22.8	−1.0
37. Other Leisure	21.9	16.7	11.5	−5.2
TOTAL	1,440	1,440	1,440	0

An instance of a much smaller projected percentage reduction may be illustrated as follows: Robinson's figures show that TV owners average 479.3 minutes of sleep per day whereas non-TV owners average 491.8, a difference of 12.5 minutes. Our projections estimate that interactive TV users will average 12.5 minutes less sleep daily than people presently owning conventional one-way TV do. This 12.5 minutes represents a reduction of only 2.6%.

From our time budget projections it appears that people will get the time to use interactive TV primarily by reducing the time they presently devote to one-way television, sleep, and social activity away from home. Modest reductions in time spent in reading books, leisure travel, animal care and gardening, laundry, personal care, conversation, and miscellaneous leisure will also provide some of the time needed for using interactive TV.

Relatively little time for using interactive TV will come from reductions in the time devoted to active sports, other media (newspapers, magazines, and theater movies), religious activity, community and professional organizations, and formal study. This conclusion is based on the fact that citizens en masse already spend relatively little time on these activities so that there is not much room for furher reductions and on the fact that one-way TV has not made much inroad into the time that consumers spend on most of these activities.

In the long run the time for using interactive TV could conceivably be made available as the workweek shortens and people spend less time in gainful employment. However, the limited available evidence does not indicate that the time for watching one-way TV has come from this source. Nor does it appear likely that a reduction in the workweek will be a major source for time for using interactive TV, because:

1. A shortening in the average work hours is a rather slow process. Between 1900 and 1950 the U.S. chopped five hours off the workweek and, as productivity increases, it is expected that another five hours will be taken from the workweek by the year 2000. However, the amount of reduction in the workweek between 1973 and 1980 is not likely to average more than one hour.

2. Many activities, such as other media, active sports, community affairs, travel and vacations, gardening, etc., will compete with interactive TV for that extra hour of the worker's free time.

Summary

To sum up, we have used the time-honored techniques of historical analogy and simple extrapolation of existing trends to project how interactive TV may ultimately affect the way man lives.

Our projected time budget analysis suggests that most people will get the time to use interactive TV by slightly reducing the time they now spend in watching one-way TV, in sleeping, and in social activity away from home. Moderate reductions in time spent in reading books, leisure travel, animal care and gardening, laundry, personal care, conversation, and miscellaneous leisure will also provide some of the time needed for using interactive TV.

EXERCISES

VOCABULARY

interactive	monochrome	telecommunications
priority	gauge	projection
magnitude	referendums	ramifications
analysis	forecasting	analogy
extrapolations	benchmark	

QUESTIONS

1. The first six paragraphs in this essay develop one main idea. What is it? What organizational strategy does the writer use to present the information? What type of paragraph development is dominant?

2. After paragraph 6 another main idea is introduced. What is it?

3. Why are we given the first six paragraphs before getting on to the writer's main point?

4. This article forecasts the future. Do you think the author offers adequate evidence that the future can be forecast with some accuracy?

5. Does this article give us a "sales pitch" convincing us to purchase or subscribe to an interactive cable television system?

6. What organizational strategy is most prevalent in this essay?

7. Do you think the author's analysis of how people spend their time is adequately supported by evidence? From your own experience can you provide more details to support some of his statements: for example, "consumers . . . will willingly spend more money *and* at the same time accept a lower quality product in order to save time."

8. What organizational strategies discussed in Unit II of this book resemble the method of "analogy forecasting"?

WE'RE DOING SOMETHING ABOUT THE WEATHER
Walter Orr Roberts

As a boy in Massachusetts, I would often go down on gray mornings to the dock at Cuttyhunk Island and watch Capt. Frank Veeder head his stubby swordfishing boat out to sea. I would wonder what kind of weather lay ahead of him on the open Atlantic.

In those days, people depended a great deal on weather lore. For clues that bad weather was coming, they paid attention to the twinges in the rheumatic joints of older folk, or watched the erratic behavior of beasts and birds. In such rhymes as "Red skies in the morning, sailor take warning; red skies at night, sailor's delight," they distilled the experience of generations.

They may not have known, incidentally, how venerable that particular bit of lore really is. Read Matthew 16:2, 3: "When it is evening, ye say, It will be fair weather: for the sky is red. And in the morning, It will be foul weather to day; for the sky is red and lowring. O ye hypocrites, ye can discern the face of the sky; but can ye not discern the signs of the times?"

Today's mariners—and farmers, and resort owners, and construction men, and all the rest of us who watch the weather each day—seldom need depend on folklore. The National Weather Service (formerly the Weather Bureau) provides detailed forecasts covering two and three days ahead. Since February 9, 1970 (the 100th birthday of the Weather Service), less detailed five-day forecasts have been available daily. And for $3.50 a year the Weather Service will send you 30-day temperature and precipitation outlooks by mail twice a month.

Today's Forecasts: Bolder and Better

How accurate are today's two- and three-day predictions? Let the weathermen tell you.

Allen D. Pearson, Director of the National Severe Storms Forecast Center in Kansas City, points out that "forecasts are now much more precise than they used to be. They are couched in less cautious language."

Arthur Gustafson, who is in charge of San Francisco's forecast center, says, "Now we do better on two-day forecasts than we did for one day in the early '60s. And a decade ago, who would have dared tell you anything about Sunday's weather on Wednesday?"

Dr. George Cressman, Director of the National Weather Service, puts it explicitly:

FROM *National Geographic* (April 1972). Excerpted by permission.

The national average verifications show that we can forecast today's or tonight's temperature to within about 3½ degrees, and tomorrow's to within about 4½ degrees. If you count a forecast of over 50 per cent chance of rain as meaning it will rain, and under 50 per cent as meaning no rain, our national averages show about 87 per cent hits for today, and about 80 per cent hits for tomorrow.

To this Al Pearson adds a caution:

Weather forecasts are made for wide areas, not for pinpointed spots. Suppose the prediction is for 10 per cent chance of rain, yet rain falls in one corner of that area. The man who is getting drenched screams, 'Ten per cent! Don't those guys see what's up there?' He may not realize that most of the forecast area is as dry as can be.

Don't forget, a prediction of only 10 per cent chance of rain does not guarantee *no* rain. In fact, if we predict 10 per cent chance of rain on 10 different days, by all the laws of probability it should rain on one of those days!

EXERCISES

VOCABULARY

erratic	verification	discern
venerable	distill	controversy
explicit	hypocrite	
vigorous		

QUESTIONS

1. Roberts begins this essay with a personal anecdote (a story). Is this beginning effective? How does it tie in with the rest of the essay?

2. Is this essay mainly a discussion of folklore about the weather? What sentence signals the true topic of the essay?

3. What technique does Roberts use to demonstrate how accurate weather forecasts are?

4. In the end, are you convinced that scientific weather forecasts are an improvement over folklore?

5. We have excerpted part of a longer essay here. Are there any hints as to what topics the rest of the essay will discuss?

THE ENERGY CRISIS AND ITS MEANING FOR AMERICAN CULTURE

Boyd Keenan

THE so-called energy crisis cuts to the heart of American culture. But our preoccupation with it tends to blind us to the fact that it is but one aspect of a global problem facing all mankind—the problem, namely, of the universal scarcity of natural resources. Our own country finds itself in an unprecedented situation.

In the first comprehensive assessment of the nation's mineral resources since 1952, the U.S. Geological Survey declared (May 8, 1973) that of 64 vital minerals many already are or soon will be in short supply. This shortage, it warned, puts "not merely U.S. affluence, but world civilization . . . in jeopardy."

The energy dilemma, then, cannot be considered alone. But energy is the immediate question, and we must come to grips with it. Our politicians know as much. Thus every conceivable candidate for presidential nomination in 1976 has made dramatic speeches about the matter. Not atypical were grim predictions of one aspirant, Indianapolis Mayor Richard Lugar, who told an audience in Peoria, Illinois, on May 13 that the energy crisis—not Watergate or today's other headlines—would be the crucial issue in 1976. "People think somehow we're going to muddle through," he said. "They expect to wake up someday now and read a headline that says the energy shortage is over and everything is okay. But it isn't okay. We're plunging on day by day, uncertain about what is to occur."

Categories of Concern

The issues relating to the energy dilemma are so complex as to boggle the mind. Can they be clustered into any rational grouping? Probably not. Let us try nevertheless to discern broad categories of concern. Three such categories suggest themselves: (1) national security, (2) domestic inflation and related economic questions, and (3) possible adjustments in life style.

National Security. Though some of our best minds decry it, the sovereign "nation state" is still the basic unit of power in world politics. Virtually everywhere, "national well-being" is measured by the availability of energy sources. In the U.S. those who govern believe that they just cannot allow the nation to be without energy for driving the engines of our technological system. Therefore they will have to see to it that, whatever the costs, energy is supplied. This requirement was not frightening so long as prospects appeared good that we would be able to furnish the fuel needed. But now the experts are telling us that we overestimated the potential of nuclear energy and that foreign oil must pick up much of the slack resulting from the miscalculation.

Worse, at the very time when the nuclear dream is being shattered, the dependable fossil fuels long abundant at home have become scarce for one reason or another. The high sulphur content of much of our coal prohibits its use in many areas where ecology-minded lawmakers have set up stringent standards. Geologists generally assert that natural-gas reserves are low. And—perhaps most important politically—the oil corporations insist that they cannot afford to locate and extract crude oil at today's prices. Thus almost all knowledgeable observers agree that over at least the next decade the U.S. will have no alternative to importing oil from foreign ports, notably the Middle East. In that case, we shall find our national security—broadly defined—dependent on a politically unstable region of the world.

Add to this the fact that most of the countries allied with us since World War II are themselves increasingly dependent on Middle Eastern oil. Hence our friends have become our competitors in the search for energy fuel, and our desire for national security puts us potentially in conflict with our allies. The frustrating stinger in the total national-security picture is our future posture toward Israel and the oil-producing Arab states in the Middle East. No wonder that the U.S. defense establishment is haunted by the question: Over the next decades will we possess the petroleum products necessary to satisfy the thirst of the huge military apparatus which, as the cliché goes, is our "first line of defense"?

Further, nations are teaming up around the international oil market as they have not done since World War II. Distinguished students of world affairs differ in their analyses, but they all agree that unprecedented power blocs are forming. The power of the producing lands is centered in the Organization of Petroleum Exporting Countries (OPEC), a consortium of 11 nations. Complex cross-relationships have discouraged the consuming countries from creating equally powerful consortia.

In short, it takes little imagination to devise international scenarios that have frightening implications for the U.S. That is why alert presidential aspirants have identified the energy crisis as the major issue for 1976.

Inflation and Related Economic Issues. The complexity of the energy dilemma becomes even more evident when one considers the relation of the international situation to domestic problems. World monetary experts tell us that the increasing U.S. payments to foreign countries for oil exacerbate our own inflationary spiral. It doesn't take a professional economist to understand that a scarcity of fuel would cause ripples in every sector of American life. For instance, if our steel manufacturers lacked fuel to fire their furnaces, hundreds of other manufacturers would have to cut down production at once and lay off thousands of workers. The result might be political chaos of a scope never before experienced in this country.

Life-Style Changes. As gasoline prices soar and the threat of rationing looms, a tired cliché is sounded: "The situation requires nothing less than a total refashioning of life styles." Even the oil companies that peddle petroleum products and the utilities firms that sell electric power have taken up this cry. On their part, our philosophers and theologians attempt to trace the energy dilemma to ideological roots. Some of them argue that Western religion is the culprit. They point to pronouncements in "holy" writings which—so they say—have encouraged Western man to build extravagant industrial systems that gulp up the world's resources. Lynn White and Alan Watts (to cite only two distinguished scholars) contend that a "conquer the earth" syndrome, deriving chiefly from Judeo-Christian Scriptures, is somehow a uniquely Western characteristic. Therefore, they suggest, one hope for world civilization lies in Eastern religions, which emphasize meditative as opposed to material rewards. This approach seems apt in view of the fact that the United States, with about 6 per cent of the world's population, is now consuming over 35 per cent of the planet's total energy production. The average American uses as much energy in a few days as does each of half of the world's people in a year.

The basic question here is whether U.S. consumption is a function of its philosophical and theological underpinnings or whether many other complex factors are critical variables. Put this way, the question may seem abstract, but in the effort to understand the world energy chain it may be the most practical question yet faced by world civilization. In less cosmic terms, it has significance for every American who pulls his automobile into a service station or flips an electric light switch. Yet to anyone who has observed businessmen from the Orient in hot pursuit of Western technological dollars, a theory that fastens total responsibility for the world energy problem on Judeo-Christian ideologies appears inadequate.

Where then can we find help in making sense of what is clearly a world problem, not just an issue affecting American culture? The psychological pressure for comfort tempts us to accept at face value the propagandistic pronouncements of various interest groups. And indeed it is far too early to assess the sincerity or wisdom of either the huge corporations or the militant spokesmen for ecological concerns.

But it is not too early—in fact, it is already past time—to ask if we are at the mercy of these groups which offer such bizarrely diverse interpretations of the problem. We shall betray the best of our political traditions if we blindly accept the explanations of either the newly emerging total-energy conglomerates or the recently aroused environmentalists. After all, the energy dilemma did not come upon the U.S. full-blown late in the 1960s. For years American writers had been predicting a time when our materialistic society would succeed in enlisting the nation's economic, technological and even moral forces in an almost worshipful search for energy sources. Many of these thinkers were as confused as we seem to be about solutions to the energy dilemma. But if we had heeded their warnings, we might not now be so paralyzed with shock that we cannot think clearly about our predicament.

Henry Adams as Major Prophet

Outstanding as a prophet of today's dilemma was Henry Brooks Adams (1838–1918), great-grandson of John Adams, revolutionary hero and second President of the United States, and grandson of John Quincy Adams, fifth President of the U.S.

It was late in his life, as he experienced a sense of failure in not achieving a status befitting a member of one of America's "first families," that Adams conceived a theory of history centering on the role of energy in civilization. Of his many books, his autobiographical *The Education of Henry Adams* (first printed only for his friends in 1907) was probably the most eerily prophetic. The following passage from this book should be read in the light of certain events of May 11, 1972: President Nixon's energy message and some of the most dramatic of the Watergate disclosures.

The work of domestic progress is done by masses of mechanical power—steam, electric, furnace, or other—which have to be controlled by a score or two of individuals who have shown capacity to manage it. . . . The work of internal government has become the task of controlling these men, who are socially as remote as heathen gods. . . . Most of them . . . are forces as dumb as their dynamos, absorbed in the development or economy of power. They are trustees for the public, and whenever society assumes the property, it must confer on them that title; but the power will remain as before, whoever manages it, and will then control society without appeal, as it controls its stokers and pitmen. Modern politics is, at bottom, a struggle not of men but of forces. The men become every year more and more creatures of force, massed about central power-houses. The conflict is no longer between the men, but between the motors that drive the men, and the men tend to succumb to their own motive forces [*op. cit.* (Random House, 1931), pp. 421–22].

"Dumb as their dynamos"—a striking phrase. To Adams, the dynamo was a symbol of an accelerating industrial society. His interest in this symbol dated from Chicago's Columbian Exposition in 1893, at which he spent a fortnight studying the exhibits of new and powerful engines. "Chicago was the first expression of American thought as a unity," he wrote later. "One must start there" (*ibid.*, p. 343).

Exactly 80 years after Adams identified Chicago as the symbolic home of the energies America adored, that city remains the focal point for new dynamos. Commonwealth Edison, the city's electric public utility, has built the world's largest nuclear power plant at nearby Zion, and is now besieging the U.S. Atomic Energy Commission for a license to make the plant fully operative. Meanwhile, numerous environmental groups have filed suits to prevent the plant from operating at all until there is proof that it can do so safely. Thus the battle between Adams's "dumb dynamos" and people who fear them continues at the very spot where he envisioned energy as a common denominator for the various forces at work in the universe.

Oil corporation executives, environmentalists, political leaders and indeed all of us would do well to read about the agonies Adams experienced in developing his idea of energy as an almost universal factor that could explain the march of civilization. It took him seven years to realize that the dynamo—that ingenious channel for "conveying somewhere the heat latent in a few tons of poor coal"—was in truth a symbol of infinity and that, as such, it took on the characteristics of a moral force, much as the cross did for the early Christians. He even predicted that, ultimately, men would pray to the dynamo.

Energy and the Agonies of Eugene O'Neill

Like Henry Adams, Eugene O'Neill sensed the quality of infinity in energy, and in his play *Dynamo* he labored to give it spiritual and intellectual content. The plot revolves around a boy in his late teens, the son of an overbearing clergyman, who rebels against the religious teachings of his childhood and embraces the religion of electricity. Driven mad by the conflict between his lust for a girl and his desire to attain oneness with the god Electricity, he murders the girl and, flinging himself upon the dynamo, is electrocuted.

Dynamo was produced on Broadway in 1929, but closed after a few performances. Reviewers panned it mercilessly, to the playwright's deep disappointment. In an unsigned letter to the *Times Literary Supplement* (May 8, 1937), he said his intention had been to get at the roots of a sickness involving "the death of an old God and the failure of science and materialism to give any satisfying new one for the surviving religious instinct."

Many lines in *Dynamo* seem to draw heavily on Henry Adams. Today, 40 years after O'Neill failed to get his point across to the intelligentsia, ambitious politicians are drawing on ideas very similar to his to appeal to the general electorate. Tracing the circuitry of ideas from seminal thinker to artist to politician represents an intriguing intellectual exercise. In 1907 Adams could say that following the track of energy was the historian's main business. But both he and O'Neill, if they were alive today, would probably join those who say that tracking energy is the chief business of government. For technological experts are virtually unanimous in asserting that there is no real scarcity of energy resources; that there is, rather, a crisis in the management of energy, both within and among nation-states, that only governments can deal with.

Ironically, the heads of the big American oil companies have always protested against any government intervention in energy affairs. Actually, of course, these same companies have themselves functioned as governments, singly or collectively. Several of them are larger, in terms of wealth, than many nations; and their long-standing cooperative networks possess great political power. So they are indeed "governments" by any imaginable criterion.

Theories and Faith for an Energy Age

That aside, however; if the energy issue is worthy of a top spot on the agenda for debating the merits of 1976 presidential candidates (and most aspirants have declared it is), our society has an unprecedented task on its hands. The chore of educating thinking people to the enormity and complexity of the energy question will be the most demanding ever undertaken by a democratic system. Our failure to succeed in this assignment will no doubt be interpreted by world intellectuals as final evidence that a representative system of government cannot control technology. And unless our leaders can create the kind of passion felt by Adams and O'Neill, the educational effort will fail.

The problem we face is not a bureaucratic one requiring only a bureaucratic mentality. Instead, we shall be thrashing about in a thicket of ignorance in an attempt to understand what are perhaps the most mysterious characteristics of the universe. We need to devise theories that both explain the industrial and technological revolutions and project approaches for a supersensuous age of energy acceleration. In other words, we need to construct a dynamic formula of history.

Never before has world civilization been called upon to sustain itself while fashioning such a cosmic program. But hitherto the tests have never been programmatic or technological; they have been tests of faith. At times it may have been provincial or even perverse faith; yet the happenings of history were inspired by it. From the days when Constantine set up the cross through World War II days when American scientists built the atomic bomb, a blending of political and religious ideologies provided much of the faith undergirding Western political achievements. Now, however, the very term "Western civilization" is an anachronism. As a result of technology, there is only one civilization: world civilization. If there is one distinguishing characteristic to the energy crisis, it is its worldwide scope. Hence faiths built only on Western foundations are, by definition, inadequate for the challenge posed by the energy dilemma.

Let me quote Adams once more, for he offers hints concerning the character of the faith required to attack energy problems. In 1907 he wrote that the forces of energy represent "a sort of God compared with any former creature of nature" (*op. cit.*, p. 496). A heady and perhaps heretical point of view. But it is what the energy crisis is all about and what American culture must ponder if it is to survive.

EXERCISES

VOCABULARY

precedent	consortium	ideology
dilemma	scenarios	bizarre
inflation	exacerbate	dynamo
decry	syndrome	common denominator
sovereign	variables	seminal
cliché	propaganda	anachronism
power blocs	cosmic	

QUESTIONS

1. Reread the first three paragraphs, and state Keenan's main point in your own words.

2. The third paragraph uses one of the methods of paragraph structure discussed in Unit I. What is it?

3. In the section "Categories of Concern," what strategy does Keenan use to organize his discussion?

4. In the subsection "National Security," Keenan makes clear transitions between paragraphs. Identify the devices he uses to make

transitions between paragraphs. Identify the devices he uses to make transitions both within each paragraph and between them.

5. Does Keenan agree that the answer to the energy crisis is "a total refashioning of life styles"? What life styles provide an alternative? Why does Keenan mention "businessmen from the Orient"?

6. What are the "bizarrely diverse interpretations of the problem" Keenan refers to? Why do you think he rejects these interpretations?

7. Why does Keenan suddenly start talking about Henry Adams, a man who has been dead for half a century? Does this destroy the unity of the essay?

8. Keenan shifts from a discussion of energy problems to talking about history, literature, and religion. How do references to religion and worship fit in an essay about oil and other natural resources?

9. How do the final three paragraphs relate to the introductory paragraphs?

10. Look up the definition of metaphor. Keenan uses metaphors in this essay. Identify them. Are metaphors out of place in an essay about a scientific or technical subject?

A SCIENTIST COMES UP WITH A "PERFECT CAR"; DETROIT JUST YAWNS

Charles B. Camp

IMAGINE it. The perfect car.

It is small and lightweight, easy to maneuver and park. It's practically silent, yet has all the pep and power of any of today's big cars. And it costs a mere fraction of what current cars cost to operate.

What's more, no pollution of any kind comes out of the tailpipe. Indeed, it doesn't even have a tailpipe.

What powers this new miracle car? Electric batteries? A steam engine? An exotic chemical fuel cell? Wrong on all counts, friends. It's a wind-up car.

That's right. A small group of scientists is currently conducting studies that they're convinced will lead to hordes of adult-sized wind-up cars humming around cities and suburbs in future years without the slightest trace of fumes. And despite the complete rejection of their idea by an amused auto establishment here, they've already won a $190,000 government contract to help them prove it can be done.

Though they haven't built any of these dream cars yet, there's no question they are serious. "Every day this concept looks better and better, which usually doesn't happen in this kind of research," enthuses David W. Rabenhorst, supervisor of special projects for Johns Hopkins University's applied physics laboratory in Silver Spring, Md. "We've proved the principle already and are anxious to get on with the hardware engineering," he says.

Being a scholarly sort, Mr. Rabenhorst discourages the comparison of his pollution-free car concept with a child's toy. For example, he insists there'll be no big brass keys sticking out of the backs of his wind-up cars. And, in fact, in describing the system he studiously avoids the phrase "wind-up car" in favor of the more impressive sounding term "flywheel energy storage."

But a description of Mr. Rabenhorst's system makes one thing clear: It *is* a wind-up car. The principle is identical to the one behind the dimestore model car that is wound up by some brisk strokes of its wheels on the floor before being released to zoom about the room. It's just that Mr. Rabenhorst's version is a bit more sophisticated and a lot more efficient.

The grown-up wind-up would contain a large free-spinning disc, or fly-wheel, to store the energy needed to drive the car. When not in use, such as during the night, the car would be connected to an electrical outlet and a small electric motor would gradually spin the heavy flywheel up to very high speeds, or wind it up. Then to drive the car, the owner would merely unplug it and throw a switch that would allow the spinning motion of the flywheel to be gradually converted back into electricity that would in turn drive the car's wheels. The flywheel would slow down, or unwind, after up to 110 miles of driving or so and would stop gen-erating enough electricity to run the car. It would then have to be spun back up again during a 20-minute rewind.

It is so simple that as far as Mr. Rabenhorst and his Johns Hopkins associates are concerned, the system is just about unbeatable. For one thing, the car wouldn't carry any kind of fuel on board, so there'd be no burning, no exhaust and thus no pollution. On top of that, it would be amazingly cheap to run, Mr. Rabenhorst says, costing about one-tenth of a cent per mile, compared with about two cents a mile in gasoline costs for current cars. It would be reliable, he claims, since the wind-up power system would have relatively few moving parts and needs no trans-mission, clutch, drive shaft, starting system, fuel system or ignition system.

The elimination of all these parts, in turn, would save weight, which means a small two or three-passenger wind-up car could be built that would still have enough pickup to stay even with a large-engined Detroit behemoth belching away from traffic lights. Top speed would be in the vicinity of 70 miles per hour, enough for freeway cruising.

In fact, there seems to be only one over-riding problem: the auto-mobile makers think the whole idea is nuts. Only one Detroit engineer—from Ford Motor Co.—has even visited Mr. Rabenhorst's labs. Engineers at General Motors Corp. say one look at the flywheel power concept on paper was enough to cause them to rule it out as an alternative to today's auto engines. "It just won't work," snorts one top GM engineer. "Anyone pursuing that course is unfortunately misplacing his energies."

Mr. Rabenhorst, of course, challenges that view. "It's already been done," he counters. And it's true that flywheel power has been used for some 5,000 years in such varied jobs as driving machinery, starting air-craft engines and propelling military torpedoes. In the 1950s, he says, a Swiss company built a wind-up, or flywheel-driven, locomotive and a fleet of 35-seat urban buses powered by flywheels. Though less sophisticated than Mr. Rabenhorst's proposed cars, the buses ran regular routes in some Swiss and African cities daily for more than a decade, he says, clearly proving the principle of wind-up power. (The big problem with these buses was inefficiency. They required a quick 30-second "rewind" at bus stops every half mile or so.)

But auto makers contend the flywheel concept is a patently unsafe idea. To develop the required power, the 222-pound flywheel in Mr. Rabenhorst's car would be whirling so fast its outer edge would be moving at more than 2,000 miles an hour, or three times the speed of sound. Detroit engineers say they get the willies thinking about a fly-wheel traveling at that speed breaking loose from its moorings, as they contend could happen in a traffic collision.

Mr. Rabenhorst scoffs at such fears. He points to engineering papers that indicate flywheel failures in the Swiss buses were rare, even in traffic accidents, and when they occurred they were noisy but generally harmless. He says in laboratory tests his new super-flywheel disintegrates in bits and pieces without danger, rather than in a violent explosion. "We have high hopes of making the system completely failsafe," he adds.

Some auto men find fault with even the underlying premise that such a car would help solve pollution problems. Wind-up cars wouldn't elim-inate air pollution, they charge, but simply move it from the city street to the powerhouse smokestack. Some suggest that a switch to wind-up cars would even increase air pollution. They note the energy to spin the cars' flywheels up in the first place is electricity, and the creation of vast amounts of additional electric power for this job could mean a sharp increase in pollution from electric generating stations.

Mr. Rabenhorst disputes that. He contends there is more hope of controlling power station fumes concentrated in one spot than of con-trolling countless individual cars. And, he says, electric generating sta-tions can be intentionally located in low-pollution areas, while cars spew out exhaust everywhere they go. He sees this aspect in particular a boon to urban areas now choked by automobile emissions.

Of course, Mr. Rabenhorst concedes some problems. Since no one has even started to build a prototype of his wind-up car, its success depends on some components not yet fully developed. One is the special "super-flywheel" itself, composed of a new generation of high-strength materials, and another is a hermetically sealed vacuum chamber inside which the flywheel will whirl, transmitting its motion to the outside through an as-yet-untested magnetic coupling. All these problems must be solved with readily available, nonexotic materials and simple manufacturing methods, he admits, or else costs of a wind-up car would soar, making all other arguments academic.

But he's still undaunted. "This is the ideal urban car," he says. "That is where the greatest pollution problems are. Right now we don't expect it to replace the big gasoline burning car that the family takes from here to California." But since some 20% of the country's cars are concentrated in a dozen or so major cities, filling urban streets with wind-up cars is no small goal.

Though Detroit engineers currently pooh-pooh the idea of wind-up cars, there's some cause for optimism from other quarters. For example, Mr. Rabenhorst says the New York Metropolitan Transportation Authority may experiment with flywheel systems on some subway cars, and San Francisco might try them on some electric buses. In both cases they would supplement rather than replace electric motors, but could provide experience useful in the future, Mr. Rabenhorst believes.

Some non-Detroit automotive experts have at least been keeping an eye on Mr. Rabenhorst's progress, too. One is Ernest S. Starkman, noted former engineering professor and a past adviser to both California and federal auto pollution regulators. Rating alternate automotive power systems recently as to promise on a declining scale from 10, he gave a "4" —behind steam engines, electrics and turbines, but not completely out of contention.

Mr. Starkman has since been named vice president for environmental affairs for GM. It isn't known if that appointment will have any bearing on the future of Mr. Rabenhorst's wind-up car.

EXERCISES

VOCABULARY

principle	patently	hermetically
alternative	moorings	supplement
premise	concede	transmit
prototype	component	undaunted
exotic	optimism	

QUESTIONS

1. Describe the "voice" speaking to you in this article. Is it pompous, friendly, casual, concerned, humorous? Does the author take the idea of a wind-up car seriously?

2. Which arguments are more convincing: those of the Detroit engineers or those of Mr. Rabenhorst? Who has the best evidence?

3. Mr. Camp's description of the car is intended to make a point. What is the point? How does this influence the words he uses in writing the description?

4. In telling us about this new automobile, Mr. Camp uses a device we discussed in the section on description. What is this device?

5. The controversy between the inventor and the engineers is arranged so that Rabenhorst's arguments appear after the negative comments. What is the effect of this arrangement? What would happen if the order were reversed?

6. Read the introduction to the article again. Does the author supply facts and details to support the points made in the opening lines?

HUMANE TECHNOLOGY

Amitai Etzioni

IN COCKTAIL party sociology, where slogans serve as substitutes for thinking, technology is often depicted as anathema to a humane, just, "liberated" society. The defense made by the friends of technology is equally simplistic: "Technology is a set of neutral means; whether it is used to good or evil purposes is not determined by the technology itself."

Both of these viewpoints are as valid as half-truths usually are. In fact, most technologies do have fairly specific uses; no one has yet been killed by a cable television. And, while some technological developments do promote an impersonal, efficiency-minded, mass-production society, other technologies are essential for a more humane society.

Some recent technological developments take over routine and repetitive jobs, freeing people from the drudgery of counting, calculating, remembering numerous dull details. It is also true that these same technologies, those of the computer for instance, generate such routine work as key punching. But they eliminate more drudgery than they impose. Automatic switchboards of telephones do routine work which would require several million people, while generating little menial work. And, the way to combat remaining and newly created routines is to advance technology—to create, for example, computers that understand spoken English—surely not to condemn the machines.

Beyond this, new technological developments contribute to the solution of societal problems very close to the hearts of the deriders of technology, often making progress precisely where nontechnological attempts have failed. Thus, one of the barriers to arms limitation was the demand for human, on-site inspection, a demand quite unacceptable to the U.S.S.R. and unattractive to U.S. corporations worried about their trade secrets. The development of powerful inspection satellites made this issue obsolete. Another example: a cost-effectiveness study made by the Department of Health, Education and Welfare shows that it is much more economical to avert a death by means of seat belts, a technological innovation, than driver education. The birth control pill, a chemical technology, is much more potent in reducing family size than are efforts to educate people to have smaller families. Instructional television saves teachers the time often used to repeat exercises to their classes ad nau-

FROM *Science*, Vol. 179, No. 4077 (March 9, 1973), p. 959. Copyright 1973 by the American Association for the Advancement of Science. Reprinted by permission.

seum; it allows pupils to view the lesson when they choose, as often as they need to, and, soon, at the pace they wish; and it is as effective as or more effective than live teaching—tune in "Sesame Street" some time.

As for the future, pollution will be reduced through the development of less polluting, substitute technologies, not by a return to the pretechnological age. Distance and isolation will be further bridged through technological means such as two-way cable television and more suitable housing patterns. More and more people will be able to enjoy increased free time, culture, education, and each other because more of their chores will be done by machines and supervised by machines, whose excesses are corrected largely by other machines.

All of this is surely less romantic than the world depicted by the advocates of a return to nature, but it is also more likely to be realized, and it promises a *more* livable world, by practically any humane standard, than our Stone Age past. The task before us is to marshal more of technology to the service of human purposes, not to put technology into a self-destruct, reverse-thyself gear. This will not be achieved by a blind, wholistic approval of technology, but by carefully developing those tools which can be geared to advance our true values.

EXERCISES

VOCABULARY

technology	drudgery	innovation
sociology	menial	ad nauseum
anathema	deride	romantic
humane	obsolete	wholistic

QUESTIONS

1. What is the writer's main purpose in this essay? Is it to give us some new facts? Is it to persuade us to accept an idea or opinion? Does the writer prompt us to take action? State the writer's purpose in a short, succinct sentence of your own.

2. Pick out three key sentences that show the writer's purpose.

3. What is the dominant strategy used to organize this essay?

4. Identify the topic sentence and controlling idea in paragraphs 3, 4, and 5.

5. In paragraphs 3, 4, and 5 describe the method of paragraph development most dominant in each.

6. Does the writer provide adequate details and facts to support his points? Rewrite one of the main paragraphs, substituting details of your own.

7. Use Etzioni's details to construct a paragraph or essay that develops a different idea or an opposing opinion to that expressed here.

NORMATIVE ETHICS AND PUBLIC MORALITY IN THE LIFE SCIENCES
Daniel Callahan

THE topic of this essay, normative ethics and public morality in the life sciences, contains many dirty words. "Normative ethics," as we all know, disappeared some time ago, dying what was thought a richly deserved death at the hands of linguistic analysis, pluralism, and the "hard data" of the social sciences. "Public morality," that foul invention of Inquisitors, Comstockians, and assorted thin-lipped religious dogmatists, has been no less decisively put to death—at least in the better circles—by a combination of individualism, libertarianism, affluence, and all forms of "liberation."

Yet it is necessary to revive these old and dirty corpses because of emerging ethical problems in the life sciences, in medicine and biology. Increased longevity and highly sophisticated devices for the artificial maintenance of life, for example, have engendered a whole range of issues centering on the control of death, and thus on the quality of life of those approaching death. Genetic counseling and improvements in the technique of amniocentesis, the imminence of mass screening for genetic defects, the prospect of in-vitro fertilization, genetic surgery, and cloning, all raise questions of individual genetic welfare and the future of the human gene pool. The ever-broadening scope of behavior-control techniques, including operant conditioning, drug therapy, psychosurgery, and electrical stimulation of the brain, have momentous consequences for the future of human freedom, political life, and individual and public welfare.

Most people are only dimly aware of the social meaning and implications of medical and biological developments. Genetics, in particular, could have a powerful impact on the lives of future generations. Because two or three generations may be required to determine the consequences of genetic manipulation, the choices we make now may either increase the freedom of future generations or seriously, and perhaps irreversibly, limit it. Moreover, it is increasingly difficult to judge whether a particular scientific advance or technology is good or bad, both in the short and long run, and this is complicated by the possibility of different and discrepant ethical standards existing between the medical and scientific community . . . and the larger community. . . .

This article first appeared in *The Humanist* (September/October 1972) and is reprinted by permission.

There is already some evidence, for example, that a majority of physicians believes that most dying patients *do not* want to be told they are dying, while a majority of the public says that they do want to be told. In many cases, since patients are dimly aware of these different standards, the result is a distrust of the physician, whom they suspect may not be telling the truth. Another difficulty is that much of the medical experimentation on human subjects necessary to develop future technologies will be carried out on a "voluntary" basis. Social consequences of these experimentations, regardless of the absence of coercion, raise serious problems that cannot be ignored simply because some subject voluntarily signed a consent form.

Why do these problems raise issues of "normative ethics" and "public morality"? The first step in answering this question is to make some observations about the way many people in the scientific and medical community appear to make ethical decisions. My observations are based on a reading of scientific literature and on personal experience, not on hard survey data.

A number of schools of popular ethical thought can be distinguished. In the "religious" school, ethical decisions are made out of the context of a tradition of religious morality. If asked for a reason why he thinks some particular act is "right" or "good," a person in this school is likely to reply, "because I am a Christian," or, "because I am an Orthodox Jew," and so on. The "emotive" school believes that certain acts are right or wrong because they "feel" they are. "Gut reactions" are taken to be normative. The "conventionalist" judges acts to be right or wrong on the basis of accepted conventions or mores. An acceptable reason for a certain type of behavior is, for instance, because "that's what everyone does," or "it's always been done that way." Another school might be called "empirical conventionalism," which relies on the results of public-opinion surveys. If a majority of people thinks something is right, then it must be right. "Simple utilitarians" believe that acts are good because they are conducive to the greatest good for the greatest number.

If these are representative of the kinds of reasons given for personal behavior, another related cluster of schools can be found to classify judgments about public behavior and social conflicts. For example, the "barefoot civil-liberties" school allows everyone to be free "to do his own thing" or "to make up his own mind." It is not necessary for people to justify their conduct; it is enough if they are honest, sincere, or authentic. Another school, "gross majoritarianism," judges public acts and laws as right if they command majority support. If it is legal, then it must be morally acceptable. Still another criterion of judgment is "primitive cost-benefit analysis," which says that if the public will save *x* dollars by carrying out a certain policy, then that must be the ethically correct policy.

Finally, there are some expressions that are variants of "professional ethics": "That's not our responsibility"; "If we don't do it, then someone else will"; "I'm not a philosopher or theologian"; and "That's a political (or ethical, or social, or theological) question."

These descriptions are not parodies. Every one is an expression I have either heard repeatedly in discussions with scientists and physicians, or found in scientific and medical literature. Moreover, the kinds of expressions I have quoted often represent total ethical positions.

I do not mean to be entirely condemnatory here, because even professional philosophers who can speak knowingly and critically of different schools of ethical thought are not always articulate when explaining why they think some specific act that involves them is right or wrong. My main point is to call attention to the great diversity of popular ethical opinion and to the fact that, philosophically speaking, much of this ethical opinion is acted upon without any sense of need to provide a full rationale for holding an opinion. Most people seem to justify actions with an ethical slogan or a one-sentence general principle.

In a sense, of course, it is a tribute to the freedom available in our society that there can be such diversity and so little pressure to justify ethical decisions. At the same time, we need to ask whether this incredible welter of opinion, together with the absence of pressure to defend and justify it, provides an adequate method for coping with ethical issues in the life sciences. The ethical premise that one position is as good as another is an easy going geniality that is politically serviceable in our pluralistic society, up to a point. The problem is defining where that point is. While history has taught us the hazards of suggesting that there is a limit beyond which ethical diversity, informality, and freedom cease to be valuable, it is no less true that few of us are willing really to follow through in allowing everyone to act as he sees fit. Most of us do not find freedom served by a "live-and-let-live" tolerance toward anti-Semites, racists, government manipulators, or industrial polluters. We are *forced* into this position because it is rarely possible to honor all values simultaneously.

Reflecting on the possibility of present genetic interventions that may significantly and irreversibly influence the constitutions of future humans, how are we to determine and act upon our obligations to future generations? Whatever we do, it will not be with the consent of those future generations. Nonetheless, they will have to live with the fruits of our choices, hopefully good, but possibly bad. Is it sufficient in this kind of situation to let the matter be decided by individual scientists technically capable of making the decision? And what would be a good ethical reason for running unknown genetic risks with the welfare of future generations? Is it sufficient that some people "feel" it would be acceptable, or that it would contribute to "the greatest good for the greatest number"? Since the topic is controversial, perhaps each scientist should be allowed to make up his own mind. Or should the matter be put to vote?

I am not interested at the moment in judging the validity of any of these possible responses. More fundamentally, I am concerned with whether the "ethical geniality" I mentioned above would constitute responsible behavior on our part as a community, in light of our possible obligations to the unborn. Future generations would have grounds for condemning our behavior if they discovered that the matter had been decided on the basis of unexamined "feelings" of a small minority. A solution that allowed each scientist to make up his own mind, willy-nilly affecting the lives of others who will have no choice about the consequences, seems no less capricious.

The question of different and discrepant ethical judgments between physicians and patients poses no less vexing difficulties. Different standards of what is good for the individual can result in a conflict between a patient's judgment of his case and the judgment of his physician. A problem can also stem from a conflict between a physician's judgment of what he owes society and the claims of individual patients. It is increasingly common among genetic counselors, for instance, to worry about whether their obligation to the genetic welfare of society and the species should take precedence over their traditional obligation to individual sufferers from genetic disease. Some patients might believe themselves victimized if chance should drop them in the waiting room of a physician who gives the benefit of doubt to society—at their cost.

The care of terminal patients provides another example. Some physicians are willing to cease useless treatment, to allow "death with dignity." Others, however, feel compelled to use every piece of technology to the bitter end, despite the wishes of patients and their families. Is it proper that, once again, chance may dictate which kind of physician one gets, or that the choices will be the physician's rather than the patient's?

In my opinion, the most difficult problem is the extent to which society ought to rely upon the norm of "voluntary consent" as an ethical justification for medical experimentation on human subjects. At one level, to be sure, that norm is a valuable protection of individual rights of potential experimental subjects. Their bodies may not be tampered with, no matter how worthy the scientific cause, without their permission. There are abuses, of course, and the pervasive skepticism about the possibility of truly voluntary consent is sensible.

At quite another level, however, one must ask whether every experimentation to which consent might voluntarily be given is necessarily good for the individual giving the consent, or for the society. Is it ethical that some people should allow psychosurgery to be performed on them at the price of irreversible personality changes, or that they should allow the implantation of electrodes that permit their behavior to be controlled? Is it morally desirable that some women should be allowed to consent to contraceptive·experimentation that may result in deformed children? I am citing very uncommon cases, but each raises serious questions of the extent to which a pure ethic of free choice should be allowed to determine the outcome. Unfortunately, we live in a society where, with enough diligence, one can find someone who will consent to anything. Do we want this? Various methods of biological warfare, we recall, could not have been developed had there not been willing experimental subjects.

Naturally, each of the cases presented here has its other, more beneficent face. In the case of some genetic disease, it is quite possible that the physician has a greater obligation to society than to the individual patient. It may be good that physicians are not always obliged to do what their patients ask. And if an earlier generation of experimental subjects had not freely consented to some hazardous medical experimentations, many of us would not be alive today. Nothing I have said should be construed to suggest any clear-cut ethical resolution of the problems raised. The entire dilemma is more fundamental than the particular issues. How should we as a society cope with these problems? Moreover, can these problems be solved by means of a do-it-yourself ethic?

One commonly proposed solution is that there be public review and discussion of actual or potential scientific developments. "Technology assessment" has emerged as one response, together with various schemes to improve scientific "peer-review" procedures that would consider ethical and social implications. The general concern is that the public should have a greater role in the establishment of scientific policy, in the determination of desirable lines of research, in the application of new technologies, and in the development of professional codes of conduct. This spirit is commendable; the public should be consulted far more than it has been. "Science for the people" is not a meaningless slogan.

Realism demands, however, a recognition of the limitations of these possibilities. Considerable education and sophistication are often required to understand what is or may be at stake in biomedical developments. When scientists in different branches cannot keep up with or understand what colleagues in other specialties are doing, it is asking a lot to expect the ordinary citizen to do any better. One should realize that a very formidable education program would be needed. Moreover, much scientific work is often hotly debated among scientists themselves. Try, for instance, to get any consensus among biologists on whether and when it will be possible to "clone" human beings. Another limitation is that the results of "the people" controlling science might be deleterious for the quality of scientific work. Even now, basic research has been harmed in this country by popular pressure in and on Congress to fund only "relevant" research. Still another limitation is that, unless careful thought is given to the ethical issues before decisions are made by the public, there is no guarantee that the decisions will be wise ones.

In handling the ethical problems of the life sciences, it is quite possible that the democratic political method is the best we have and all that we should aspire to. It does provide a procedure for resolving public disputes and, together with the courts, ways of adjudicating conflicting values. If that is the case, then the best path to follow would be to attempt to maximize public information and debate, submit vexing issues to courts and legislators, and hope for the best.

Yet, if we are concerned not only with using the best available political methods, but also with trying to act toward the ethical problems themselves in a wise and responsible manner, then something additional is needed. In fields as intimate as biology and medicine, good laws and professional codes will not suffice to produce sensitive ethical behavior. Everything cannot be legislated and, in any case, science and medicine might be badly crippled if an attempt were made to bring all acts under legal control. Barring that kind of control, by what philosophical methodology should individuals and professional groups try to work through the ethical problems? Questions of this kind—which imply that good political and legal procedures alone do not suffice—ineluctably raise normative questions such as what should be counted as good and desirable behavior, and how such behavior is to be facilitated and encouraged. Normative concerns push us into the problem of public morality: the standards governing private acts that have social implications. It is simply not enough to say, for example, that the only ethical requirement for the physician is that he act according to his conscience, or that he be allowed to make a free choice. His acts will cure or kill us; as far as possible, we want his decisions to be right, and not simply conscientious. Future generations will care less about the procedural impeccability of our present decisions than they will about the quality of the decisions.

The very idea of a normative ethics entails at least two important assumptions. The first is that society, particularly in confronting ethical issues of the life sciences, would profit from an attempt to develop some common core of ethical standards and to set limits to acceptable answers. If this attempt succeeded, even in part, elements of a public morality might be found. I assume also that the effort would not be in vain and that the attempt would be valuable. We cannot claim ethical seriousness or responsibility if we do no more than blithely and passively accept the ethical geniality I pointed out above. There are certain values most people share, even if they do not always agree on their meaning and application. We do know more than earlier generations about what people need, both at the physical and psychological level. There still exist many traditions that may need some refurbishing, but are by no means dead. We have had some very bad experiences that might tell us a thing or two. These are some starting points. Where they will take us we will not know until they have been followed through.

EXERCISES

VOCABULARY

normative	conducive	pervasive
pluralism	criterion	beneficent
dogmatist	theology	consensus
genetic	parody	ineluctable
cloning	articulate	impeccable
amniocentesis	diversity	refurbish
coercion	welter	skepticism
mores	premise	construe
capricious	discrepancy	formidable
compel	norm	deleterious
facilitate	blithe	

QUESTIONS

1. One sentence in the first two paragraphs tells us what Callahan's position is. What is this sentence?

2. At what point in the essay do we get Callahan's answer to the dilemmas he discusses? Would it have been more effective to explain his position earlier—say, in the first paragraph or so?

3. Explain Callahan's strategy for developing his essay. Is there any evidence that he feels the people reading this essay might not all agree with him? Does the answer to this question help explain the way he goes about organizing the essay?

4. In the first half of the essay what organizational strategy does Callahan rely on extensively?

5. What kind of evidence does Callahan use to develop his essay? Does he need more "facts"?

6. What is Callahan trying to establish in the main text of his essay? Why does he devote only the last two paragraphs to his own position?

7. What kind of paragraph structure does Callahan rely on most often: detail, reason, or example?

SOCIAL BENEFIT VERSUS TECHNOLOGICAL RISK
Chauncey Starr

THE evaluation of technical approaches to solving societal problems customarily involves consideration of the relationship between potential technical performance and the required investment of societal resources. Although such performance-versus-cost relationships are clearly useful for choosing between alternative solutions, they do not by themselves determine how much technology a society can justifiably purchase. This later determination requires, additionally, knowledge of the relationship between social benefit and justified social cost. The two relationships may then be used jointly to determine the optimum investment of societal resources in a technological approach to a social need.

Technological analyses for disclosing the relationship between expected performance and monetary costs are a traditional part of all engineering planning and design. The inclusion in such studies of *all* societal costs indirect as well as direct) is less customary, and obviously makes the analysis more difficult and less definitive. Analyses of social value as a function of technical performance are not only uncommon but are rarely quantitative. Yet we know that implicit in every nonarbitrary national decision on the use of technology is a trade-off of societal benefits and societal costs.

In this article I offer an approach for establishing a quantitative measure of benefit relative to cost for an important element in our spectrum of social values—specifically, for accidental deaths arising from technological developments in public use. The analysis is based on two assumptions. The first is that historical national accident records are adequate for revealing consistent patterns of fatalities in the public use of technology. (That this may not always be so is evidenced by the paucity of data relating to the effects of environmental pollution.) The second assumption is that such historically revealed social preferences and costs are sufficiently enduring to permit their use for predictive purposes.

In the absence of economic or sociological theory which might give better results, this empirical approach provides some interesting insights into accepted social values relative to personal risk. Because this methodology is based on historical data, it does not serve to distinguish what is "best" for society from what is "traditionally acceptable."

FROM *Science*, Vol. 165 (September 19, 1969), pp. 1232–1238. Copyright 1969 by the American Association for the Advancement of Science. Reprinted by permission.

Maximum Benefit at Minimum Cost

The broad societal benefits of advances in technology exceed the associated costs sufficiently to make technological growth inexorable. Shef's socioeconomic study (1) has indicated that technological growth has been generally exponential in this century, doubling every 20 years in nations having advanced technology. Such technological growth has apparently stimulated a parallel growth in socioeconomic benefits and a slower associated growth in social costs.

The conventional socioeconomic benefits—health, education, income —are presumably indicative of an improvement in the "quality of life." The cost of this socioeconomic progress shows up in all the negative indicators of our society—urban and environmental problems, technological unemployment, poor physical and mental health, and so on. If we understood quantitatively the causal relationships between specific technological developments and societal values, both positive and negative, we might deliberately guide and regulate technological developments so as to achieve maximum social benefit at minimum social cost. Unfortunately, we have not as yet developed such a predictive system analysis. As a result, our society historically has arrived at acceptable balances of technological benefit and social cost empirically—by trial, error, and subsequent corrective steps.

In advanced societies today, this historical empirical approach creates an increasingly critical situation, for two basic reasons. The first is the well-known difficulty in changing a technical subsystem of our society once it has been woven into the economic, political, and cultural structures. For example, many of our environmental-pollution problems have known engineering solutions, but the problems of economic readjustment, political jurisdiction, and social behavior loom very large. It will take many decades to put into effect the technical solutions we know today. To give a specific illustration, the pollution of our water resources could be completely avoided by means of engineering systems now available, but public interest in making the economic and political adjustments needed for applying these techniques is very limited. It has been facetiously suggested that, as a means of motivating the public, every community and industry should be required to place its water intake downstream from its outfall.

In order to minimize these difficulties, it would be desirable to try out new developments in the smallest social groups that would permit adequate assessment. This is a common practice in market-testing a new product or in field-testing a new drug. In both these cases, however, the experiment is completely under the control of a single company or agency, and the test information can be fed back to the controlling group in a time that is short relative to the anticipated commercial lifetime of the product. This makes it possible to achieve essentially optimum use of the product in an acceptably short time. Unfortunately, this is rarely the case with new technologies. Engineering developments involving new technology are likely to appear in many places simultaneously and to become deeply integrated into the systems of our society before their impact is evident or measurable.

This brings us to the second reason for the increasing severity of the problem of obtaining maximum benefits at minimum costs. It has often been stated that the time required from the conception of a technical idea to its first application in society has been drastically shortened by modern engineering organization and management. In fact, the history of technology does not support this conclusion. The bulk of the evidence indicates that the time from conception to first application (or demonstration) has been roughly unchanged by modern management, and depends chiefly on the complexity of the development.

However, what *has* been reduced substantially in the past century is the time from first use to widespread integration into our social system. The techniques for *societal diffusion* of a new technology and its subsequent exploitation are now highly developed. Our ability to organize resources of money, men, and materials to focus on new technological programs has reduced the diffusion-exploitation time by roughly an order of magnitude in the past century.

Thus, we now face a general situation in which widespread use of a new technological development may occur before its social impact can be properly assessed, and before any empirical adjustment of the benefit-versus-cost relation is obviously indicated.

It has been clear for some time that predictive technological assessments are a pressing societal need. However, even if such assessments become available, obtaining maximum social benefit at minimum cost also requires the establishment of a relative value system for the basic parameters in our objective of improved "quality of life." The empirical approach will require an explicit scale of relative social values.

For example, if technological assessment of a new development predicts an increased per capita annual income of x per cent but also predicts an associated accident probability of y fatalities annually per million population, then how are these to be compared in their effect on the "quality of life"? Because the penalties or risks to the public arising from a new development can be reduced by applying constraints, there will usually be a functional relationship (or trade-off) between utility and risk, the x and y of our example.

There are many historical illustrations of such trade-off relationships that were empirically determined. For example, automobile and airplane safety have been continuously weighed by society against economic costs and operating performance. In these and other cases, the real trade-off process is actually one of dynamic adjustment, with the behavior of many portions of our social systems out of phase, due to the many separate "time constants" involved. Readily available historical data on accidents and health, for a variety of public activities, provide an enticing stepping-stone to quantitative evaluation of this particular type of social cost. The social benefits arising from some of these activities can be roughly determined. On the assumption that in such historical situations a socially acceptable and essentially optimum trade-off of values has been achieved, we could say that any generalizations developed might then be used for predictive purposes. This approach could give a rough answer to the seemingly simple question "How safe is safe enough?"

The pertinence of this question to all of us, and particularly to governmental regulatory agencies, is obvious. Hopefully, a functional answer might provide a basis for establishing performance "design objectives" for the safety of the public.

Voluntary and Involuntary Activities

Societal activities fall into two general categories—those in which the individual participates on a "voluntary" basis and those in which the participation is "involuntary," imposed by the society in which the individual lives. The process of empirical optimization of benefits and costs is fundamentally similar in the two cases—namely, a reversible exploration of available options—but the time required for empirical adjustments (the time constants of the system) and the criteria for optimization are quite different in the two situations.

In the case of "voluntary" activities, the individual uses his own value system to evaluate his experiences. Although his eventual trade-off may not be consciously or analytically determined, or based upon objective knowledge, it nevertheless is likely to represent, for that individual, a crude optimization appropriate to his value system. For example, an urban dweller may move to the suburbs because of a lower crime rate and better schools, at the cost of more time spent traveling on highways and a higher probability of accidents. If, subsequently, the traffic density increases, he may decide that the penalties are too great and move back to the city. Such an individual optimization process can be comparatively rapid (because the feedback of experience to the individual is rapid), so the statistical pattern for a large social group may be an important "real-time" indicator of societal trade-offs and values.

"Involuntary" activities differ in that the criteria and options are determined not by the individuals affected but by a controlling body. Such control may be in the hands of a government agency, a political entity, a leadership group, an assembly of authorities or "option-makers," or a combination of such bodies. Because of the complexity of large societies, only the control group is likely to be fully aware of all the criteria and options involved in their decision process. Further, the time required for feedback of the experience that results from the controlling decisions is likely to be very long. The feedback of cumulative individual experiences into societal communication channels (usually political or economic) is a slow process, as is the process of altering the planning of the control group. We have many examples of such "involuntary" activities, war being perhaps the most extreme case of the operational separation of the decision-making group from those most affected. Thus, the real-time pattern of societal trade-offs on "involuntary" activities must be considered in terms of the particular dynamics of approach to an acceptable balance of social values and costs. The historical trends in such activities may therefore be more significant indicators of social acceptability than the existent trade-offs are.

In examining the historical benefit-risk relationships for "involuntary" activities, it is important to recognize the perturbing role of public psychological acceptance of risk arising from the influence of authorities or dogma. Because in this situation the decision-making is separated from the affected individual, society has generally clothed many of its controlling groups in an almost impenetrable mantle of authority and of imputed wisdom. The public generally assumes that the decision-making process is based on a rational analysis of social benefit and social risk. While it often is, we have all seen after-the-fact examples of irrationality. It is important to omit such "witch-doctor" situations in selecting examples of optimized "involuntary" activities, because in fact these situations typify only the initial stages of exploration of options.

Quantitative Correlations

With this description of the problem, and the associated caveats, we are in a position to discuss the quantitative correlations. For the sake of simplicity in this initial study, I have taken as a measure of the physical risk to the individual the fatalities (deaths) associated with each activity. Although it might be useful to include all injuries (which are 100 to 1000 times as numerous as deaths), the difficulty in obtaining data and the unequal significance of varying disabilities would introduce inconvenient complexity for this study. So the risk measure used here is the statistical probability of fatalities per hour of exposure of the individual to the activity considered.

The hour-of-exposure unit was chosen because it was deemed more closely related to the individual's intuitive process in choosing an activity than a year of exposure would be, and gave substantially similar results. Another possible alternative, the risk per activity, involved a comparison of too many dissimilar units of measure; thus, in comparing the risk for various modes of transportation, one could use risk per hour, per mile, or per trip. As this study was directed toward exploring a methodology for determining social acceptance of risk, rather than the safest mode of transportation for a particular trip, the simplest common unit—that of risk per exposure hour—was chosen.

The social benefit derived from each activity was converted into a dollar equivalent, as a measure of integrated value to the individual. This is perhaps the most uncertain aspect of the correlations because it reduced the "quality-of-life" benefits of an activity to an overly simplistic measure. Nevertheless, the correlations seemed useful, and no better measure was available. In the case of the "voluntary" activities, the amount of money spent on the activity by the average involved individual was assumed proportional to its benefit to him. In the case of the "involuntary" activities, the contribution of the activity to the individual's annual income (or the equivalent) was assumed proportional to its benefit. This assumption of roughly constant relationship between benefits and monies, for each class of activities, is clearly an approximation. However, because we are dealing in orders of magnitude, the distortions likely to be introduced by this approximation are relatively small.

In the case of transportation modes, the benefits were equated with the sum of the monetary cost to the passenger and the value of the time saved by that particular mode relative to a slower, competitive mode. Thus, airplanes were compared with automobiles, and automobiles were compared with public transportation or walking. Benefits of public transportation were equated with their cost. In all cases, the benefits were assessed on an annual dollar basis because this seemed to be most relevant to the individual's intuitive process. For example, most luxury sports require an investment and upkeep only partially dependent upon usage. The associated risks, of course, exist only during the hours of exposure.

Probably the use of electricity provides the best example of the analysis of an "involuntary" activity. In this case the fatalities include those arising from electrocution, electrically caused fires, the operation of power plants, and the mining of the required fossil fuel. The benefits were estimated from a United Nations study of the relationship between energy consumption and national income; the energy fraction associated with electric power was used. The contributions of the home use of electric power to our "quality of life"—more subtle than the contributions of electricity in industry—are omitted. The availability of refrigeration has certainly improved our national health and the quality of dining. The electric light has certainly provided great flexibility in patterns of living, and television is a positive element. Perhaps, however, the gross-income measure used in the study is sufficient for present purposes.

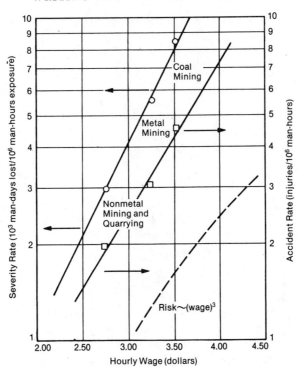

FIGURE 1. *Mining accident rates plotted relative to incentive.*

Information on acceptance of "voluntary" risk by individuals as a function of income benefits is not easily available, although we know that such a relationship must exist. Of particular interest, therefore, is the special case of miners exposed to high occupational risks. In Fig. 1, the accident rate and the severity rate of mining injuries are plotted against the hourly wage (2, 3). The acceptance of individual risk is an exponential function of the wage, and can be roughly approximated by a third-power relationship in this range. If this relationship has validity, it may mean that several "quality of life" parameters (perhaps health, living essentials, and recreation) are each partly influenced by any increase in acceptance of risk is exponentially motivated. The extent to which this relationship is "voluntary" for the miners is not obvious, but the subject is interesting nevertheless.

Risk Comparisons

The results for the societal activities studied, both "voluntary" and "involuntary," are assembled in Fig. 2. (For details of the risk-benefit analysis, see the appendix.) Also shown in Fig. 2 is the third-power

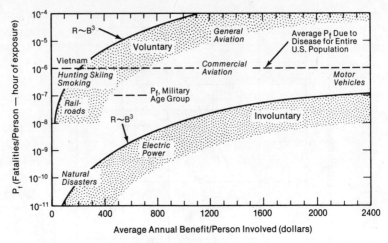

FIGURE 2. *Risk* (R)*-plotted relative to benefit* (B) *for various kinds of voluntary and involuntary exposure.*

relationship between risk and benefit characteristic of Fig. 1. For comparison, the average risk of death from accident and from disease is shown. Because the average number of fatalities from accidents is only about one-tenth the number from disease, their inclusion is not significant.

Several major features of the benefit-risk relations are apparent, the most obvious being the difference by several orders of magnitude in society's willingness to accept "voluntary" and "involuntary" risk. As one would expect, we are loathe to let others do unto us what we happily do to ourselves.

The rate of death from disease appears to play, psychologically, a yardstick role in determining the acceptability of risk on a voluntary basis. The risk of death in most sporting activities is surprisingly close to the risk of death from disease—almost as though, in sports, the individual's subconscious computer adjusted his courage and made him take risks associated with a fatality level equaling but not exceeding the statistical mortality due to involuntary exposure to disease. Perhaps this defines the demarcation between boldness and foolhardiness.

In Fig. 2 the static for the Vietnam war is shown because it raises an interesting point. It is only slightly above the average for risk of death from disease. Assuming that some long-range societal benefit was anticipated from this war, we find that the related risk, as seen by society as a whole, is not substantially different from the average nonmilitary risk from disease. However, for individuals in the military-service age group (age 20 to 30), the risk of death in Vietnam is about ten times the normal mortality rate (death from accidents or disease). Hence the population as a whole and those directly exposed see this matter from different perspectives. The disease risk pertinent to the average age of the involved group probably would provide the basis for a more meaningful comparison than the risk pertinent to the national average age does. Use of the figure for the single group would complicate these simple comparisons, but that figure might be more significant as a yardstick.

The risks associated with general aviation, commercial aviation, and travel by motor vehicle deserve special comment. The latter originated as a "voluntary" sport, but in the past half-century the motor vehicle has become an essential utility. General aviation is still a highly voluntary activity. Commercial aviation is partly voluntary and partly essential and, additionally, is subject to government administration as a transportation utility.

Travel by motor vehicle has now reached a benefit-risk balance, as shown in Fig. 3. It is interesting to note that the present risk level is only slightly below the basic level of risk from disease. In view of the high percentage of the population involved, this probably represents a true societal judgment on the acceptability of risk in relation to benefit. It

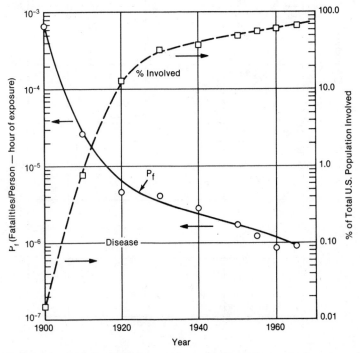

FIGURE 3. *Risk and participation trends for motor vehicles.*

also appears from Fig. 3 that future reductions in the risk level will be slow in coming, even if the historical trend of improvement can be maintained (4).

Commercial aviation has barely approached a risk level comparable to that set by disease. The trend is similar to that for motor vehicles, as shown in Fig. 4. However, the percentage of the population participating is now only 1/20 that for motor vehicles. Increased public participation in commercial aviation will undoubtedly increase the pressure to reduce the risk, because, for the general population, the benefits are much less than those associated with motor vehicles. Commercial aviation has not yet reached the point of optimum benefit-risk trade-off (5).

For general aviation the trends are similar, as shown in Fig. 5. Here the risk levels are so high (20 times the risk from disease) that this activity must properly be considered to be in the category of adventuresome

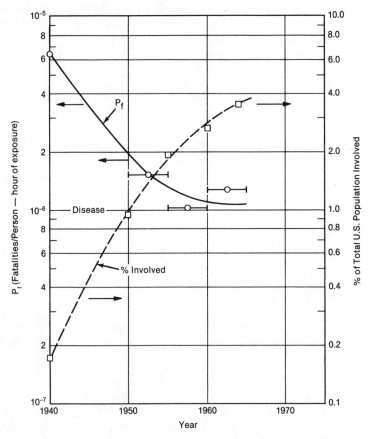

FIGURE 4. *Risk and participation trends for certified air carriers.*

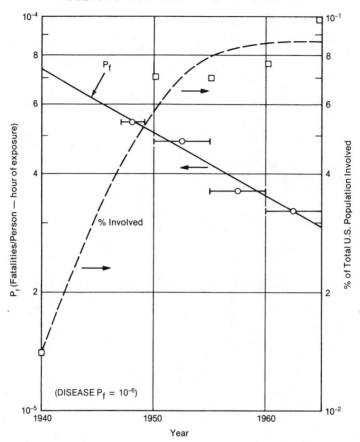

FIGURE 5. *Risk and participation trends for general aviation.*

sport. However, the rate of risk is decreasing so rapidly that eventually the risk for general aviation may be little higher than that for commercial aviation. Since the percentage of the population involved is very small, it appears that the present average risk levels are acceptable to only a limited group (6).

The similarity of the trends in Figs. 3–5 may be the basis for another hypothesis, as follows: the acceptable risk is inversely related to the number of people participating in an activity.

The product of the risk and the percentage of the population involved in each of the activities of Figs. 3–5 is plotted in Fig. 6. This graph represents the historical trend of total fatalities per hour of exposure of the population involved (7). The leveling off of motor-vehicle risk at about 100 fatalities per hour of exposure of the participating population may be

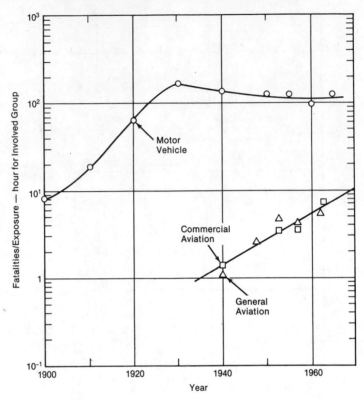

FIGURE 6. *Group risk plotted relative to year.*

significant. Because most of the U.S. population is involved, this rate of fatalities may have sufficient public visibility to set a level of social acceptability. It is interesting, and disconcerting, to note that the trend of fatalities in aviation, both commercial and general, is uniformly upward.

Public Awareness

Finally, I attempted to relate these risk data to a crude measure of public awareness of the associated social benefits (see Fig. 7). The "benefit awareness" was arbitrarily defined as the product of the relative level of advertising, the square of the percentage of population involved in the activity, and the relative usefulness (or importance) of the activity to the individual (8). Perhaps these assumptions are too crude, but Fig. 7 does support the reasonable position that advertising the benefits of an activity increases public acceptance of a greater level of risk. This, of course could subtly produce a fictitious benefit-risk ratio—as may be the case for smoking.

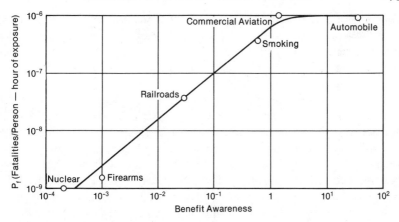

FIGURE 7. *Accepted risk plotted relative to benefit awareness (see text).*

Atomic Power Plant Safety

I recognize the uncertainty inherent in the quantitative approach discussed here, but the trends and magnitudes may nevertheless be of sufficient validity to warrant their use in determining national "design objectives" for technological activities. How would this be done?

Let us consider as an example the introduction of nuclear power plants as a principal source of electric power. This is an especially good example because the technology has been primarily nurtured, guided, and regulated by the government, with industry undertaking the engineering development and the diffusion into public use. The government specifically maintains responsibility for public safety. Further, the engineering of nuclear plants permits continuous reduction of the probability of accidents, at a substantial increase in cost. Thus, the trade-off of utility and potential risk can be made quantitative.

Moreover, in the case of the nuclear power plant the historical empirical approach to achieving an optimum benefit-risk trade-off is not pragmatically feasible. All such plants are now so safe that it may be 30 years or longer before meaningful risk experience will be accumulated. By that time, many plants of varied design will be in existence, and the empirical accident data may be applicable to those being built. So a very real need exists now to establish "design objectives" on a predictive-performance basis.

Let us first arbitrarily assume that nuclear power plants should be as safe as coal-burning plants, so as not to increase public risk. Figure 2 indicates that the total risk to society from electric power is about 2×10^{-9} fatality per person per hour of exposure. Fossil fuel plants contribute about $\frac{1}{5}$ of this risk, or about 4 deaths per million population per year. In a modern society, a million people may require a million kilowatts of power, and this is about the size of most new power stations. So, we now have a target risk limit of 4 deaths per year per million-kilowatt power station (9).

Technical studies of the consequences of hypothetical extreme (and unlikely) nuclear power plant catastrophes, which would disperse radioactivity into populated areas, have indicated that about 10 lethal cancers per million population might result (10). On this basis, we calculate that such a power plant might statistically have one such accident every 3 years and still meet the risk limit set. However, such a catastrophe would completely destroy a major portion of the nuclear section of the plant and either require complete dismantling or years of costly reconstruction. Because power companies expect plants to last about 30 years, the economic consequences of a catastrophe every few years would be completely unacceptable. In fact, the operating companies would not accept one such failure, on a statistical basis, during the normal lifetime of the plant.

It is likely that, in order to meet the economic performance requirements of the power companies, a catastrophe rate of less than 1 in about 100 plant-years would be needed. This would be a public risk of 10 deaths per 100 plant-years, or 0.1 death per year per million population. So the economic investment criteria of the nuclear plant user—the power company—would probably set a risk level 1/200 the present socially accepted risk associated with electric power, or 1/40 the present risk associated with coal-burning plants.

An obvious design question is this: Can a nuclear power plant be engineered with a predicted performance of less than 1 catastrophic failure in 100 plant-years of operation? I believe the answer is yes, but that is a subject for a different occasion. The principal point is that the issue of public safety can be focused on a tangible, quantitative, engineering design objective.

This example reveals a public safety consideration which may apply to many other activities: The economic requirement for the protection of major capital investments may often be a more demanding safety constraint than social acceptability.

Conclusion

The application of this approach to other areas of public responsibility is self-evident. It provides a useful methodology for answering the question "How safe is safe enough?" Further, although this study is only exploratory, it reveals several interesting points. (i) The indications are that the public is willing to accept "voluntary" risks roughly 1000 times greater than "involuntary" risks. (ii) The statistical risk of death from disease appears to be a psychological yardstick for establishing the level of acceptability of other risks. (iii) The acceptability of risk appears to be crudely proportional to the third power of the benefits (real or imagined). (iv) The social acceptance of risk is directly influenced by public awareness of the benefits of an activity, as determined by advertising, usefulness, and the number of people participating. (v) In a sample application of these criteria to atomic power plant safety, it appears that an engineering design objective determined by economic criteria would result in a design-target risk level very much lower than the present socially accepted risk for electric power plants.

Perhaps of greatest interest is the fact that this methodology for revealing existing social preferences and values may be a means of providing the insight on social benefit relative to cost that is so necessary for judicious national decisions on new technological developments.

Appendix: Details of Risk-Benefit Analysis

Motor-vehicle travel. The calculation of motor-vehicle fatalities per exposure hour per year is based on the number of registered cars, an assumed 1½ persons per car, and an assumed 400 hours per year of average car use [data from 3 and 11]. The figure for annual benefit for motor-vehicle travel is based on the sum of costs for gasoline, maintenance, insurance, and car payments and on the value of the time savings per person. It is assumed that use of an automobile allows a person to save 1 hour per working day and that a person's time is worth $5 per hour.

Travel by air route carrier. The estimate of passenger fatalities per passenger-hour of exposure for certified air route carriers is based on the annual number of passenger fatalities listed in the *FAA Statistical Handbook of Aviation* (see 12) and the number of passenger-hours per year. The latter number is estimated from the average number of seats per plane, the seat load factor, the number of revenue miles flown per year, and the average plane speed (data from 3). The benefit for travel by certified air route carrier is based on the average annual air fare per passenger-mile and on the value of the time saved as a result of air travel. The cost per passenger is estimated from the average rate per passenger-mile (data from 3), the revenue miles flown per year (data from 12), the annual number of passenger boardings for 1967 (132×10^6, according to the United Air Lines News Bureau), and the assumption of 12 boardings per passenger.

General aviation. The number of fatalities per passenger-hour for general aviation is a function of the number of plane hours flown per year, and the average number of passengers per plane (estimated from the ratio of fatalities to fatal crashes) (data from 12). It is assumed that in 1967 the cash outlay for initial expenditures and maintenance costs for general aviation was 1.5×10^9. The benefit is expressed in terms of annual cash outlay per person, and the estimate is based on the number of passenger-hours per year and the assumption that the average person flies 20 hours, or 4000 miles, annually. The value of the time saved is based on the assumption that a person's time is worth $10 per hour and that he saves 60 hours per year through traveling the 4000 miles by air instead of by automobile at 50 miles per hour.

Railroad travel. The estimate of railroad passenger fatalities per exposure hour per year is based on annual passenger fatalities and passenger-miles and an assumed average train speed of 50 miles per hour (data from 11). The passenger benefit for railroads is based on figures for revenue and passenger-miles for commuters and noncommuters given in *The Yearbook of Railroad Facts* (Association of American Railroads, 1968). It is assumed that the average commuter travels 20 miles per workday by rail and that the average noncommuter travels 1000 miles per year by rail.

Skiing. The estimate for skiing fatalities per exposure hour is based on information obtained from the National Ski Patrol for the 1967–68 southern California ski season: 1 fatality, 17 days of skiing, 16,500 skiers per day, and 5 hours of skiing per skier per day. The estimate of benefit for skiing is based on the average number of days of skiing per year per person and the average cost of a typical ski trip [data from "The Skier Market in Northeast North America," *U.S. Dep. Commerce Publ.* (1965)]. In addition, it is assumed that a skier spends an average of $25 per year on equipment.

Hunting. The estimate of the risk in hunting is based on an assumed value of 10 hours' exposure per hunting day, the annual number of hunting fatalities, the number of hunters, and the average number of hunting days per year [data from 11 and from "National Survey of Fishing and Hunting," *U.S. Fish Wildlife Serv. Publ.* (1965)]. The average annual expenditure per hunter was $82.54 in 1965 (data from 3).

Smoking. The estimate of the risk from smoking is based on the ratio for the mortality of smokers relative to nonsmokers, the rates of fatalities from heart disease and cancer for the general population, and the assumption that the risk is continuous [data from the *Summary of the Report of the Surgeon General's Advisory Committee on Smoking and Health* (Government Printing Office, Washington, D.C., 1964)] The annual intangible benefit to the cigarette smoker is calculated from the American Cancer Society's estimate that 30 per cent of the population smokes cigarettes, from the number of cigarettes smoked per year (see 3), and from the assumed retail cost of $0.015 per cigarette.

Vietnam. The estimate of the risk associated with the Vietnam war is based on the assumption that 500,000 men are exposed there annually to the risk of death and that the fatality rate is 10,000 men per year. The benefit for Vietnam is calculated on the assumption that the entire U.S. population benefits intangibly from the annual Vietnam expenditure of 30×10^9.

Electric power. The estimate of the risk associated with the use of electric power is based on the number of deaths from electric current; the number of deaths from fires caused by electricity; the number of deaths that occur in coal mining, weighted by the percentage of total coal production used to produce electricity; and the number of deaths attributable to air pollution from fossil fuel stations [data from 3 and 11 and from *Nuclear Safety* 5. 325 (1964)]. It is assumed that the entire U.S. population is exposed for 8760 hours per year to the risk associated with electric power. The estimate for the benefit is based on the assumption that there is a direct correlation between per capita gross national product and commercial energy consumption for the nations of the world [data from Briggs, *Technology and Economic Development* (Knopf, New York, 1963)]. It is further assumed that 35 per cent of the energy consumed in the U.S. is used to produce electricity.

Natural disasters. The risk associated with natural disasters was computed for U.S. floods (2.5×10^{-10} fatality per person-hour of exposure), tornadoes in the Midwest (2.46×10^{-10} fatality), major U.S. storms (0.8×10^{-10} fatality), and California earthquakes (1.9×10^{-10} fatality) (data from 11). The value for flood risk is based on the assumption that everyone in the U.S. is exposed to the danger 24 hours per day. No benefit figure was assigned in the case of natural disasters.

Disease and accidents. The average risk in the U.S. due to disease and accidents is computed from data given in *Vital Statistics of the U.S.* (Government Printing Office, Washington, D.C., 1967).

References and Notes

1. A. L. Shef, "Socio-economic attributes of our technological society," paper presented before the IEEE (Institute of Electrical and Electronics Engineers) Wescon Conference, Los Angeles, August 1968.
2. *Minerals Yearbook* (Government Printing Office, Washington, D.C., 1966).
3. *U.S. Statistical Abstract* (Government Printing Office, Washington, D.C., 1967).
4. The procedure outlined in the appendix was used in calculating the risk associated with motor-vehicle travel. In order to calculate exposure hours for various years, it was assumed that the average annual driving time per car increased linearly from 50 hours in 1900 to 400 hours in 1960 and thereafter. The percentage of people involved is based on the U.S. population, the number of registered cars, and the assumed value of 1.5 people per car.
5. The procedure outlined in the appendix was used in calculating the risk associated with, and the number of people who fly in, certified air route carriers for 1967. For a given year, the number of people who fly is estimated from the total number of passenger boardings and the assumption that the average passenger makes six round trips per year (data from 3).

6. The method of calculating risk for general aviation is outlined in the appendix. For a given year, the percentage of people involved is defined by the number of active aircraft (see 3); the number of people per plane, as defined by the ratio of fatalities to fatal crashes; and the population of the U.S.

7. Group risk per exposure hour for the involved group is defined as the number of fatalities per person-hour of exposure multiplied by the number of people who participate in the activity. The group population and the risk for motor vehicles, certified air route carriers, and general aviation can be obtained from Figs. 3–5.

8. In calculating "benefit awareness" it is assumed that the public's awareness of an activity is a function of A, the amount of money spent on advertising; P, the number of people who take part in the activity; and U, the utility value of the activity to the person involved. A is based on the amount of money spent by a particular industry in advertising its product, normalized with respect to the food and food products industry, which is the leading advertiser in the U.S.

9. In comparing nuclear and fossil fuel power stations, the risks associated with the plant effluents and mining of the fuel should be included in each case. The fatalities associated with coal mining are about ¼ the total attributable to fossil fuel plants. As the tonnage of uranium ore required for an equivalent nuclear plant is less than the coal tonnage by more than an order of magnitude, the nuclear plant problem primarily involves hazard from effluent.

10. This number is my estimate for maximum fatalities from an extreme catastrophe resulting from malfunction of a typical power reactor. For a methodology for making this calculation, see F. R. Farmer, "Citing criteria—a new approach," paper presented at the International Atomic Energy Agency Symposium in Vienna, April 1967. Application of Farmer's method to a fast breeder power plant in a modern building gives a prediction of fatalities less than this assumed limit by one or two orders of magnitude.

11. "Accident Facts," *Nat. Safety Counc. Publ.* (1967).

12. FAA *Statistical Handbook of Aviation* (Government Printing Office, Washington, D.C., 1965).

EXERCISES

VOCABULARY

quantitative	jurisdiction	perturb
implicit	facetious	impute
spectrum	assessment	demarcation
paucity	diffusion	judicious
empirical	parameters	mantle
inexorable	intuitive	caveats
exponential	optimize	pragmatic
subsequent	cumulative	methodology
socioeconomic	correlation	

QUESTIONS

1. This essay is the most "technical" of our selections. The unit of this book called "Writing on the Job" should give you some background

regarding the organization of this essay. In some ways this essay is like a proposal. What is the author proposing?

2. Starr says the historical empirical approach to balancing technological benefit and social cost is inadequate for "two basic reasons." What method of development does he use to explain these two reasons?

3. What kind of data does Starr use to perform his analysis of benefit and cost?

4. Look at Starr's discussion of "voluntary" and "involuntary" social activities. This section is like a smaller essay within the larger essay. What organizational strategy is used in this discussion?

5. Why is it necessary for the author to explain so carefully the reasons for using particular standards of measurement?

6. Compare Starr's explanations of his charts with the structure we suggest for an example paragraph. Does he generally follow that structure?

7. Starr engages in quite a bit of speculation and analysis based on his figures, particularly when discussing people's motives. Does this detract from his case?

IV

Job-Related Writing

WRITING ON THE JOB

THIS section, Unit IV, introduces you to some practical uses for the writing techniques explained in earlier chapters. Much of the writing you will do on a job will fall into the category of informal reports. Most organizations have established formats for longer, formal reports; but the day-to-day writing tasks demanded by memos, progress reports, proposals, and trip reports assume whatever form best suits the purposes of the individual on the job. The reports discussed here are usually sent within a company.

Informal reports of every type share certain features.

1. Reports are precise and clear. They contain an explicit statement of purpose and scope, stick to that purpose, and stay within defined limits.
2. Good reports have a logical order, and this order is often signaled by headings.
3. A good report is accurate in its presentation of facts.
4. A good report makes a clear distinction between information and opinion.

Most reports have six basic sections or some modification of this basic pattern. These sections are

1. Introduction.
2. Summary.
3. Body.

4. Conclusions.
5. Recommendations.
6. Appendix.

In the introduction, the purpose of the report is explained. The summary condenses the information in the report. In a progress report, the summary is usually just that—a summary of work done to date. In brief reports the summary and the introduction can be one and the same. The body of the report presents the factual information relevant to the purpose of the report. Any conclusions drawn by the writer must be based on the information presented in the body; conclusions that do not grow from the information presented have no place in the report. The recommendations are based on the conclusions the writer has drawn from the information. The appendix, attached at the end of the report, will generally present facts and figures or additional data to supplement the body of the report.

Memorandum Report

Memorandum reports have become an essential communication tool in all types of companies. The tone of a memorandum (*memo*, for short) is often informal, but a memo usually has the serious purpose of communicating vital facts or information. The information contained in a memorandum is intended for personnel within the same company. Although the memorandum can be informal in tone, facts and observations must be precise and accurate. The success of an organization depends on clear communication among its various levels of operation. The general organizational pattern for reports applies to memorandum reports; and description, exposition, and argument are valuable tools in organizing an effective memorandum.

A memorandum report filed by a field representative sent out to investigate the potential advantage of one company's buying another is our first example. The need for information is immediate, and the investigator's conclusions are important in helping to make the final decision. Mr. Wilson will be asked to write a formal report on his findings, but the memorandum supplies his employers with the immediate essentials. Mr. Wilson divides his report into *observations* and *recommendations*. The recommendations follow logically from the activities he observed while visiting the factory.

The form provided for memoranda varies in appearance from company to company; but there is always a place for the name of the party to whom the memo is directed, a place to indicate who else has received this information, the name of the writer, and the date. Most important, memorandum forms include a space in which to specify the subject of the memorandum.

```
To: John Epstein                        From: Anthony Wilson
Subject:  Peoria Manufacturing Co.      Date:  June 22, 1972

          Here are some of my observations and recommendations
          resulting from the visit.

          The potential for profit is obvious.

          I was very impressed by the good housekeeping practices
          prevalent. The operators seem to work at a very
          productive pace and without too much direct
          supervision. Their methods, especially those used in
          presenting work to the machines, are good. However, the
```

flow of work is haphazard and needs immediate
modification.

The caliber of the senior personnel I met was
unfortunately not up to par. I was not satisfied with
the bookkeeping procedures, nor was I happy with the
inefficient loading system. The loading procedure
involves a great deal of downtime owing to periodic
lags in production. We must establish an even rate of
production through the factory to eliminate the time
wasted on the loading dock.

I recommend the following:

1. Very close functional supervision from Chicago.

2. Planning of production from a sales forecast.

3. Installation of a Kardex type record-keeping system
   for both raw and finished goods on site.

4. Design a more efficient loading procedure. Too
   many men presently spend too much time with nothing
   to do.

To sum up, the operation should be turned round, given
a gentle kick in the pants, and sent on its way to
what I am confident will be a profitable destination.

Companies use the memorandum format for many different
kinds of reports. Mr. Wilson's trip report analyzed the situation in
Peoria. The memorandum that follows is primarily an informa-
tional progress report. This example illustrates why the telephone
is sometimes inadequate for precise communication. The large
amount of detail in this memorandum could never be communicated effectively over the telephone. Mr. Carson, the plant foreman,
organizes his report chronologically. His superiors have expressed
dissatisfaction with delays in completing an assignment, so Mr.
Carson has written a progress report to explain the delays and persuade his boss that the job has been worthwhile to the company.
The informality of the memorandum and other informal reports
allows the writer a great deal of leeway in choosing a strategy to
suit a specific purpose. But the requirements of precision, clarity,
and order supersede the temptation to be flippant, humorous, or
self-justifying.

Copy to: Don Hutchins

To: John Martin   From: Herb Carson

Subject: Boiler Conversion re   Date: October 12, 1972
         your memo dated Aug. 21/72.

John, we finally have the conversion boiler in action! I realize
from your memo you assumed the conversion was completed, but we

were delayed until this week, waiting for a low pressure safety valve and other parts.

I thought I would take the time to lay out in chronological order what has transpired during this project.

1970–1971	Received numerous complaints from the Department of the Environment regarding "excessive smoke emission."
Dec. 1971	Received letter from Department of Environment to take action "or else."
Jan. 1972	Contacted gas and oil companies regarding installation of an afterburner that would burn off hardwood smoke emission and can also switch to high fire and carry the heating load when no firewood is available. We also included in this contract a conversion from high to low pressure steam, which means we do not have to guard the boilers physically 25 hours per day.
May 1972	Received approval certificate from Department of Environment to proceed.
June 1972	Issued purchase order to Kennedy's Heating in Portland for $9,000.00 to install above equipment.
Sept. 1972	We investigated the possibility of hauling scrap hardwood away and not burning it at all. This would allow us to run with only one engineer on day shift. However, this did not prove out as we would not gain anything by hauling the scrap away. Hardwood has a heat content of approximately 5,000 BTU per lb. and coal approximately 13,800 BTU per lb. Coal costs $26.00 per ton, so a ton of hardwood would reduce our fuel bill approximately $10.00. We are burning approximately 10 tons per week, which is $100.00. It also would cost $90.00 per week to haul the scrap away. We would still need a man to load the scrap; so he might as well fire the boiler. The savings in fuel plus the cost of hauling scrap covers one man's wages per week.
Oct. 1972	The three men that covered the boiler 7 days a week are now reduced to two men 5 days per week. The third man will be used in our direct labor force.

In summary, we will recover some hidden costs because, with the high pressure system, we could not leave the boiler unattended. In the 1972 fiscal year we spent $7,000 overtime dollars in this area to cover vacation periods and sickness.

We do not feel it is within the scope of our purpose to provide examples and directions for every type of report you may ever be required to write. The sample memos demonstrate not only a specific format but also two different types of reports: one, in effect, a trip report; the other, basically a progress report. Both examples illustrate the type of information that usually constitutes the body of a report: precise facts and data.

The other sections of a report (introduction, summary, recommendations, and conclusion) need some further illustration. The following paragraphs appear in a book on occupational safety. The first paragraph could be the introduction to a memo suggesting methods of increasing worker safety. The introduction tells what the problem is and specifies a solution. The summary capsulizes the content of the proposal and anticipates its method of organization.

Introduction

Our study leads us to the conclusion that mere tinkering with traditional approaches to job safety and health will eventually lead to the same old frustrations. What is necessary is an entirely fresh focus by all sectors of the movement. In our view, the key to real progress lies in the cultivation of worker involvement.

Summary

The employee's own life and health are at stake in the workplace. Truly adequate protection will not develop until the individual worker becomes aware of all the dangers of the workplace, their dimensions, and the alternatives that can furnish reasonable safeguards. The challenge, therefore, is to make occupational safety and health a vital, central part of the worker's everyday life, rather than an outside force generated by others, sweeping periodically through the plant, and then disappearing. The usual approaches to the problem have always smacked of paternalism, with workers being admonished and taken care of by company, government, and union officials. Our conviction is that the worker must be encouraged to take care of himself and participate in the control of the quality of his or her own occupational environment.[1]

Proposals

Proposals can be extremely formal pieces of writing, submitted, perhaps, to a funding agency asking for support in a project. The type of proposal writing useful to you, though much less formal, is no less demanding in organization and detail than the formal one. In our example of an introduction and summary, a technician sees a way to solve an important problem as well as save the hospital a significant amount of money. In order to gain an audience for the idea and get it implemented, the technician took the time to organize his data and ideas into a proposal that specifies the problem, supplies the supporting data, and offers the solution. The proposal growing from the introduction and summary cited earlier helps the

[1] Joseph A. Page and Mary-Win O'Brien, *Bitter Wages* (New York: Grossman Publishers, 1973), p. 242.

hospital and benefits the employee who took the time to develop a good idea in writing. If you work anywhere for very long, you will hear employees voice complaints and suggestions that never go beyond the lunchroom or coffeepot. A good idea deserves to be heard, and the best way to have it heard and then acted on is to write a proposal. In an informal proposal sent to a supervisor or administrator, all you need do is state the problem, present the data, and then offer your solution based on the data. The following proposal used this format to improve patient care at a large hospital.

Problem

The main medical surgical floor at Kelsey Hospital has a problem communicating doctors' orders that are new, changed, or discontinued. The team leader has to find each specific worker to carry out these orders. If the team leader is busy, the order may be delayed or forgotten.

Data

At Mercy Hospital, the team leader writes new, changed, and discontinued orders on a special sheet located at the nurses' station. Each time a nurse walks by, she checks the sheet for orders concerning her patients. If the doctor has ordered a change in treatment for one of her patients, she initials the order, thus showing she has acknowledged it. After carrying out the new order, she crosses it from the sheet so that the team leader knows the order has been carried out.
Hurley Medical Center uses a sheet similar to this. The team leaders write new, changed, and discontinued orders on this sheet; and when the team members go to coffee or lunch, they check the sheet, and the team leader explains the orders to them.

Solution

A special sheet will be made and placed on the desk at the nurses' station. The team leaders, who note orders, will put all orders on this sheet pertaining to the nurses who are doing patient care. These nurses will check this sheet frequently and initial each order intended for any of their patients. After the order has been completed, they will cross it off the sheet and report any important information to the team leader. The team leader will be able to use this sheet when giving a report to the next shift.

Work Specifications

There are two basic approaches to specifying work responsibilities. One is to write *performance* specifications. Performance specifications do not stipulate the means used to accomplish a goal or manufacture a product; they simply state what is desired and leave the means to the worker or workers involved. Job descriptions and sales quotas are examples of performance specifications. The performance or product to issue from a job must be specified in precise, objective terms. If you write a careless work order, you cannot very well object when the completed product fails to match what you had in mind.

Performance specifications are written by service managers, for example, who have a team of skilled mechanics available to do the work. The service manager translates the customer's complaints into performance specifications:

> Replace front brake shoes.
> Repair oil leak in front of engine.

An architect or engineer faces a more complex task in writing performance specifications. In working with a contractor to build, say, an office building, the engineer may want to leave such things as dimensions, materials, and finishes to the judgment of the contractor; but the engineer also wants the final structure to meet certain standards. A performance specification for office buildings might contain the following guidelines: "Door frames shall withstand a pressure of 2000 pounds per square inch. The doors shall be fire resistant. All glass components shall be shatterproof and withstand wind forces at the level specified for exterior windows."

Work procedure specifications, as opposed to work performance specifications, state the exact quantity and quality of material to be used and stipulate the methods for achieving the end product. Unlike the preceding example, a work procedure specification for an office building identifies every material, carefully describes the structure, specifies methods of fastening, and lists the steps in construction. Work procedure specifications use the techniques described earlier under "Process." The following procedure specification tells a homeowner how to cure a common problem:

> In another type of faucet, the big nut is not visible. The handle covers the shaft. To disassemble this, first use a Phillips screwdriver (made to fit into screws with crisscross slots rather than one straight slot) to take out the screw holding the handle on. Lift the handle off. If it balks, just tap upward on the bottom with a screwdriver handle, then lift off. With the handle off, you will see the big nut. Using a wrench (or pliers, in a pinch) loosen this nut. Then replace the handle on the shaft and turn as if you were turning the faucet ON. The shaft will come up and out; on the end, of course, will be the washer. Replace with one of the same size.

Some faucets look like they can't be taken apart: there doesn't seem to be anything to turn. But there is. With a screwdriver, or a fingernail, whichever works, pry up the little disc on the top of the handle. When you do you'll see a screw. Just take this out, pry off the handle—and there will be the big nut, ready for turning.[2]

Writing Instructions

Everyone at some time or other, whether a technician or a father assembling a Christmas bicycle, has experienced the frustration of confusing and unclear assembly instructions. In his book *Zen and the Art of Motorcycle Maintenance* Robert Pirsig explains why some instructions are so annoying, confusing, and frustrating. According to Pirsig, the boss goes out into the factory and finds the only man who isn't busy, probably because he has very little responsibility, and gives him the job of writing the instructions on how to operate or assemble a carefully manufactured device. Pirsig says the persons who really know and care about the manufacture of the product, who understand the principles behind the assembly and operation of the product, are usually too busy and too valuable to spend time writing instructions.

If Pirsig's observations contain some truth, no wonder instructions often confuse and frustrate. Telling someone how to operate a sophisticated device demands both writing skill and a thorough knowledge of the device or product. Some practical suggestions can improve the quality and the clarity of operating and assembly instructions. Some instructions are simple, one-sentence statements that define the work to be done but leave the details of time and method to the reader. Most often, however, instructions describe step-by-step procedures that lead the reader through an unfamiliar operation.

What makes a good set of instructions? Much depends on the basic technical competence of the reader, and you should be aware of the technical knowledge of your reader before writing the instructions. Can you assume that the instruction "Open the cover plate" will be read by someone who knows how to find the cover plate? In some cases, it may be necessary to specify the tools needed to perform a certain operation (such as using an insulated

---

[2] *Consumer Guide* (New York: New American Library, 1974), pp. 375–76.

screwdriver to test the spark on a sparkplug). To write effective, clear instructions, you must know your potential reader; a good rule of thumb is to write for the lowest skill level you can anticipate. Remember that the clarity of maintenance or operating instructions may determine the consumer's satisfaction with a given product.

The language of instructions should be direct and unambiguous. Exact measurements and precise numbers provide clarity and instill confidence in your reader. Consider these examples:

> *Vague:* Some insulation should be stripped from the ends of a fairly long piece of wire. The wire is connected to the second terminal from the bottom and the other end to the pin on the other side.
>
> *Clear:* Cut an 18-inch length of 10-gauge wire, and strip one inch of insulation from each end. Solder one end of the wire to terminal 7 and the other end to pin 49.

The first example is ambiguous and imprecise. It leaves far too much for the reader to figure out and could very well result in time wasted in trial and error. The second example is crisp and assertive. It supplies precise information in a way that gives even the unskilled reader confidence to perform the task. Good instructions are written as commands: "Remove the cover." "Unsolder the four wires that connect to the power supply circuit cord." The same information can be conveyed in different words, but the tone of crispness and confidence would be missing.

Good instructions avoid ambiguous language. The difference between "the head bolts should be fairly tight" and "apply 90 pounds of torque to each head bolt" can mean the difference between a successful job and a disaster. The command to "take the cover off" is ambiguous and can lead to wasted time. "Lift the cover off" or "remove the cover by inserting a screwdriver into the narrow slot just above the fringe" tells the reader not only what to do but saves the time of figuring out how to do it. Precise commands are time-savers; they also prevent unnecessary damage to a sensitive mechanism through erroneous use of the improper tool or method.

Most instructions are written as a series of numbered steps, each step containing the necessary information for one procedure. It should be possible for a technician to read the instruction at a glance while working in cramped quarters. The following example combines numbered procedures with added explanatory and descriptive information to aid the technician who might be working on this particular device for the first time.

Access to the Display Unit Circuitry

For access to the circuits within the Terminal, remove the two screws on each side of the cover, and the two in back one inch from the top. Then lift the cover off.

Keyboard Information

Perform the following procedure to get at the keyboard circuits:

1. Remove the Terminal cover.

2. Remove the three larger screws from the top rear of the keyboard.

3. Remove the three screws from the bottom-front of the keyboard panel.

4. Pull the keyboard forward, then up and out as far as the cables will allow. Then turn the keyboard over.

5. The top surface of the circuit board can be reached by removing the eight screws that hold the keyboard assembly to the keyboard panel.

Key caps can be removed by pulling them directly away from the keyboard. Using a large pair of tweezers or a forceps is recommended.

Keys utilize reed switches whose solder contacts are accessible on the underside of the keyboard circuit board. Once the wires are unsoldered, the reeds can be extracted through the holes. Reverse the procedure for replacement.

Groups of keys are installed in assemblies that can be removed once the nuts are removed from the underside of the circuit board.[3]

These instructions keep the reader precisely located in space through directional terms such as "side," "top," "top rear," "bottom-front," "underside," "top surface." Words like these are essential to writing clear instructions and are a way of orienting the reader. Even though these instructions are written for skilled technicians, the writer offers suggestions on the proper tools for the job and also some potentially timesaving hints for those unfamiliar with this particular operation: "the reeds can be extracted through the holes." Notice the large amount of white space between each step in the process. Each instruction can be read at one quick glance without confusing it with the next step or the previous step.

---

[3] *Tektronix Service Manual* (Beaverton, Oregon: Tektronix, Inc., 1973), p. 35.

Operating instructions differ only slightly from assembly or disassembly instructions like those just discussed. Precise operating instructions are a vital part of any product that may be damaged by incorrect operating procedures or not utilized to full efficiency because the user does not understand the operating procedure. Operating instructions can also be effectively written as numbered steps, but frequently the user must understand not only what to do but why certain steps are necessary. The example that follows helps the user feel comfortable with the device and explains the reasons for following certain procedures:

Before turning the power on, set the LOCAL/ON LINE switch to LOCAL to isolate the 4023 from the computer. Set the DIRECT BUFFER switch to BUFFER. Set both auxiliary switches 1 and 2 OFF to prevent typed data from accidentally being sent to any auxiliary units that may be connected to the Terminal. The above switch settings completely isolate the 4023 from the components of your company's data-processing system. Set the DIRECT/BUFFER switch to BUFFER. You are now ready to turn on the power.

Turn the power on. Fig. 1–11 shows the location of the switch. Note the POWER indicator is lighted. After about 30 seconds, the cursor will appear in the upper left-hand corner of the display. This is the first character position of the first line and is called the HOME position. If the cursor does not appear after about one minute, turn up the BRIGHTNESS control (see Fig. 1–11) until most of the screen is dimly lit. Adjust the CONTRAST to make the cursor more clear, then turn down the brightness to your liking. With the cursor displayed, type in a few characters from the keyboard. Now, using the BRIGHTNESS and CONTRAST controls, adjust the display for a viewing level that is most comfortable for you.[4]

These operating instructions illustrate a useful stylistic device in writing good, clear instructions. Using phrases and clauses as sentence openers gets more information into your sentences. Sentence openers signal the stages in an operating procedure and show the relationship of these stages to each other. Notice how sentence openers contribute to a clear understanding of the procedures in the preceding example:

[4] Ibid., p. 9.

Before turning the power on, . . .
After about 30 seconds, . . .
If the cursor does not appear, . . .
With the cursor displayed, . . .

Operating instructions that involve manipulating switches identify the switches and controls exactly as they appear on the equipment. In our example capital letters identify the various switches and controls.

Whether writing assembly or disassembly instructions or operating procedures, be clear, concise, and definite. Even a nonspecialist should recognize that the instructions are easy to follow; the reader should feel that you knew exactly what you were doing when writing the instructions and should feel confident that following the instructions will produce the desired results.

Writing for Employment

The first major test of your writing skills will be in the search for a job. Even if you have a job lined up, very few people in any career field ever cease looking for a better job or seeking more responsibility in the job they have. This is healthy ambition, and the career person who becomes complacent in a job is probably not working at peak ability. Further, jobs change and people's interests change; many jobs that existed ten years ago can no longer be found. Very few people, after five or more years with an employer, are working on the job for which they were originally hired. Job seeking is a continuing process, and exploring new job possibilities contributes to your economic well-being and personal growth.

Competition for most job openings today is fierce; the recent college graduate often must compete for a job with people who have significant work experience beyond their education. All of your education, preparation, and fine personal qualities will be of little value unless you can sell them to an employer. Perhaps a few people can walk off the street into a company or an employer's office and receive an immediate interview or even a job; but, in reality, such good fortune rarely occurs. The telephone offers an efficient means of presenting your qualifications, if you can get past the secretary, but the most you can realistically hope for is a request for your résumé. The essential tools for finding a job are the résumé and covering letter, both of which demand careful and imaginative preparation.

The Résumé

A résumé is an objective presentation of the facts about you. In your attempt to reach the first positive stage in job hunting, the interview, the résumé is your personal advertisement. If it doesn't sell effectively, you will never have a sound opportunity to convince the employer that you are the right person for the position. Although most companies have their own employment application forms, these forms often do not offer the opportunity to include all your important personal qualifications for the job. A résumé, on the other hand, is prepared by you, so it emphasizes the most important facts about you, as well as demonstrating your abilities to evaluate, organize, and display vital information. In addition, a résumé can help in filling out the application form, because most of us can't remember offhand all the necessary dates and other facts often required. A well-prepared résumé also helps us take advantage of the information about job openings in the classified section of a newspaper. Because as many as half of the "Help Wanted" ads list only a post office box number, a good résumé is vital in gaining access to those employers.

A résumé allows an employer to see your qualifications at a glance and to decide from them whether you are worth interviewing. The résumé must be objective; long passages of persuasion or personal anecdotes interfere with a potential employer's appraisal of your qualifications. The effectiveness of the résumé depends on three qualities only: content (the facts about you), organization, and appearance.

The content of the résumé should give the employer specific information demonstrating your qualifications for the position. Much of the information included in a résumé will, of course, depend on your background; but the following items should be incorporated:

1. Heading.
2. Statement of job objective.
3. Details of work experience.
4. Educational background.

5. List of activities and organizations.
6. Personal data.
7. Names of references.

Heading

The heading should include a title (for example, Résumé, Data Sheet, Vita) and your name, current address, and phone number. If you are close to graduation or anticipate a move for some other reason, supply the future address and the date you can be reached there.

Career Objective

The statement of your career objective or personal goals is an extremely important part of the résumé. The career objective may have to be written to accord with a specific company's needs; but it should state clearly and concisely the job for which you are suited by training, temperament, and experience. The career objective should also indicate what your personal goals are for yourself: Are you interested in moving into management or sales? Are you interested in field work or research? Specific, clearly defined career objectives show your confidence in your own abilities and potential.

CAREER OBJECTIVE: Seek position in drafting with opportunity to move into design.

CAREER OBJECTIVE: Retail sales clerk with ultimate goal of becoming a buyer.

Details of Work Experience

List your most recent employment first, followed by previous employment in reverse chronological order. Include starting and leaving dates, the position you held, and the company's address. The salary you earned at these jobs should not be mentioned except indirectly to show promotion or advancement (the mention of a merit raise, for example). A brief description of your responsibilities and, of course, accomplishments in each job should also be included. If you have held many jobs with complex responsibilities, add an amplification page to provide more detail about your employment history. An employment entry like the following has little value for an employer:

EMPLOYMENT

| 1968 | Standard Oil of California |
| 1967 | A & P Supermarkets |

The lack of detail is suspicious. This person could have been employed as a gas station attendant or a grocery clerk; it is also possible that he or she held important executive responsibilities. In either case, the employer has to guess for himself or herself. The dates are vague, also; these may well have been summer jobs or temporary employment, or the movement from A & P to Standard Oil may represent professional advancement. Don't make the employer guess; supply adequate information and accurate beginning and ending dates for previous employment. The employer should also know why you left these previous jobs.

May 1968–September 1968	Joe's Standard Station
	615 Lake Drive
	Eugene, Oregon 97405
	Service Station Manager.
	Resigned to attend college.
May 1967–May 1968	A & P Supermarket
	220 River Road
	Corvallis, Oregon 97301
	Check-out clerk.
	Resigned to accept better position.

In some cases, the title you held in the job might be of more significance than the name of the company you worked for. If so, mention the position first and then the name of the company. But be consistent and follow the same pattern for the other entries. If a past employment experience has no relationship to the job for which you are applying, the duties of that job need not be specified in detail; but you can show how the job benefited you. For example, a job as a check-out clerk may have given you valuable experience in relating to customers and other employees, although the job itself contributed little to your training in a specialized technical field.

Educational Background

If you have an excellent educational record and employment has been sporadic or relatively unimportant, then reverse the order of these two categories. The further away an applicant is from school, the less educational detail is necessary. However, a recent graduate usually has nothing else but education to offer an employer; consequently, this area should be covered thoroughly, listing major and minor fields along with all subjects related to the field of interest. Grades and class standing can also be mentioned if they are better than average. Important courses should be listed by name, especially those directly related to the position you are seeking. Again use reverse chronological order, and include accurate dates of attendance or graduation. If you received a degree or certificate, name the degree and the field in which you received it.

EDUCATION

1976—	Certified as Medical Laboratory Technician.
1973—1975	Ferris State College, Big Rapids, Michigan. Associate degree in Medical Laboratory Technology.
1969—1973	Big Rapids High School; Big Rapids, Michigan.
Important courses	Inorganic Chemistry. (B+) Qualitative Analysis. (A−) Microorganisms and Man. (A) Medical Lab. Techniques—8 hrs. (A)

Activities and Organizations

This section will show the employer that you can work with others. Your participation in activities (sports, plays, fund-raising drives, community service work) and membership in organizations, especially well-known organizations, offer important evidence that you will be a desirable employee. You should mention any offices you have held or honors received in recognition of your fine work. This section, along with the section on personal data, helps the employer see you as an individual, as a person rather than a set of qualifications.

ACTIVITIES AND ORGANIZATIONS

President of Student Government, 1974–1975, Delta College.
Chairman, Student Entertainment

Committee, 1973–1974, Delta College.

Member National Honor Society, 1972–1973.

Varsity football, 1973–1975, Delta College (elected co-captain).

Active in Drama Club, Clare High School, 1970–1973.

Personal Data

Personal data introduce you to the employer. Much of this information has little bearing on your qualifications for a job, but employers and everyone else are interested in the person behind the qualifications. In a more practical vein, there may be something about you as a person that attracts an employer's attention and makes your résumé stand out slightly from the many others examined. Usually, personal data will include a physical description (age, height, and weight) and an honest statement about your health. You should also declare your marital status and the number of dependents you may have. Employers are interested to know whether you own a home and if you are willing to relocate. Details about your military service record, if you have one, should also be included here. Special hobbies or interests also have a place if you feel they show something important about you as a person.

PERSONAL DATA

Birth date:	December 10, 1946.
Place of birth:	Glasgow, Scotland.
Height:	6 feet, 1 inch.
Weight:	185 pounds.
Health:	Good.
Married:	Carol Barnett, September 16, 1968.
Children:	Elizabeth Anne, born May 15, 1970.
Residence:	Rent an Apartment; free to relocate.
Service:	USAR: three years' inactive duty until discharge.
Hobbies:	Music (play organ); collect antiques.

References

If you name people who are willing to provide references, list the name, title, and address of the references (perhaps a teacher in your field, an employer, and a personal acquaintance). Be certain to ask the people you wish to list if you may give their names as references. This is not only good manners, but it may also save you some embarrassment if anyone does not want to be a reference. References can be omitted from your résumé if you are answering a "blind" advertisement and do not want anyone involved with your present job to know you are seeking other employment. You may also not be sure whether you are truly interested in the job, and so do not want to have your references waste their time answering inquiries about you.

Appearance

The résumé should be balanced and uncrowded. You should make the headings stand out by capitalizing all the letters or underlining the heading. Use phrases rather than complete sentences; this allows more information to be given in limited space and lends a tone of objectivity to the résumé. A sample résumé follows to illustrate many of the points made in this section.

RÉSUMÉ

```
    Name:  Herbert John Nichols

 Address:  416 South Columbia
           Hadley, Massachusetts 01035

   Phone:  (616) 832-6061
```

Career <u>Objective</u>   Retail sales position with
                                        opportunity to move into
                                        management.

<u>Employment</u> <u>History</u>

    August 1974–present   Assistant Manager ''Coffee Cup''
                                        Restaurant, 620 Oak Street,
                                        Hadley, Massachusetts 01035
                                        Part-time work while attending
                                        college. Responsible for three
                                        employees and daily supply
                                        orders.

  June 1973–August 1974   Clerk
                                        Towne and Country Men's Store
                                        213 Mecosta Avenue
                                        Rodney, Michigan 49201

Gained valuable experience in
dealing with the public.

Educational Background

September 1974–present   Hopkins College
                                      Northhampton, Massachusetts 01035

                                      Will receive B.S. degree in
                                      Marketing, November, 1976.

1970–1973   West Shore Community College
                                      Ludington, Michigan 48211

                                      Associate of Arts degree

1963–1967   Morley–Stanwood High School
                                      Morley, Michigan 49301

Important Courses   Consumer Behavior (A)
                                      Salesmanship (A)
                                      Principles of Advertising (B)
                                      Retail Management (B)
                                      Purchasing (A)

Activities and Organizations   Vice–president of Student
                                      Government, Hopkins College,
                                      1975–1976.

                                      Member, Society for the
                                      Advancement of Management,
                                      Hopkins College, 1974–1975.

                                      Varsity football team, Hopkins
                                      College, 1974–1975.

Personal Data

Birthplace: January 10, 1949.

Place of birth: Detroit, Michigan.

Height: 5 feet, 10 inches.

Weight: 190 pounds.

Health: Excellent.

Married: Julia Stevens, June 1976.

Children: None.

Residence: Rent apartment; free to
                                      relocate.

Service: United States Army, 1967–1970;
                                      honorable discharge.

Hobbies and Interests   Individual and group sports;
                                      fishing, hunting.

References   Available on request.

The Covering Letter

Accompanying your résumé should be a *covering letter* that introduces your résumé and gets the employer to read it. The covering letter can show the employer a great deal about you, your interest in the job, and your qualifications for the job. The covering letter relates your special qualifications to the demands of the job in question. The organization and content of your covering letter will vary with circumstances and should change to suit each job opportunity for which you apply. Nothing could be more devastating to your chances for a job than a form letter designed to cover every situation.

The letter of application has perhaps more potential for affecting your life than any other you'll ever write. Only the good letter can survive the competition for jobs even in prosperous times. Many "Help Wanted" ads bring literally hundreds of responses. Under these circumstances the advertiser reads all of them very rapidly, selects the best of the lot for serious consideration, and disposes of the rest. A good letter of application will insure that you are among the applicants given serious consideration.

Before writing such a letter, analyze the position open and ask yourself if you have the qualifications for it. Recent college or community college graduates with little or no work experience feel at a disadvantage in applying to employers who specify experience as a necessary qualification. A good covering letter can emphasize qualities that compensate for lack of specific work experience. Put yourself in the position of the employer. What type of person would you hire for the job? What qualities would make up for lack of work experience? In this case, the covering letter relies on the techniques of persuasion to overcome your disadvantage. Little can be gained by lying or avoiding the fact you lack experience; the best policy calls for an honest, direct approach.

```
Mr. Joseph E. Hastings
Hastings Machine Shop
Beaverton, Oregon 97001

Dear Mr. Hastings:

    The position of managerial assistant now available at Hastings
Machine Shop fits my personal qualifications and educational
background. One of your former employees, Mr. Frank Cary,
suggested I seek an interview for the position.
```

I do not have the two years' machine shop experience your ad in the <u>Gazette</u> asks for, but I have other qualifications that give evidence of my ability to do the job. My first two years of college include many trade-technical courses with an emphasis on machinist training. The sophisticated facilities at Rock Creek Community College simulated actual machine shop conditions. I transferred to the School of Business and will receive a B.S. degree in Marketing at the June commencement. This combination of practical training and business education has prepared me to assume a responsible position in a company such as yours. The offices I have held in student government at Rock Creek show my ability to get along with others and to assume a position of leadership.

I would appreciate the opportunity for an interview. Your office can reach me by telephoning 353-6000.

Sincerely,

Curtis Cole

Assuming you have the proper qualifications for a job, how do you write the type of letter that gains attention?

1. Have a realistic conception of the sort of competition your letter will meet.
2. Bear in mind that the purpose of your letter is to *get an interview*.
3. Think of the letter as one in which you are trying to *sell your services*. Therefore, you should use the techniques of sales letters in your application letter. By that it is meant that you should design your letter to
   a. Attract the reader's attention.
   b. Create a desire for the product or service.
   c. Convince the reader that the product or service is the best of its kind.
   d. Motivate action.

The opening lines of your covering letter are crucial. The first few lines demonstrate your interest in a specific job and in a specific employer. If at all possible, establish some contact with a particular employer. Suitable contacts range from having grown up near the company to knowing someone who works for the company to reference to a published notice of an opening.

Attract *attention* by making a general statement of the services you can render or naming an outstanding qualification you possess. There are three types of openings you can use to get attention:

1. The *Summary* Opening:

Because of my three years' experience as an engineer for the White Company, I feel I can qualify for the position which you advertised in this morning's *Herald Tribune*.

Avoid the colorless opening:

I would like to be considered as an applicant for a position of laboratory technician with your firm.

Be surer to avoid such openings as the following:

I happened to be reading the *Minneapolis Tribune* and saw your advertisement for a secretary.

Some authorities suggest that the covering letter avoid beginning too many sentences with *I*. Mentioning the employer or company first shows consideration and helps give the letter a more objective tone.

2. The *Name* Opening:

A *name* opening mentions the name of a person who has told you about the job. This opening is effective because the use of a person's name constitutes a recommendation by him or her.

Mr. James Johnson, one of your customers, has told me you are in need of another draftsman for your design department. Mr. Johnson knows my record as a student in the Acme Trade School and was my immediate supervisor during two years of summer employment as a draftsman.

3. The *Challenging Question* Opening:

Opening a cover letter with a challenging question has, perhaps, become a slightly overused technique to attract attention. It should be used with care and reserved for applications submitted for an unadvertised position. If a company has not advertised a specific position, the opening question technique can immediately introduce an employer to your outstanding qualities.

Can your company use someone with 12 years' experience in designing specialized heating and air-conditioning systems for office buildings?

Create desire and conviction of superiority. Make detailed statements that amplify the quality featured in the first lines. Present your qualifications in terms of how they can be of most use to the prospective employer. Emphasize those aspects of your background that you feel the employer would be most interested in. For a student or newly graduated person, these would probably fall in the following order: (1) course of study, (2) grades, (3) extracurricular activities, and (4) work experience. Samples of work may be offered and outstanding accomplishments cited.

Motivate action. Suggest emphatically that the prospective employer respond or *act* in some way.

> May I come in for an interview? You may reach me at the address or telephone number given at the top of my personal record sheet.
>
> May I show you actual examples of my work? Just sign the enclosed card, and I shall call for an appointment at your convenience.

Never write an employment letter in terms of

> How badly I need work.
> How intensely I dislike my present job.
> How much I would like to work for a company like yours.

Write it in terms of

> *What I can do for you.*

Here is an effective opening paragraph:

> Mr. Joe Weber of your technical writing department informed me recently that a technical writing position is available at Tektronix. My B.S. degree in engineering and minor in English provide excellent background for a technical writing position. Working as an assistant to Mr. Weber last summer familiarized me with the demands of the job.

The covering letter should not repeat the detailed information contained in the résumé, but the middle paragraphs must convince the employer that you can do the job. Put another way, the covering letter gives you the chance to show the relationship between the career objective stated on the résumé and your qualifications.

Throughout the covering letter establish a tone of self-confidence, demonstrating your assurance that you can do the job. Try to be concise; because you are, in effect, doing a selling job, the tendency is to include too much detail. Analyze to the best of your knowledge the individual situation, and use the middle section of your letter to focus on these qualities most appealing to a specific employer.

I have examined several of the service and maintenance manuals relating to Tektronix products. My educational background in engineering enables me to understand the technical detail. My article on solar power in the July 1976 issue of *Consulting Engineer* demonstrates my ability to write clearly and effectively. My technical expertise will contribute to the satisfaction of Tektronix customers who rely on service and maintenance manuals.

In the final paragraph of the covering letter the applicant asks for an interview and tries to motivate the employer to give one. A tone of sincere interest in the job and an indication of your availability for an interview form an effective closing paragraph.

Tektronix is a growing, progressive company, and I would like to grow with it. I have many samples of my writing that are available on request, but I would like to discuss them with you personally, Mr. Eppick. My home is nearby, so I am available for an interview at your convenience.

The covering letters following can serve as models:

330 Fourth Street
Big Rapids, Michigan 49307

Mr. Richard Williams
P.O. Box 542
Reed City, Michigan 49201

Dear Mr. Williams:

Your recent advertisement in the Detroit Free Press for a public health official in Reed City interests me very much. My training and experience qualify me for such a position as my résumé indicates.

I will receive the BS degree in health administration from Ferris State College in June 1976. While working for this degree, I organized, then administered, the Planned Parenthood office in Big Rapids, Michigan. This office serves both students and citizens; our clientele averaged three hundred per month for three years. My interest in the public health field began with my participation in several flood relief projects in neighboring states, work that I found both challenging and satisfying. I had the privilege of working with public health officials in Pottstown, Pennsylvania, to establish emergency medical facilities and disease control procedures. This experience motivated me to pursue a career in public health administration.

I have demonstrated the ability to organize and work with people, and my training has equipped me to be an effective administrator in the public health field. I am available for an interview on any afternoon to discuss the contribution I can make to Reed City's public health program.

Sincerely,

Joseph Case

411-D Hillcrest Village
Freeman, Illinois 60592
January 29, 1975

Mr. George Rouman
Calhoun County Health Department
Coldwater, Michigan 48712

Dear Sir:

Mr. Jack Chapman, departmental head of Environmental Quality at Southwestern State College, has informed me that you have an opening for a sanitarian. I feel my training and experience in this field fully qualify me to apply for this position.

In May 1975, I shall complete a Bachelor of Science degree at Southwestern State. The Southwestern Environmental Quality provides a thorough grounding in sanitary science, public health, and environmental control, as well as training in supervisory and administrative functions.

In order to pay for my college education, I have worked during most of my high school and college years. In doing so, I have held two jobs in health-allied fields and was also a volunteer at a public clinic for one summer. This experience has provided me with qualifications that will enable me to work in harmony with others.

For two years I participated in intramural athletics and have held office in the student government. As an athlete most of my life, I have learned the importance of competition and a winning attitude.

I am a member of the National Environmental Health Association and the Southwestern Environmental Health Association.

If you have any questions about my capabilities, I would be happy to answer them. I can free myself at any time for an interview at your convenience. Please call TW 3-8896, or write me at the above address.

Sincerely,

Sally E. Harmon

630 Clark Street
West Bend, Massachusetts
May 14, 1975

Mr. Harold Griffith
Bright Wholesale Distributors
14 East Polk Street
University Heights, Massachusetts 02109

Dear Mr. Griffith:

My ten years' experience as a salesman for the Green Wholesale
Grocery Company should qualify me for a position as sales
manager with your company.

I have traveled in western Massachusetts for the past six
years, and my wide acquaintance among grocers and food buyers
in that section should be valuable to you in marketing the new
line of Premex Foods you are introducing. My record as a
salesman has been excellent, as my resume will show; as a sales
manager, I could use my own experience in training personnel
rapidly but efficiently.

As the enclosed personal record indicates, I am a college
graduate and have taken several graduate courses in marketing
and sales organization. I am widely known among businessmen in
this city, for I have been active in many civic and fraternal
organizations.

May I have an interview to answer any questions you might
have? You can reach me by calling OXford 3-1500.

                                        Sincerely,

                                        Robert F. Bellinger

Enclosure

EXERCISES

Write a letter of application setting forth your own qualifications for
a position that you might reasonably apply for. Let it be assumed that
you definitely know an opening exists and that the reader knows little
if anything about you until he or she reads your letter.

In stating your qualifications, assume you are about to complete or
have just completed the courses you are taking. Mention any experience
with summer jobs, part-time employment, full-time employment, and
so on, that you might have had. (You can *make up* a summer job or
part-time or full-time job for this letter.)

V

A Glossary of Frequent Errors

AGREEMENT OF SUBJECT AND VERB

ETTING the verb to agree with the subject in a sentence can be troublesome at times. Some simple rules can help you avoid spoiling your writing or speech by using the wrong verb form. To help you make the right decisions about verb forms, refresh your memory by examining the forms of the present tense of a regular English verb:

PERSON	SINGULAR	PLURAL
First	I work	We work
Second	You work	You work
Third	He works	They work

Only one of these verb forms is not like the others—*works*. This verb form, third person singular, has an -*s* ending, which the others do not have. The -*s* form of the verb is used with a third person *singular* subject. Notice that this is the reverse of the situation whereby many nouns form the *plural* by adding an -*s* ending (*duties, machines, pulleys*).

The -*s* form of the verb is used when the subject is any singular pronoun except *I* and *you,* as in

He *works.*
She *delivers.*
It *runs.*
Each *uses* his or her own tools.
Each of the mechanics *uses* his or her own tools.
Everyone *depends* on skilled technicians.
Neither of the men *admits* his mistake.
Neither of the male contractors *admits* his mistake.

Of course, the -*s* form of the verb is also used with a singular *noun.*

His job *involves* electronics.
This product *demands* promotion.
One error in calculation *causes* a series of mistakes.

Forms of the verbs *be, have,* and *do* also take the *-s* ending with a singular subject in the third person.

The solar *cell is* simple, light, and reliable.
The nineteenth *century was* an era of great progress in medicine.
This cassette *player has* a piece of rubber underneath the tape head.
Everybody *was* urged to offer a solution.

Looking back at the forms of the verb *work* listed earlier, notice that the plural forms of the verb have no endings, but consist of the bare verb—*work.* In the present tense, verb forms without endings are used with plural subjects:

The *carpenters promise* completion by the end of May.
Production *workers* often *go* right to supervisors and *skip* their immediate superiors.
Some of the men *refuse* to work overtime.

The plural forms of *be, have,* and *do* are often neglected; and the result is substandard constructions such as *they was, the man have,* or *it do.* Here are some examples of these verb forms with plural subjects. Notice that in each case the form of *be, have,* or *do* is used as an *auxiliary* with another verb (*are made, have become, do hold*).

The *fasteners are* made of aluminum alloy.
Fluorescent *lamps have* become the preferred type of lighting in kitchen-ceiling and undercabinet fixtures.
Air *conditioners* for truck campers *do* hold promise as a new product line.

There are nine situations in which many people mismatch singulars and plurals. If you can master these nine situations, you can avoid most subject-verb agreement problems.

1. Compound subjects joined by *and* require a plural verb regardless of the number of each subject.

   The low down payment and low interest rate *make* the house a good buy.

2. Sometimes a compound subject names one company or object that is regarded as a unit. In this case, use the singular verb.

Liggett and Myers *is* a very large company.
The block and tackle *hangs* from the ceiling of his garage.

3. Words and phrases that come between the subject and the verb do not influence the form of the verb. You must be certain the verb agrees with its subject, not with intervening words regardless of their number.

> The *duties* of a salesman *are* described in this brochure.
> *Difficulties* with maintenance *require* modifications in the engine.
> *Methods* of application *have* improved tremendously.

4. Clauses that begin with relative pronouns (*who, which, that*) often cause problems with agreement. Remember that relative pronouns replace another word in the sentence, and this word is considered the subject of the verb.

> My father has two *motorcycles* in his garage that *have* won several motocross championships.
> Herman Bigelow is one of the *auditors* who *were* called in to examine our books.

5. Another source of agreement problems is sentences like this one. The word *sentences* almost compels us to use *are* instead of *is*, but the subject of the sentence is the singular word *source*.

6. Sentences that begin with *there* can cause agreement difficulties. *There* has no number; it is simply a function word that gets the sentence started. In *there* sentences the subject follows the verb.

> There *are* three new *products* on the market.
> There *are* a distributor, a generator, and a toolbox missing from the supply room.

7. Collective nouns can be either singular or plural, depending on whether you are referring to a group as a whole or to the individuals in the group.

> A number of people *have* offered to help the flood victims.
> The Personnel Department *is* not functioning efficiently.

8. Pronouns that refer to individual units take a singular verb. The most common are *nobody, somebody, everybody, anybody, either, neither, everyone, everything, each,* and *every.*

> Each *wants* his or her own way.
> Each of the students *wants* his or her own way.
> Everyone *hopes* to go to the party.
> Neither of the performers *is* nervous.
> Either of the vehicles *is* satisfactory.

9. If two or more subjects are joined by *or* or *nor,* the verb agrees with the subject closest to it.

> Either the poor road conditions or his poor driving *is* at fault.
> Neither Bill nor Harry *has* the answer.

Antecedents: Pronoun Reference

Pronouns are rather harmless looking little words, but their misuse can bring chaos to an otherwise clear paragraph or sentence. A pronoun must have a clear antecedent; in other words, there should be no question as to which noun the pronoun replaces.

1. Pronouns must have definite antecedents. Here is an example of faulty pronoun reference:

> The humidifier has two pulleys. *It* must be oiled before operating *it.*

The pronoun *it* is especially susceptible to vague and careless usage. The preceding direction could cause a great deal of confusion, for the first *it* seems to refer to the humidifier itself and not to the pulleys. Rewritten for clarity, the sentence could avoid pronouns altogether without awkwardness:

> The pulleys must be oiled before operating the humidifier.
> or
> *They* must be oiled before operating *it.*

2. Many writers depend too much on the indefinite *it* to begin sentences, as in

> It is uncertain when he will arrive.

The first position in the sentence can nearly always be filled by a noun to make the sentence much more concise:

> His time or arrival is uncertain.

3. Most cases of faulty pronoun reference are the result of the pronoun's having no definite antecedent to refer to, as in this example:

> Five safety experts were hired to test the new aircraft design. *They* have a maximum speed of 1,500 miles per hour.

The confusion here is amusing, but rather embarrassing to the writer, who let his thoughts get ahead of his pen. A good rule of thumb is to use nouns rather than pronouns as much as possible:

> Five safety experts were hired to test the new aircraft. The new planes have a maximum speed of 1,500 miles per hour.

4. The pronouns *this* and *which* are the occasion for much vague and unclear writing. These words are often used without a definite antecedent, sometimes with this result:

> Thompson suggested a new assembly procedure. *This* made it more efficient.

Writers who do not make the effort to summarize their ideas or look for a more precise word will use *this* several times in a paragraph. As a result, the reader is often uncertain as to precisely what the writer means or else has to stop for a moment to figure out the meaning of a sentence like the one in our example. Usually, the confusion can easily be avoided:

> Thompson suggested a new assembly procedure. His suggested changes made it more efficient.

The pronoun *which* is often tacked on to the end of a sentence to refer to a preceding idea. Once again, this practice can lead to imprecise writing:

Joe purchased new speakers for his stereo system, *which* improved the sound quality a great deal.

The reader must pause for a moment to decide on the exact antecedent for *which*. Again, a little care on the writer's part can eliminate any possibility of confusion:

Joe purchased new speakers for his stereo system; as a result, the sound quality has improved a great deal.

or

Joe purchased new speakers for his stereo system; the new components have improved the sound quality a great deal.

Fragments

Fragments are pieces of a sentence presented in the form of a complete sentence, that is, with a capital letter at the beginning and a period at the end. A habitual use of sentence fragments destroys the quality of writing much as frequent misspellings ruin otherwise fine work. Fragments assume many forms, but there are five main types:

1. Failing to provide the subject or the complete verb in a sentence causes fragments:

   FRAGMENT: divided into four sections
   FRAGMENT: the foreman angered by the breakdown

Fragments of this type can be made into complete sentences simply by adding the missing words:

The land was divided into four sections.
The foreman was angered by the breakdown.

2. Relative pronouns are often substituted for the subject of a sentence; this procedure results in a fragment.

   FRAGMENT: The supervisor made a suggestion.
               Which solved the problem.
   FRAGMENT: The company has moved to Peterborough.
               Where the market potential is greater.
   FRAGMENT: The executive committee selected a new vice-president.
               Who was the last man to leave the meeting.

Relative pronouns introduce dependent clauses that must be joined to a complete sentence in clear relationship with an antecedent. The problem is easy to correct:

> The supervisor made a suggestion that solved the problem.
> The company has moved to Peterborough, where the market potential is greater.
> The executive committee selected a new vice-president, who was the last man to leave the meeting.

Many fragments are a result of failure to complete a sentence containing a dependent clause headed by a relative pronoun.

FRAGMENT: The heart, which is a hollow, muscular organ.
CORRECTION: The heart, which is a hollow, muscular organ, pumps blood to the body.
FRAGMENT: The physical handicaps *that were the cause of his dismissal.*
CORRECTION: The physical handicaps that were the cause of his dismissal could have been improved through therapy.

3. Subordinating conjunctions introduce dependent clauses that must be linked to a complete sentence. A common type of sentence fragment results from careless use of subordinating conjunctions like *when, while, although, if, as, such as.*

FRAGMENT: The company's profits are decreasing steadily. *Although sales are higher than ever before.*
CORRECT: The company's profits are decreasing steadily, although sales are higher than ever before.
FRAGMENT: More and more companies will be faced with the problem of energy rationing. *As America's natural gas and fuel oil sources continue to dwindle.*
CORRECT: More and more companies will be faced with the problem of energy rationing as America's natural gas and fuel oil resources continue to dwindle. .
CORRECT: As America's natural gas and fuel oil resources continue to dwindle, more and more companies will be faced with the problem of energy rationing.
FRAGMENT: The salesman should see that someone is available to assist the consultant in correcting the problem. *If the equipment does malfunction.*

CORRECT: If the equipment does malfunction, the salesman should see that someone is available to assist the consultant in correcting the problem.

4. Word structures formed around verbs ending in *-ing* (*being, working, selling, producing*) are sometimes allowed to stand alone as sentence fragments. These fragments can also be joined to a complete sentence, but some care must be taken in deciding where to put them. The word *being* is probably one of the most abused words in the English language in this regard.

FRAGMENT: The same *being* true of service industries.
CORRECT: The same is true of service industries.
FRAGMENT: The makeup line will be capable of delivering 60 million gallons of water per day to the reservoir. *Consisting of 18,000 feet of 60-inch pipe.*
CORRECT: The makeup line, consisting of 18,000 feet of 60-inch pipe, will be capable of delivering 60 million gallons of water per day to the reservoir.
FRAGMENT: As with other engineering work, a strong contract is the best defense against client problems. *Clearly assigning the various responsibilities to the parties involved.*
CORRECT: As with other engineering work, a strong contract, clearly assigning the various responsibilities to the parties involved, is the best defense against client problems.

5. Prepositional phrases are often written as complete sentences, especially when they are fairly long and complex.
FRAGMENT: Haskell has had a very successful career as a consultant. *First in New York and then in Los Angeles.*
CORRECT: Haskell has had a very successful career as a consultant, first in New York and then in Los Angeles.

Misplaced Modifiers

Modifiers (words, phrases, or clauses used to change, limit, or qualify the meaning of other words) should be placed as close as possible to the words they modify. A misplaced modifier can completely change or obscure the intended meaning of a sentence. Some problems with misplaced modifiers are the result of carelessness on the part of the writer, whereas others reflect the writer's uncertainty about what he or she wants to say.

1. Adverbs can easily be misplaced in a sentence if the writer does not take care. Notice the different meanings created simply by moving the adverb *only* in the following sentences:

> He works on Saturday *only*.
> He *only* works on Saturday.
> He works *only* on Saturday.

An apparently insignificant placement of a word in a sentence can have serious consequences. Consider the following sentence, which might be part of an urgent memo:

> I need the parts for the generator that broke down *today*.

The writer's message is unclear: Did the generator break down today, or are the parts needed today? Simply moving the word *today* causes the message to take on a different meaning:

> I need the parts *today* for the generator that broke down.

2. Misplaced phrases and clauses not only confuse the meaning of a sentence but result in embarrassment for the writer. As a general rule, phrases and clauses should be placed as close as possible to what they modify without creating unnecessary awkwardness.

MISPLACED MODIFIER: The cords are pulled intact from the walls, *each weighing about 1,000 pounds*. (The walls do not weigh 1,000 pounds; the cords do.)

CLEAR: The cords, each weighing about 1,000 pounds, are pulled intact from the walls.

or

CLEAR: Each weighing about 1,000 pounds, the cords are pulled intact from the walls.

MISPLACED MODIFIER: *By talking to employers in the Boston area,* the information summarized in the following graph was developed by a research group. (The information obviously did not do the talking. Revision of this sentence involves changing the main sentence or moving the modifying phrase to the end of the sentence, which would sound awkward.)

CLEAR: By talking to employers in the Boston area, a research group developed the information summarized in the following graph.

MISPLACED MODIFIER: The factory resumed operation after a monthlong strike on July 1. (The confusion here can be remedied by simply moving the prepositional phrase to another position in the sentence.)

CLEAR: The factory resumed operation on July 1 after a monthlong strike.

Parallelism

Parallelism means keeping the various parts of a sentence structure in balance. Similar ideas demand similar structures. Failure to maintain parallelism creates rough reading and may also place undue emphasis on one idea at the expense of others. Similar parts of a sentence should be expressed in parallel form.

1. Items in a series should be kept parallel:

NOT PARALLEL: His duties include *maintenance* of equipment and *to keep* the costs down.

PARALLEL: His duties include *maintenance* of equipment and *cost control.*

NOT PARALLEL: It should not be used *in concrete* where sulfate resistance is needed, *where* magnesium or aluminum will be contacted, or *mixed* with prestressed concrete.

PARALLEL: It should not be used in concrete where sulfate resistance is needed, in concrete that will be in contact with magnesium or aluminum, or in prestressed concrete.

NOT PARALLEL: There will be major demands upon engineers *to assist* and *advising* in identifying unsafe buildings.

PARALLEL: There will be major demands upon engineers *to assist* and *advise* in identifying unsafe buildings.

2. Parts of compound sentences should be parallel in structure, and compound verbs should be parallel in form.

NOT PARALLEL: Production workers often *take* problems right to their supervisors and *skipped* their immediate superiors. (The verbs are not parallel in form. One is in the present tense, whereas the other is in the past tense.)

PARALLEL: Production workers often take problems right to their supervisors and skip their immediate superiors.

Passive Voice

Much of your writing will concern work completed or a job being performed. This type of writing tends to rely a great deal on the passive voice, which often results in a dull, lifeless writing style. Sentences written in the active voice are much more direct, interesting, and lively. Although you cannot avoid the passive voice at times, you should be aware of opportunities to revise your passive sentences into active ones. Each of the following sentences contains the same message:

PASSIVE: The road was repaired by the construction crew.
ACTIVE: The construction crew repaired the road.

In the passive construction the subject acted upon (the road) comes first in the sentence, whereas the construction crew, who did the job, is mentioned last in a prepositional phrase. This is the reverse of the way things actually happened. Notice that the passive construction uses more words than the active; good writing uses as few words as possible to make a point. Passive constructions contain a helping verb (*is, are, was, were*) and a prepositional phrase, often beginning with *by* or *with*. Notice the difference between the following pairs of sentences:

ACTIVE: The house was damaged by the flood.
ACTIVE: The flood damaged the house.
PASSIVE: The old ship was covered with rust.
PASSIVE: Rust covered the old ship.

Many writers fall into the habit of relying too much on the verb *to be* even in active constructions. The verb carries much of a sentence's meaning and action, so use good, active verbs instead of *is* or *are* or *was* or *were*—these verbs add little to a sentence's message.

ORIGINAL: Fluorocarbons are harmful to the earth's ozone layer.
REVISED: Fluorocarbons damage the earth's ozone layer.

Point of View

A writer who suddenly and without reason changes *tense* or *person* or *number* is shifting what is called *point of view*. Such shifts should be avoided because they make it difficult to read and understand the writer's thought.

TENSE
INCORRECT: We *finished* our homework and *turn* on the radio.
CORRECT: We *finished* our homework and *turned* on the radio.

In the first example, the tense is changed from past to present incorrectly. In the second example, only the past tense is used.

PERSON
INCORRECT: *One* must remember to be careful, or *you* will have an accident.
CORRECT: *One* must remember to be careful, or *he* (or *she*) will have an accident.

or

You must remember to be careful, or *you* will have an accident.

In the first example, the person is changed abruptly from third to second. This is confusing. In the second example, only the third person is used; and, in the third example, the second person is used consistently.

NUMBER

INCORRECT: *Each* boy carried *their* own books.

CORRECT: *Each* boy carried *his* own books.

In the first example, the number shifts incorrectly from the singular *each* to the plural *their*. In the second example, the singular *each* agrees in number with the singular *his*.

USAGE PROBLEMS

A, an

Use the article *a* before words beginning with a consonant sound, even if it is a vowel: *a useful product*. The article *an* is used with words beginning with a vowel sound: *an hourly wage; an optimistic projection*.

Accept, except

The word *accept* means to receive something, such as a gift or an honor, voluntarily: They decided to *accept* the report.

Accept is used many times in the context of something being attached to or inserted into something else: The hopper will not *accept* metal objects.

Except is often confused with *accept*. *Except* means to leave out or exclude: The committee accepted every proposition *except* the last.

Advice, advise

Advice is a noun; *advise* is a verb: The lawyer *advised* the strikers to follow the *advice* of the union leadership.

Affect, effect

Affect is used as a verb meaning "to influence": Heat *affects* the viscosity of oil.

Effect is a noun in its most common meaning of result: The *effects* of poor maintenance are expensive. *Effect* can also be a verb meaning "to bring about": The new foreman *effected* several changes in procedure.

Alot

The term *alot* has crept into the vocabulary of many writers in place of *a lot*, which is two words. *Alot* is not an English word.

All ready, already

Already is an adverb meaning "previously." *All ready* means "completely prepared."

Construction has *already* begun.
The new engine is *all ready* for testing.

All together, altogether

Altogether means "wholly," "completely," "entirely." *All together* is a phrase meaning "in a group."

Our sales representatives contacted twelve companies *altogether*.
Our sales representatives were *all together* at the meeting this morning.

Allusion, illusion

Allusion means "to make reference to" or "mention briefly": The personnel manager made an *allusion* to my lack of experience.

An *illusion* is something that deceives or creates a false impression:

Though ill, she was able to give an *illusion* of health.

Alright, all right

Alright is often incorrectly used instead of the accepted form, which is *all right*.

Among, between

Among refers to more than two persons or things; *between* implies only two.

The profits were divided *among three* companies.

Between is always followed by *and*, not *or:* The choice is *between* quality and quantity.

Amount, number

Amount refers to the quantity of a thing viewed as a whole. *Number* refers to individual, countable units.

The *amount* of gasoline that leaked from this pump exceeds forty gallons.
A *number* of new devices have been developed to make this operation more efficient.

As, like

As should be used to introduce clauses.

INCORRECT: The pump does not operate *like* it should.
CORRECT: The pump does not operate *as* it should.

As a method of

The phrase *as a method of* is often used in connection with a gerund, creating a needlessly wordy construction:

> WORDY: The factory uses sand filtration *as a method of* wastewater treatment.
>
> BETTER: The factory uses sand filtration for wastewater treatment.

At about, at around

The expressions *at about* and *at around* are unnecessary and can result in vague writing.

> INEXACT: Shut down the boiler *at about* 300 degrees.
>
> EXACT: Shut down the boiler at 305 degrees.

Awhile, a while

The words *awhile* and *a while* should not be confused. *Awhile* is an adverb, as in

> She read *awhile* before going to sleep.

A while consists of an article and a noun, as in

> She read for *a while* before going to sleep.

Bad, badly

The words *bad* and *badly* are often confused. *Bad* is an adjective, as in

> The patient felt *bad*.

Badly is an adverb, as in

> The applicant performed *badly* in the interview.

Before . . . first

Using *before* and *first* together produces needless redundancy.

> REDUNDANT: *Before* he left for work, he *first* called the phone company.
>
> BETTER: Before he left for work, he called the phone company.

Being, being that, being as

Try to avoid constructions involving the word *being*. The result is usually a clumsy or redundant sentence.

> *Being* left without a job, he visited the employment office.

Being should be omitted from the preceding sentence. *Being that* and *being as* frequently replace *because:*

INCORRECT: *Being that* he has a Ph.D., he thinks he knows everything.
CORRECT: Because he has a Ph.D., he thinks he knows everything.

Beside, besides

The words *beside* and *besides* should be distinguished. *Beside* is a preposition and indicates position, as in

He stood *beside* her at the dance.

Besides is an adverb with the meaning of "in addition," as in

We played checkers and other games *besides.*

Between each, between every

Between implies two items; so it should not be joined to the singular adjectives *each* and *every.*

INCORRECT: Fireproof insulation was installed *between each* wall.
CORRECT: Fireproof insulation was installed *between* the walls.

Between you and I

The construction *between you and I* is always wrong. *Between* is a preposition requiring the objective case: *between you and me.*

Burst, bust, busted

Bust and *busted* are incorrect forms of the verb *to burst.* The principal parts of *burst* are *burst, burst, burst.*

INCORRECT: That line has *bursted* five times.
CORRECT: That line has *burst* five times.

But that, but what

The expressions *but that* and *but what* are clumsily used for *that,* particularly following the word *doubt.*

CLUMSY: We don't doubt but that your company can do the job.
IMPROVED: We don't doubt that your company can do the job.

Can, may

The following distinction between *can* and *may* should be observed. *Can* refers to ability, whereas *may* indicates both possibility and permission.

Yes, you *may* go to the dance.

I *may* not be able to drive you to the airport tomorrow.

He *can* play tennis better than anyone I know.

Informally, however, *can* is sometimes used to express permission, as in

Yes, you *can* go to the dance.

Cause, reason

The words *cause* and *reason* do not have similar meanings. A cause produces an effect:

The frequent power failures *caused* a decrease in production.

A *reason* is someone's motive for action:

A prolonged illness was the *reason* for his resignation.

Compliment, complement

The words *compliment* and *complement* sound alike but have different meanings. *Compliment* means "to praise," as in

I *compliment* you on a job well done.

Complement means "to complete or make perfect." It is used in contexts such as

Radial tires will *complement* your car's performance.

Continual, continuous

The words *continual* and *continuous* differ slightly in meaning, but the difference is significant for accurate writing. *Continual* means "at intervals":

The technician has had *continual* problems with that display unit.

Continuous carries the sense of "uninterrupted":

The unit emits a *continuous* buzz when operating.

Correspond to, correspond with

Correspond to means that one thing matches another:

The bearings on the new model *correspond to* those on the old.

Correspond with means to exchange letters with someone.

Facet

The word *facet* is so overused that it should be avoided entirely.

Farther, further

Farther is best used when physical distance is involved; *further* covers most other situations.

Denver is *farther* than St. Louis.
The inspector made no *further* comments.

Factor

The word *factor* finds its way into so many sentences that we tend to forget that it means "contributing to a result." Consequently, the phrase *contributing factor* is redundant because a factor is already contributing.

Fewer, fewer in number, less

Fewer in number is a redundant phrase because *fewer* already implies number. Whereas *fewer* denotes number, *less* concerns value and amount.

Fewer people came to the party than had been expected.
It takes *less* time than you think.

Hopefully

The word *hopefully* is too often used incorrectly, as in

Hopefully, our team will win Saturday.
Hopefully, I won't have to go.

An example of the correct use of the adverb *hopefully* is

He looked up *hopefully* when he heard the phone ring.

Imply, infer

The words *imply* and *infer* are often confused; *infer* is often used when *imply* is correct. To *imply* is to give or leave an implication; to *infer* is to draw out or take an implication.

The memo *implied* the parts had been ordered.
Because the parts were not in the stock room, we *inferred* they had not been ordered.

Irregardless

The word *irregardless* is a mistake for *regardless, irrespective,* or *nevertheless.*

Its, It's

Its is the possessive form, whereas *it's* is a contraction for *it is*.

> The full-scale range of an ammeter is a measure of *its* sensitivity.
> *It's* time we received a progress report.

Lie, lay

If you mean stretching yourself out somewhere for a nap or some other purpose, *lie* is the right word. *Lay* means to set something else down.

> Tell the dog to *lie* down.
> Don't *lay* that heavy package on the table.

Number

A general rule for dealing with numbers is to write out numbers of two digits or less and use numerals for numbers of more than two digits.

> More than *twenty* men waited for their orders.
> There are *365* days in a year.

However, it is wise to use numerals when decimal points are involved or when the material is highly precise or technical:

> A *15*-ampere fuse will allow *15* amperes of current to flow through it.
> The inductive reactance is *676.8 ohms*.

It is not considered good form to begin a sentence with a numeral.

> *One hundred and fifty* (*not* 150) people applied for the job.
> *Nineteen seventy-six* (*not* 1976) was an election year.

Per cent, percentage

Both *per cent* and *percentage* mean "rate per hundred." Use *per cent* with numbers (*20 per cent*), and use percentage without numbers (*a small percentage*).

Personal, personnel

Personal, which means "pertaining to an individual" is often substituted for *personnel,* which refers to all the people engaged in a particular work or service. A letter addressed to *Director of Personal* creates a poor impression.

Principal, principle

Principal means "the first or highest in importance or value." A principle, on the other hand, is a rule or law.

His *principal* difficulty is a lack of training in mathematics.
It is this *principle* upon which the familiar "neon lamp" operates.

Precedence, precedents

Precedence means "priority in rank or order of importance."

The secretary asked which job had *precedence*.

Precedents means "going before in time." Usually, a precedent will provide a model for present action or decision making.

There are no *precedents* to guide me in this matter.

Rational, rationale

Rational refers to the activities of the mind, meaning "reasonable" or "sensible."

The explanation seemed *rational*, but it did not solve the problem.

Rationale means "a statement of reasons" or "a reasoned exposition of principles."

What is your *rationale* for suspending operations?

Since

Strictly speaking, *since* is a time word. It should be restricted to its time sense and not used causally. *Because* is preferable for causal use.

I have been waiting for you *since* three o'clock.
I shall go to the meeting *because* (not *since*) I think it is an important one.

Than, then

The words *than* and *then* are frequently confused. *Than* is used for comparison, as in

She is prettier *than* her sister.

Then refers to time, as in

First he bought a house; *then* he bought a new car.

Theirselves

Themselves is the proper form.

There, their, they're

Confusion of the words *there, their,* and *they're* is a common result of carelessness.

There refers to a place or a point in an action: Dump the sand *there.*

Their is the possessive form of *they: Their* thermostat is located in the hallway.

They're is a construction for *they are: They're* concerned about the revised price list.

There is often used to begin a sentence or clause in which the subject appears after the verb: *There* is another advantage for the multipolar generator.

To, too, two

To, a preposition, indicates direction; *too,* an adverb, means "also"; and *two* is a numeral. The following examples illustrate their correct use:

I went *to* Florida for my vacation.
She, *too,* will do volunteer work in the hospital.
Mr. and Mrs. Booth have *two* sons and one daughter.

Try and

Try and is a common mistake for *try to.*

INCORRECT: We will *try and* be there in the morning.
CORRECT: We will *try to* be there in the morning.

Which, that

A fine point in style is the use of *that* (instead of *which*) in relative clauses that restrict the meaning.

LESS DESIRABLE: The book *which* I just bought is about Mexico.
BETTER: The book *that* I just bought is about Mexico.
ALSO CORRECT: *This* book, *which* I just bought, is about Mexico.

In the first two examples, the relative clause restricts the meaning. For this reason, *that* is preferable to *which.* However, in the last example, *this* restricts the meaning, and the relative clause merely adds information; therefore, *which* is correct in the last example. Note also that in the first two examples, commas are *not* used to set off the relative clause *because* it *restricts* the meaning. Commas to set off the relative clause are all right in the last example because the clause does *not* restrict the meaning but simply supplies additional information.

While

The use of *while* should be limited to the time sense. Other senses for which *while* is sometimes used are best represented by *although* and *whereas*.

While it is raining, I shall stay indoors.
John is a painter, *whereas* (not *while*) Mary is a musician.
Although (not *while*) it is true, I still cannot believe it.

PUNCTUATION PROBLEMS

Apostrophe

The apostrophe is used to show possession:

This is the point struck by the *tube's* electron beam.
The *factories'* waste products cause thermal pollution.
James's novel was read in class.

The apostrophe also shows we have left out part of a word:

it's = it is
doesn't = does not
five o'clock = five of the clock

The apostrophe helps form the plurals of letters and figures:

His 7's look like 9's.
Watch your *p*'s and *q*'s.

Comma

The comma is the most frequently used punctuation mark and the most frequently misused. Many problems with commas are caused by using them when they are not needed in the sentence. Commas help clarify the meaning of your sentences and should be used with care and precision. A few hints can assist you in making more effective and correct use of commas in your writing.

1. Try reading your sentences aloud. Sometimes you need a comma to indicate a pause your voice would make for clarity if you were speaking rather than writing.

   UNCLEAR: Inside the fire had gutted the living room.
   CLEAR: Inside, the fire had gutted the living room.

2. Use commas to separate words and phrases in a series:[1]

   WORDS IN A SERIES: Control units are mounted in a metal module that keeps each unit intact for installation, removal, and testing.
   PHRASES IN SERIES: Thermostats should be installed in the hallway, in the kitchen, and in each bedroom.

---

[1] Newspapers omit the comma before the *and*, however.

The typical large corporation shows a net profit just under 5.0 per cent of its total sales, earns about a 12.0 per cent return on its equity capital, and turns over its capital 2.5 times a year.

3. In sentences containing two or more whole or independent clauses, commas are often necessary before the conjunctions *and, or, nor, for,* or *but:*

Peak firing temperatures of 725°–780°C can be used, but best results are generally obtained between 730°C and 760°C.

4. Use commas to set off introductory words, phrases, and clauses when there is danger of confusion.

A comma is often used after an introductory adverb or transitional word:

Finally, the parts arrived.
However, signs now indicate a reduction in prices.

A comma is used to set off introductory phrases, especially when they are fairly long or complex.

In terms of jobs alone, we estimate that between 155,000 and 193,000 on-site and related off-site construction jobs are being filled through current construction activities.

Introductory clauses often require a comma to set them off from the main clause.

When relative humidity is properly maintained, people feel better and work better.

5. Commas set off parenthetical elements that interrupt normal sentence flow. These interrupting elements may be words, phrases, or entire clauses.

PHRASES: If we disregard, *for the moment,* the series field winding, we have, *in effect,* a shunt wound generator.

WORDS: Construction of the parking areas has been delayed, *however,* by problems with the final grades.

CLAUSES: The architect's plans, *although they did provide the dimensions of the glass panels,* did not provide particular specifications for the type and thickness of the glass.

Relative clauses present some difficulties when one has to decide whether or not to set them off with commas. If the relative clause is essential to identifying or defining its subject, then it *should not* be enclosed in commas:

> The employee *who was injured* claimed the contractor was negligent.

Here the relative clause *who was injured* identifies the particular employee. In the following example, the relative clause is not essential to identifying *the owner* but merely offers additional information.

> The work was accepted by the owner, *who had the power of final approval of all specifications.*

Relative clauses beginning with *that* are never set off with commas.

6. Commas are used with appositives that do not restrict the meaning.

> The manufacturer, *Barco Construction Company,* worked two shifts a day to meet the construction schedule.

An appositive that *restricts* meaning is *not* set off by commas.

> His brother, John, is younger than he is.
> His brother John is a good athlete.

In the first example, John is his only brother; hence commas are in order. In the second example, John is *one* of several brothers, and the omission of the commas indicates this fact. In other words, in the second example, *John* restricts the meaning whereas in the first example, *John* does not restrict the meaning.

7. A comma fault or comma splice occurs when a writer joins two sentences with a comma instead of ending one with a period and beginning the next with a capital letter.

> COMMA FAULT: The pulp mill has a 130-acre waste treatment lagoon, the lagoon holds pulp liquor after processing.
>
> CORRECT: The pulp mill has a 130-acre waste treatment lagoon. The lagoon holds pulp liquor after processing.

A semicolon may also be used to join complete sentences:

CORRECT: The pulp mill has a 130-acre waste treatment lagoon; the lagoon holds pulp liquor after processing.

8. A comma should not be placed between a subject and its verb, a verb and its object, or an adjective and its noun.

INCORRECT: The books we bought, have arrived.
CORRECT: The books we bought have arrived.
INCORRECT: He studied, chemistry for the entire evening.
CORRECT: He studied chemistry for the entire evening.
INCORRECT: Mr. Taylor is a reasonable, gracious, and amiable, man.
CORRECT: Mr. Taylor is a reasonable, gracious, and amiable man.

9. A comma should not come between two words or two phrases linked by *and, but, or,* or *nor.*

INCORRECT: Do you want peas, or broccoli, or carrots for dinner?
CORRECT: Do you want peas or broccoli or carrots for dinner?

In a series, however, a comma before *or* would be correct.

CORRECT: Do you want peas, broccoli, or carrots for dinner?

Note the following, too:

INCORRECT: He intends to work hard, and to get ahead.
CORRECT: He intends to work hard and to get ahead.

10. A comma should not separate the parts of a compound predicate. Be careful to distinguish between a compound predicate and a compound sentence:

INCORRECT: He studied hard, but failed the test.
CORRECT: He studied hard but failed the test.
ALSO CORRECT: He studied hard, but he failed the test.

The first two examples illustrate the compound predicate; the third example illustrates the compound sentence.

11. Commas should not be used to set off those clauses, phrases, and appositives that restrict meaning.

INCORRECT: The man, who is laughing at you, is my uncle.
CORRECT: The man who is laughing at you is my uncle.

INCORRECT: The car, across the street, is mine.
CORRECT: The car across the street is mine.

INCORRECT: Dickens's novel, *David Copperfield,* is very popular.
CORRECT: Dickens's novel *David Copperfield* is very popular.

12. When commas are needed to set off a parenthetical clause, phrase, or word, be careful to place the commas on *both* sides of the clause, phrase, or word.

INCORRECT: I think, however that it is for the best.
CORRECT: I think, however, that it is for the best.
INCORRECT: The children, restless and noisy did not listen to me.
CORRECT: The children, restless and noisy, did not listen to me.
INCORRECT: Mr. Quinn, who is very popular may become mayor.
CORRECT: Mr. Quinn, who is very popular, may become mayor.

Colon

The most common use of the colon is to introduce a list following an introductory statement.

A comprehensive earthquake prediction program will include three elements: hazard reduction, readying emergency services, and controlling potentially disruptive consequences of the prediction.

The colon is also used to introduce quoted material.

We want our office personnel to keep in mind the following slogan: "Think ahead."

In general, the colon leads the reader to expect that something will follow: a list, a specific example, or a quotation.

Do not use a colon to separate a verb from its object.

INCORRECT: We received: four toasters, five electric blankets, and six coffee pots.
CORRECT: We received four toasters, five electric blankets, and six coffee pots.

Dash

Dashes can become addictive and, used carelessly, can become substitutes for other punctuation marks. Dashes are informal; so in many types of writing their use is inappropriate. One effective use of the dash is to supply an afterthought, much as we would in speaking:

> Thompson claims he will meet the deadline—but I don't believe him.

Dashes are also used to insert parenthetical elements into a sentence, although parentheses are more formal and usually more appropriate.

> Thompson's proposal was a well-conceived—if controversial—plan for offshore leasing and development.

Hyphens

Hyphens are troublesome punctuation marks, and many discrepancies exist even in the best dictionaries regarding their use.

1. Hyphens are used to join two or more *words* into a single, usually adjectival, unit, as in the following examples:

   > forty *fact-filled* pages
   > the *floor-to-floor* height

2. Hyphens are usually not employed when *prefixes* are added to words.

   > *reeducate*
   > *nonexistent* energy savings
   > *preeminent*
   > *antiskid* surface

   However, when the second element starts with a capital letter or is a numeral, a hyphen follows the prefix.

   > *pre-World War I*
   > *post-1970*

   When you are in doubt, consult a reputable dictionary.

3. Use a hyphen to divide words at the end of a line. There are rules covering situations that require dividing words, but mastering them is unnecessary for most writers. Simply avoid dividing words at the end of a line; or, if you must, consult a dictionary to see where the divisions are.

Parentheses

Use parentheses to enclose material that interrupts or digresses from the main point you are making.

> Motivating employees is not a matter of manipulating them, threatening them, or talking them into doing things for you (*as too many executives still think*).

Parentheses are often used to clarify terms or provide a reminder of a point made previously.

> As consulting engineers (problem solvers), we must recognize the interdependence of solutions and problems.

Parentheses can be used to insert more precise information into a sentence.

> The retail grocery business showed the highest rate (7.7 times) and railroads had the lowest (0.9 times).

Semicolon

The semicolon is subject to much abuse and misunderstanding. There are really only two circumstances that demand the use of a semicolon:

1. To separate items in a series when the series already includes commas.

   > We have decided on the starting dates for the three phases of our project: the first phase will begin on January 5, 1975; the second on July 15, 1975; and the third on August 2, 1975.

2. To join complete sentences, especially those linked by conjunctive adverbs such as *however, moreover,* and *nevertheless.*

   > Today's technology is powerful; however, its use must be balanced by respect for the environment.
   > As a rule of thumb, spandrel depth should be about half the floor-to-floor height; then only glass need be added to complete the building's skin.
   > Sunshine is an abundant, inexhaustible resource; it is free; no foreign country can control how much we get.

The semicolon is often used before a coordinating conjunction (*and, but, or, nor, for*) that joins two independent clauses when either clause is extremely long or contains other punctuation, such as commas.

> At the office, the morning began with much activity, effort, and optimism; but by afternoon a mood of pessimism, accompanied by lethargy, pervaded the atmosphere.

A semicolon is correct only when used between elements of the same level. It should not be used, for example, between a main clause and a subordinate clause or between a clause and a phrase.

INCORRECT: I am going to camp; though I don't want to.
CORRECT: I am going to camp, though I don't want to.
INCORRECT: We ran up the street; shouting with joy.
CORRECT: We ran up the street, shouting with joy.

INDEX